# The Rise and Decline of Patriarchal Systems

# The Rise and Decline of Patriarchal Systems

## An Intersectional Political Economy

Nancy Folbre

VERSO

London • New York

First published by Verso 2020
© Nancy Folbre 2021

The moral rights of the author have been asserted

1 3 5 7 9 10 8 6 4 2

**Verso**
UK: 6 Meard Street, London W1F 0EG
US: 20 Jay Street, Suite 1010, Brooklyn, NY 11201
versobooks.com

Verso is the imprint of New Left Books

ISBN-13: 978-1-78663-295-1
ISBN-13: 978-1-78663-292-0 (UK EBK)
ISBN-13: 978-1-78663-293-7 (US EBK)

**British Library Cataloguing in Publication Data**
A catalogue record for this book is available from the British Library

**Library of Congress Cataloging-in-Publication Data**
A catalog record for this book is available from the Library of Congress
Library of Congress Control Number: 2020948692

Typeset in Minion by Hewer Text UK Ltd
Printed and bound by CPI Group (UK) Ltd, Croydon CR0 4YY

# Contents

### "Myth"

Long afterward, Oedipus, old and blinded, walked the roads. He smelled a familiar smell. It was the Sphinx. Oedipus said, "I want to ask one question. Why didn't I recognize my mother?" "You gave the wrong answer," said the Sphinx. "But that was what made everything possible," said Oedipus. "No," she said. "When I asked, what walks on four legs in the morning, two at noon, and three in the evening, you answered, Man. You didn't say anything about woman." "When you say Man," said Oedipus, "you include women too. Everyone knows that." She said, "That's what you think."

Muriel Ruykeser
First published in *Breaking Open*, 1973

Acknowledgements

# Acknowledgements

I have long been drawn, like a moth to a flame, to big theoretical questions about gender inequality, social division, and collective conflict. As I worked on this manuscript, my wings began to feel singed, and I considered either changing the order of words in the title, or adding more, as in, Rise, Decline, and Rise Again. Prophecy, however, is not my goal. We have much to learn from the evolution of patriarchal institutions, whichever way they twist and turn.

The intersectional political economy developed here insists on the need to actively construct broad alliances of disempowered groups. It emerged from collaborative efforts that crossed many disciplinary and political boundaries. I am grateful to my editor Rosie Warren for her keen observations and suggestions. Several past collaborators helped me develop key ideas: Lee Badgett, Michael Bittman, Elissa Braunstein, Michelle Budig, Paula England, Ann Ferguson, James Heintz, Julie Nelson, Kristin Smith, Jooyeoun Suh, Jayoung Yoon, Thomas Weisskopf, Douglas Wolf, and Erik Olin Wright. My colleague Carol Heim gave me patient, consistent, and discerning feedback. Gerald Epstein and Robert Pollin, co-directors of the Political Economy Research Center at the University of Massachusetts Amherst, provided steadfast encouragement and support. All my colleagues at the University of Massachusetts Amherst from 1975 to the present helped me think through the ideas here.

Many friends helped me redo a frightfully confused early draft. John Stifler gently corrected many rhetorical missteps and offered helpful substantive suggestions. Haroon Akram-Lodhi, Lourdes Beneria, Sam Bowles, Carol Heim, William Ferguson, and Thomas Weisskopf offered specific suggestions. Graduate students who participated in my political economy seminar on gender, race and class took nothing for granted and asked great questions. Discussion and debate with Katherine Moos and Luiza Nassaf Pires altered my thinking on some key points. Naila Kabeer helped immeasurably with a last round of revisions.

I benefited greatly from a number of previous opportunities to present bits and pieces of the ideas here, including the Festschrift Conference for Thomas Weisskopf, organized by the Political Economy Research Institute (thanks to Jeannette Lim); the David Gordon Lecture sponsored by the Union for Radical Political Economics (thanks to Fred Moseley); several Amherst College classes in Women and Gender Studies (thanks to Amrita Basu); the Gender Institute of the London School of Economics (thanks to Diane Perrons); the History of Capitalism Conference at Cornell University (thanks to Jefferson Cowie); the Patten Lectureship at Indiana University (thanks to Lynn Duggan); the European University in Florence, Italy (thanks to Laura Lee Downs); session on "Patriarchy Revisited" at the meetings of the American Sociological Association (thanks to Paula England, Sylvia Walby, and Vrushali Patil); lectures at Colorado State University (thanks to Elissa Braunstein and Anders Fremstad); University of Dublin and Glasgow Caledonian University (thanks to Sara Cantillon); University of Windsor, Ontario (thanks to Erica Stevens Abbitt); Wheaton College (thanks to Brenda Wyss); the Inter-University Women and Gender Studies Institute Conference at the University of Barcelona (thanks to Lourdes Beneria); the University of Wisconsin (thanks to Erik Olin Wright); the 2018 International Association for Feminist Economics Conference (thanks to Edith Kuiper and Barbara Hopkins); and discussions around a special issue of *Daedalus* on gender inequality (thanks to Nannerl Keohane and Frances Rosenbluth).

In fall 2019, participants at meetings celebrating the work of Sam Bowles and Herbert Gintis at Columbia University (thanks to Suresh Naidu and others) and at a conference celebrating the life of Erik Olin Wright (thanks to Michael Burawoy and others) helped me think harder about what I am doing here. I am particularly indebted to Debra Satz for her feedback. I am also grateful to discussions at the meeting on Epistemologies of Care: Rethinking Global Political Economy, organized by Jocelyn Olcutt.

The Covid-19 pandemic pounced upon the world just as I was making final revisions to this manuscript, a poignant reminder of global dependence on cooperation and care for others. My research on care work emphasizes its many distinctive characteristics—among them, the difficulty of accurately assessing individual value-added. We can never know exactly what others have done for us or what, exactly, we have done for them. For better or worse, we produce and reproduce ourselves in concert.

# I

# Theoretical Tools

# 1

# Intersectional Political Economy

Social divisions can and often do morph into forms of structural inequality that are both unfair and inefficient. One might worry that attention to divisions deeply rooted in the distant past would dampen hopes for an equitable and sustainable economic future. Not so. Such a future can only be nurtured by a critical analysis of long-standing patriarchal institutions that intersect, overlap, and interact with hierarchical institutions based on other dimensions of collective identity.

Abuses of collective power are more easily redressed when we understand their evolution. Their various forms are often linked in ways that render them vulnerable to similar forms of contestation. Both the decline and the persistence of gender inequalities tell us something about the trajectory of other forms of collective conflict. Complex histories of exploitation warn of the costly consequences of gain-seeking that devalues the current and future well-being of other people.

Feminism and Marxism have been described as partners in an unhappy marriage that some believe should lead to reconciliation, others to divorce.[1] We should think less about this conjugal pair and more about their contributions to a larger meme pool. I once embraced a feminist political economy based on a concept of Patriarchy analogous to the Marxian concept of Capitalism, two big nouns that allowed for many qualifying adjectives: ageist, racist, nationalist, homophobic, and so on. In the 1980s debate raged over which noun was the bigger and more important and whether they could be combined into something called "patriarchal capitalism" or "capitalist patriarchy." Whatever their relationship, these two entities tell only part of a larger story of intersecting, overlapping forms of exploitation.

The intersectional political economy presented here retains many important insights from Marxian theory but offers a more complex account of collective conflict that draws on insights from feminist theory, institutional economics, game theory, and bargaining models. I argue that adjectives such as "patriarchal," "capitalist," "racist," and "nationalist" describe sets of social institutions that mutually influence one another, sometimes undermining but often reinforcing hierarchical relations by crippling unified opposition to them. I call attention to forms of exploitation that long predated the emergence of wage employment and were internalized, modified, and in some ways weakened by the expansion of capitalist institutions. I offer examples of the impact of patriarchal institutions on the coevolution of many forms of socially constructed inequality.

This analysis of collective identity and conflict builds on three propositions that emerged from feminist theory and seemed, initially, to pertain only to inequalities based on gender.

1. Women share some common interests.

2. Many of these common interests grow out of their historical specialization in reproductive activities, defined broadly as the production and maintenance of human capabilities and sometimes simply referred to as "care."

3. Obligations to care for dependents help reconcile tensions between individual and group welfare—and, more broadly, between self-interest and altruism—in ways that are particularly costly to women.

Each of these propositions has proved remarkably generative, extending in relevance far beyond their original domains. That women have some common interests as women implies that men have some common interests as men. Any effort to mobilize individuals around common interests almost inevitably highlights the interests that they do not have in common. If collective interests can be based on gender, they can also be based on age, sexuality, race/ethnicity, citizenship, class, and other aspects of socially assigned group membership.

Control over the means of reproduction has economic consequences just as profound as control over the means of production. The means of reproduction, however, are not just women's minds and bodies; processes of daily and generational reproduction cannot be reduced to interactions based on gender, sexuality, and age. Access to the resources required to develop and maintain human capabilities is unevenly distributed in many different ways, profoundly affected by the distribution of wealth, and mediated by access to state-financed social spending. Income is not the only currency of group advantage, especially in a global economy where paths to health care, education, social protection, and productive employment are circumscribed by many dimensions of socially assigned group membership.

Women should have as much space as men to pursue their own self-interest, but that does not mean that the total space for self-interest should expand at the expense of care for others. In order for women to gain more rights, men must shoulder more obligations. Women's historical specialization in the care of dependents has heightened awareness of the permeable boundaries of the self—the difficulties of clearly defining "self-interest" in an interdependent world. The costs, benefits, and risks of altruistic commitments should be fairly shared.

The feminist compass points toward an intersectional political economy that highlights dynamics of cooperation and conflict, applying an interdisciplinary vocabulary influenced, but not dictated by the Marxian theory of historical materialism. Like this theory, intersectional political economy interprets the broad sweep of institutional change in the past in ways that inform political strategies for the future. The following chapters add detail to the general perspective summarized below.

## Cooperation and Conflict

The economic analysis of patriarchal institutions falls largely outside the purview of both neoclassical economics (with its focus on markets) and traditional Marxian economy (with its focus on capitalism). A great deal of empirical research explores inequalities based on gender but attributes these to personal choices, outdated cultural norms, or capitalist imperatives to maximize profits.[2] The possibility that men might design, enforce, and defend social institutions that give them economic advantages over women goes largely unexplored.

This possibility is blurred by both theoretical foci: patriarchal institutions cannot be established by means of individual choices within markets, and they presuppose collective interests that are not motivated by the extraction of surplus value in wage employment. Conventional definitions of "the economy" and "economic systems" discourage economists from consideration of the institutional bases of many dimensions of social inequality, including but not limited to gender. Attention to patriarchal institutions requires a new way of thinking about economic systems—and vice versa.

Economic systems are characterized by complex forms of cooperation and conflict among both individuals and groups, mediated by a variety of social institutions. System dynamics can seldom be reduced to one axis of collective conflict such as gender, race/ethnicity, citizenship, or class; systems can be simultaneously patriarchal, racist, nationalist, and capitalist, and none of these individual adjectives fully captures their internal logic, though some are more salient than others at different points. Hierarchical institutions rely heavily on the stabilizing effect of the multiple social divisions they create. However, they can be undermined by the shifting weights of differing identities and interests, battered by the forces of technological change, social invention, and political alliance.

The rise and decline of patriarchal institutions illustrate such shifts, with implications for the evolution of the larger systems of which they are a part. Gender inequalities coexist and coevolve with other inequalities. Overlaps, intersections, and interactions among distinct structures of collective power help explain the emergence of patriarchal institutions, their alteration in the course of economic development, and their influence on welfare states. Many forms of exploitation that predated capitalist institutions have weakened over time, but some have taken new shapes.

Capitalist institutions create powerful incentives to maximize short-run profits by exploiting unpriced public goods crucial to the sustainability of the social and natural environment. The unpaid and paid care of others is one of these public goods—a source of immense social benefits that are not fully captured by those who generate them. Women's continuing specialization in the care of dependents—whether at home or in the labor market—both limits their collective bargaining power and gives them a particular stake in the development of more cooperative and sustainable economic systems.

The terms "rise" and "decline" do not imply decline and fall, but a change in the slope of a long-run line. The ragged ups and downs of political and cultural contestation remain confusing and painful. An international backlash against gender equality is evident.[3] The hypermasculinity of world leaders like Donald Trump and Vladimir Putin derogates women even as it invokes the glory of the white nation-state as a path to prosperity.[4] Yet this very backlash reveals deep-seated anxieties created by fundamental shifts in the organization of reproductive work, along with the powerful valence of overlapping privileges based on gender, race/ethnicity, citizenship, and class.

Consolidated forms of power build on their antecedents, creating complex inequalities that both hinder efforts to build political coalitions of the disempowered and create potential for sudden realignments. In January 2017, Oxfam released a report estimating that the eight richest people in the world—all white men, six from the United States—own as much net wealth as the bottom half of the global population.[5] Their personal characteristics and countries of origin hardly seem incidental.

Because patriarchal institutions are increasingly vulnerable to contestation, feminists have become the harbingers of structural change. The poster that sparked the Occupy Movement in the United States in 2011 featured an elegant ballet dancer balanced atop the bronze bull of Wall Street. In 2017, a smaller sculpture known as Fearless Girl faced that bull in the street for a few months, creating a furor because, as the mayor of New York City observed, she represented everyone willing to stand up to the rich and powerful.[6] The success of this metaphorical challenge rests on the development of theoretical tools that can help forge broad progressive coalitions based on principles of fair play.

### Systems and Structures

A patriarchal system is one that includes structures of patriarchal power, overlapping and intersecting other structures of collective power in historically specific ways. All these structures have common features: laws, ideologies, and asset distributions that create collective advantages or disadvantages. Our language reveals subliminal awareness of structural constraints: unlevel playing fields, broken ladders, poverty traps, glass ceilings, maternal walls, sticky floors.

Many of the institutional structures that shape relations between men and women also influence the reproduction and care of human beings. A patriarch is not merely a man; he is a man who wields power by virtue of his age, sexual orientation, and gender. Patriarchal laws, rules, rights, and public policies leave clear traces, and the historical record shows that they have begun to recede. Patriarchal ideologies shaping cultural norms are more resistant to change, because they are imprinted at an early age and reinforced by cultural and economic influence. Patriarchal control over financial and other assets is another durable source of gendered power.

Economic assets cannot be narrowly defined as means of capitalist production. They include all sources of future income: not just property easily denominated in dollars, but also human capital or labor power (the value of productive capabilities), natural capital (the value of environmental resources and ecological services), social capital (the value of networks of reciprocity, obligation, and mutual aid), and knowledge capital (the value of what we know, from human history to modern technology). These forms of capital, though difficult to literally own, are subject to collective control. They yield indispensable economic benefits yet can also be conducive to costly forms of exploitation.

Emphasis on the synergies between political, cultural, and economic institutions focuses attention on collective identity and action. It is often possible to ascertain the distributional effects of institutional arrangements by parsing their effects on the relative bargaining power of groups, asking "what dimension of socially assigned group membership do these institutions reward?" Some institutions facilitate the accumulation of advantages based on gender, age, or sexuality. Others facilitate the accumulation of advantages based on class, race/ethnicity, citizenship, or other dimensions of group identity such as religion.

Analogues are signaled by the very words we use. The suffix "archy" derives from the Greek words for rule and ruler. "Hierarchy," a word invented long ago to describe the ranks of angels, gradually acquired a secular meaning: a structure of inequality that is at least somewhat independent of those who occupy it.[7] The terms "patriarchy," "monarchy," and "oligarchy" reflect this semantic intent. It hardly seems incidental that most monarchies and oligarchies put fathers in charge. Economists did not invent the word "capital." It derives from Middle English: "standing at the head or beginning," via the Latin "capitalis" from "caput" or head. Capitalism is a hierarchical structure that gives owners of inherited or accumulated wealth institutional power over wage earners. Traditional Marxian theory treats it as a hegemonic mode of production that dominates—perhaps even generates—other manifestations of collective power, but when capitalism emerges, it coexists, coevolves, and interacts with other hierarchical structures. None of the causal arrows move in straight, one-way lines; they are convoluted and recursive.

All hierarchical structures are economically consequential, creating the potential for exploitation and affecting both the production and distribution of surplus. Patriarchal institutional structures allocate power by gender, age, and sexual orientation, organizing reproduction in ways that historically contributed to a distinctive form of accumulation—population growth. Likewise, the racist and nationalist institutional structures that predated capitalist ways of organizing work coordinated forms of collective action (including organized warfare) that made some groups wealthy at the expense of others. These forms of surplus creation and appropriation were not superceded by capitalist development but incorporated into it.

This historical narrative is far more tangled than the classical Marxian succession of modes of production such as feudalism-to-capitalism, revealing an ecology of power characterized by multiple and simultaneous forms of exploitation. It brings women and families into a larger picture in ways that go well beyond an analysis of gender inequality. The complexity of economic systems comprised of a large number of interlocking hierarchical structures almost certainly helps explain both their relative stability and their occasional susceptibility to change. To simply call a totality like this "capitalism" is misleading.

Democracy, in the broadest sense of rules guaranteeing both personal rights and equal participation in collective decision-making, represents an institutional structure designed to minimize exploitative outcomes. Not that democracy necessarily escapes hierarchy: even groups that forego leaders and make decisions by consensus typically enforce rules of membership and behavior, drawing boundaries that define their purview. Democracy seldom functions effectively when it remains incomplete. Still, democratic ideals provide a crucial benchmark for the critical analysis of hierarchical institutions that create arbitrary and unfair forms of inequality.

Conventional neoclassical economics locates individuals in competitive markets; classical Marxian theory focuses on class struggle within stylized modes of production. Some critics of both theories point to social institutions but stop short of a comprehensive analysis of multidimensional forms of collective conflict. Political science is generally more attentive to distributional maneuver, sociology and anthropology to normative power. These diverse approaches themselves occasionally intersect and overlap. They can all inform the conceptual project of defining institutional structures of collective power in terms of their economic consequences for collective affiliations.

### Actors and Actions

Feminists aim to understand "the patriarchal" for an obvious reason. If you want to tear down a structure, it helps to understand how it was built and what it is connected to. Collective power tends to reproduce itself or morph into resilient hybrid forms but is not invulnerable. Political realignments that weaken one institutional structure can destabilize the larger edifice. Institutional structures that promote success in one environment can prove ineffective in another, undermined by ideological inconsistencies or disrupted by technological change. Short-run gains can be abruptly reversed. The tendencies toward systemic crisis central to the classical Marxian critique of capitalism can take a more general form, applying to complex systems unable to adapt to changing circumstances such as severe threats of social and environmental disruption.

Social structures and systems do not fall from the sky. They are created and sustained by a dialectic of cooperation and competition, complicated by unforeseen events and unexpected consequences. Individuals often pursue their own self-interest in market exchange, as conventional neoclassical economics posits. Classes often struggle over the control of surplus, as Marxian political economy posits. These actors and actions, however, tell only part of a more complicated story in which unfair inequalities in bargaining power lead to coexisting forms of exploitation.

This story becomes more compelling when the definition of economic activities is expanded beyond production for market exchange to encompass appropriation (such as theft and war), reproduction (the production and maintenance of human capabilities), and the larger process of social reproduction (the creation and maintenance of social groups). All these activities require forms of coordination enforced by structures of collective power. This coordination comes at a high cost, because it creates opportunities for those in positions of power to claim an unfair share of the gains from cooperation. Effective democracy is the only safeguard, but economic inequality makes it difficult, if not impossible, to achieve.

Economic inequality cannot be defined simply in terms of market income; it must be defined more broadly in terms of differential access to financial, human, natural, and social capital. While many of us can choose whether or not to join specific interest groups, our ability to choose socially assigned groups based on characteristics such as gender, age, sexuality, race/ethnicity, class, and national citizenship is limited by distinct labels stamped upon us at birth. These labels are not necessarily culpable, but they are often deployed in ways that create economic vulnerability for some and unfair advantage for others. We can choose with which groups to align ourselves, but our agency is limited, our choices hampered by incomplete information regarding other people's virtually simultaneous decisions.

Some of us enjoy several forms of group-based advantage or suffer multiple forms of disadvantage; many of us find ourselves in mixed or contradictory positions, advantaged in some respects, disadvantaged in others. As Roxane Gay puts it, "To have privilege in one or more areas does not mean you are wholly privileged ... The acknowledgement of my privilege is not a denial of the ways I have been and am marginalized, the ways I have suffered."[8] Such complexity makes it difficult to forge agreement on principles of economic justice, much less coordinate efforts to apply them. Fear of the future often makes us cling to the past. The difficulty of predicting the consequences of possible coalitions gives theoretical narratives and cultural ideologies enormous influence over our decisions.

Neoclassical economic theory emphasizes free rider problems, instances in which the pursuit of individual self-interest undermines commitments to cooperation. Yet it often underestimates the ways in which such coordination problems are overcome. Classical Marxian theory highlights class solidarity but often leaves equally important forms of solidarity in the dark. Neither theory provides a complete account of the dialectic of cooperation and conflict that shapes social divisions. Both individuals and groups maneuver for a larger share of the gains they can garner from cooperation and exchange. Institutional structures designed to discourage free riding often exacerbate an equally serious problem: top riding or cream skimming by those in positions of power. Strong groups often find ways to exploit weak groups and to institutionalize their gains in ways that perpetuate their advantage.

We are all players in metaphorical games in which the rules and rewards are often taken as a given. The winners, in particular, are likely to resist change. Yet all players have a stake in improving the size and sustainability of the total payoff, and with it, the value of their winnings. Two important tools of political economy, bargaining models and game theory, help explain why equitable forms of cooperation can leave everyone better off in the long run. Most of the literal games we enjoy stipulate rules of fair play and put umpires into place for good reasons.

Some feminist theorists are suspicious of formal methods of economic reasoning. Audre Lorde's famous warning comes to mind: "The master's tools will never dismantle the master's house."[9] Some tools, however, cut both ways. The martial art of aikido teaches defenders to reverse the energy of attack. In medieval warfare, few successes were more impressive than those hoisting attackers on their own petards.

### Enlarging the Economic

Intersectional political economy redefines "the economic" in ways that encompass both reproduction and social reproduction, including the creation of human capabilities and the social institutions that bind people into groups with at least some common identities and interests. The first five chapters of this book conceptualize a strategic landscape in which structures of collective power create interlocking hierarchies, defining the scope for individual and collective decisions and generating coalitions that rely heavily on normative ideologies to coordinate their efforts. Interlocking structures of collective power set the stage for a multilayered process of collective bargaining among groups seeking to strengthen portfolios of privilege and those hoping to escape structural disadvantage.

This theoretical reconstruction brings patriarchal bargains to the front and center of human history, while also acknowledging their deep embeddedness in complex hierarchical systems. Because patriarchal institutions have undergone gradual, but fundamental transformation in a variety of historical and cultural contexts, they reveal some recipes for change. The proof of the pudding lies in the development of a more comprehensive explanation of intersectional dynamics.

This is a very big pudding, not one that can be fully cooked in a single pot. The last five chapters offer, instead, a taste of alterations to several central narratives of political economy: the origins of exploitation, the expansion of capitalist institutions, the development of welfare states, the persistence of gender inequality, and hopes for building progressive coalitions.

These chapters integrate analysis of demographic and economic dynamics mediated by structures of collective power that constrain individual and collective decisions. Causality works both ways: personal and social choices exert a cumulative effect on structures of collective power. These reciprocal processes fit loosely under the rubric of social reproduction but cannot be reduced to the social reproduction of capitalism as a unitary system or explained simply as the result of cultural inertia and technological change. They reflect more complex rhythms of collective cooperation and conflict.

## History, Herstory, Us-story

Capitalist development has encouraged a reallocation of human effort away from population growth toward increases in per capita income and consumption, with many positive consequences for women. These improvements, however, have been achieved in part through the exploitation of groups with relatively little bargaining power. The global North has benefited partly at the expense of the global South, and growth in gross domestic product has been purchased at the expense of future generations who lack any means to contest the degradation of natural assets, the destabilization of global climate, and the risk of social and political dysfunction. Even those singing along cannot know how this opera will end.

### Origins

Inequalities are often fractal, with small patterns replicated on a larger scale. Any understanding of unfair inequality writ large must be based on an understanding of unfair inequality writ small, in families. If the gender division of power between men and women were entirely prescribed by biological differences, it would be difficult to explain why it has been enforced—often violently—by so many social institutions. This institutional history begins long before history itself (his story, not hers or ours) was invented, challenging the Marxian assumption that societies without private property in livestock or land were largely egalitarian. Still, a more basic principle of Marxian historical materialism remains apt. Exploitative institutions can help groups seize or generate a surplus that works to their collective advantage, even though the benefits are unequally distributed within the group. Once established, such institutions remain resistant to change even when they become costly for everyone.

Patriarchal institutions initially proved complementary to the development of class- and race-based institutions of private property and status, helping ensure their social reproduction. The enslavement of women taken as prizes in war was a precursor to the later enslavement of entire families to be bought and sold like livestock. Tribes, lineages, and dynasties were conceived as families writ large, and distinctions among them provided a template for future ideologies of race. The authority of fathers became a metaphor and a model for the authority of kings. Hierarchical institutions delivered significant benefits often conditioned on military success, including the accumulation of agricultural surplus and—equally if not more important—the accumulation of population.

### Capitalist Development

Capitalist institutions ranging from debt finance to wage employment emerged slowly and unevenly within a patriarchal, racist, nationalist, and often feudal matrix that rewarded innovation but also encouraged new forms of exploitation. These institutions built upon (and may well have been dependent on) preexisting inequalities and group allegiances. One institutional form that played an important role was slave-based plantation agriculture, a profit-oriented form of coerced labor that emerged where differences in class power overlapped with differences in racial/ethnic power. Many forms of colonization took a similar turn.

Early capitalist development often proved most dynamic in countries where workers had sufficient bargaining power to pressure employers to seek profits through innovation rather than mere coercion. Indeed, where powerful groups could simply exact tribute or seize valuable natural assets, they seldom risked their wealth on forms of investment that could increase living standards. They could, instead, invest in the cooptation of local elites, a strategy perfected by the British East India Company in India.

The genesis of wage employment took variable forms. Whether workers entered factories as a last resort or eagerly sought wage employment depended in large part on their gender and their age, as well as local economic conditions. In some instances, the initial expansion of factory production had contradictory effects—making the younger generation less dependent on their parents for land and livelihood even as it locked them into a new kind of dependence on the labor market. In general, wage employment took a distinctly gendered form, with women restricted to the least remunerative jobs. Capitalists stood firmly with other men, often including their own employees, in defense of male advantage.

On the other hand, capitalist development transformed the paths to economic success. In areas where household-based production declined and family size began to shrink, it became increasingly costly for men to keep women in the home. Access to market income, as well as fertility decline, improved family living standards and increased women's ability to renegotiate patriarchal rules and norms. The institutional gains of the early feminist movement often had ideological spillover effects, weakening some patriarchal laws and norms even in areas where relatively little economic change was apparent. Imperial powers such as England often congratulated themselves on enforcing rules against child marriage or mistreatment of widows in their colonies.

Women's potential empowerment was everywhere mediated by many other dimensions of their collective identity, especially their race/ethnicity, class, and citizenship. Capitalist development and increased geographic mobility weakened family commitments. While wage employment offered economic opportunities outside the home, it did not offer any compensation for the direct care or support of family members. Some young people preferred to strike out on their own.

Here again, the consequences were contradictory. On the one hand, the increasing cost of children encouraged efforts to limit family size, reducing the enormous demands of childbearing and child-rearing. On the other hand, women were still left with primary responsibility for the care of dependents, including the growing ranks of the elderly. With increases in divorce and nonmarriage in Europe, the United States, and much of Latin America, fathers became less likely to take economic responsibility for their children, and the risk that motherhood itself would lead to poverty increased. The ethos of capitalist individualism—along with reduced incentives for family and community cooperation—left many dependents vulnerable to neglect.

**Welfare States**

Throughout much of the twentieth century, the weakening of family ties in affluent capitalist countries increased the economic pressure for state provision of care services such as education, health care, pensions, and a social safety net. State provision also offered greater efficiency through specialization, economies of scale, and pooling of risk. Working class organizations often played a key role in bargaining for increases in the "social wage," but employers also had an economic stake in the development of a healthy, well-educated, and well-cared-for labor force, and the military counted on able-bodied soldiers.

Many welfare state policies subsidized traditional breadwinner/ homemaker families, channeling pensions and other social benefits through men's hands. In racially and ethnically divided countries, such as the United States, whites acted in concert to restrict benefits to others, claiming both the profits and the wages of whiteness. Class inequalities often influenced the structure of both taxes and benefits. In Nordic countries, relatively low levels of racial and class inequality facilitated the emergence of organized women's groups that successfully fought for more generous and universal social benefits.

As the twenty-first century approached, globalization intensified the disconnect between reproduction and production. Large employers became less willing to support social spending and better able to minimize taxes and wages through offshoring and outsourcing. Both capital mobility and increased automation made employers less dependent on any one national labor force. At the same time, the proliferation of new military technologies such as unmanned drones and cyber warfare made nations less dependent on human soldiery. Neoliberal policies came to the fore: the international expansion of welfare state policies, once considered virtually inevitable, slowed considerably and, in some countries, reversed.

Changes in the realm of reproduction also put workers and taxpayers on the defensive. On the one hand, new medical technologies enhanced women's control over reproductive outcomes. On the other hand, the relative costs of raising and educating children increased— especially for mothers. Growing tensions within the welfare state echo tensions within families. Who should take care of whom? Public policies explicitly designed to support child-rearing, including family allowances, childcare provision, and paid family leaves from employment, cover a relatively small share of the costs of parenthood.

Fertility decline has tilted the population of many countries toward a larger share of elderly persons even as their life expectancy and need for medical and care services has increased. The burden of public pensions and medical services for the elderly weighs heavily on working-age adults who fear that coming generations may be unwilling or unable to provide them with the same level of support. Most of the elderly have already raised families and anticipate few direct gains from public investments in other people's children, particularly those that do not resemble their own. Such age-based divisions are exacerbated by the difficulty of understanding—and improving—the intergenerational bargain built into welfare state policies.

Poorly understood class and race/ethnicity dynamics also generate costly social division. Increased inequality in wealth and income, accompanied by a weakening of social safety nets, reduces physical and mental health and thwarts cooperative effects to respond effectively to common problems.[10] An ideological emphasis on gross domestic product and stock market returns as measures of economic success creates confusion and misunderstanding. The true cost of inequality is obscured by national income accounts that treat care for others and investments in human capabilities as just another form of consumption, rather than a fundamentally important investment in human and social capital.

Welfare states, like families, have become less reliable sources of care for dependents and investment in human capabilities. Yet people, natural assets, ecological services, and social solidarity are all important inputs into sustainable economic development, as well as wellsprings of intrinsic value. Failure to establish institutions that can effectively protect these unpriced assets is eroding capitalist structures of collective power—especially norms that legitimate the unrestricted pursuit of profit. The Covid-19 pandemic is now intensifying the resulting tensions. The putative policy trade-off between lives and livelihoods raises a big question: whose lives versus whose livelihoods?

## Care Penalties, Care Crises

The uncertain future of the welfare state resembles the uncertain future of families in an economic system that primarily rewards the production of commodities—goods and services that can easily be bought and sold in markets. Conventional neoclassical economics treats the care of children and other dependents much like the care of pets—a source of personal satisfaction, an expensive luxury good. Yet the creation and maintenance of human capabilities produces public goods—benefits for society as a whole that are diffuse, synergistic, and impossible to accurately price.[11]

Women are the primary caregivers in both the family and the labor market, and there's a reason they are called givers rather than takers. The difficulty of individually capturing the benefits of care often leaves them dependent on the good will or affections of men, without much recourse if and when such sentiments subside. Free riders often have free rein. A father who contributes little or nothing to the economic support or the hands-on care of a child can still lay claims on its affection or assistance; an employer who contributes little to public spending on education can still hire educated workers; nations that cut public spending on education can import ready-made college graduates from other countries; a woman who minimizes her care responsibilities in order to increase her market earnings can pay other women's children to help care for her in old age.

Individuals and groups who commit substantial time and effort to the unpaid care of others typically pay an economic penalty in reduced lifetime income. This penalty has been particularly well-documented in the United States, where many mothers bear primary responsibility for both the financial support and direct care of children. Childless women now earn roughly the same as men with comparable levels of education and experience; much of the gender gap in pay reflects the costs and risks of motherhood. Many public policies, including Social Security and means-tested public assistance, restrict eligibility for benefits on the grounds that family care is not really "work."

Care penalties extend well beyond unpaid work. Both men and women who work in care industries (such as health, education, and social services) and/or care occupations (such as childcare, eldercare, teaching, or nursing) often earn less than others with similar education and experience. In the United States, women represent about 75 percent of the health care workforce that is especially vulnerable to Covid-19 contagion on the job. In the face of soaring mortality from Covid-19, many hospitals in the United States ran out of money in April 2020 and cut the pay or reduced the hours of health care workers, even those serving on the frontlines.[12]

Bargaining power derives from the ability to withhold something until a satisfactory reward is offered for it. Children, individuals suffering illness or disability, and the frail elderly are often in a weak bargaining position, especially if disadvantaged by their race/ethnicity, citizenship, or class. Whether paid or unpaid, those who care for dependents share a vulnerability that increases with their level of commitment and participation; emotional attachment makes it difficult for them to threaten to withdraw their help. Many of the cultural norms and moral values that undergird care provision remain in force but require institutional support in the form of collectively agreed-upon rights to care and be cared for.

### Division and Alliance

While feminism asserts that women share common interests, effective alliances among women depend on overcoming differences among them. The intersectional political economy developed in this book emphasizes the need to recognize, theorize, and address such differences. It explains why the weakening of patriarchal institutions can improve the relative position of women but nonetheless leave predominantly women in vulnerable positions colored by differences based on race/ethnicity, citizenship, and class. It also explains why unmediated capitalist dynamics undermine environmental, demographic, and social sustainability.

Group allegiances matter. Human capabilities are public goods, but not everyone enjoys equal access to them. Some of the benefits of human capabilities are captured by the families, groups, and nations to which people belong. Women in disadvantaged or subaltern groups often find themselves in especially contradictory positions: even a partial withdrawal of their under-rewarded care services would increase their bargaining power but could reduce the ability of their families and communities to resist other forms of institutionalized exploitation.

We all share an interest in the development of institutional structures that could promote just, equitable, and sustainable economic development.

Nothing is more important than the creation of political coalitions designed to build robust democratic institutions that can effectively defend public interests and invest in the common good. The slogan "every man for himself" is both a principle of patriarchal power and a recipe for extinction.

# 2

# Defining the Patriarchal

"Patriarchy" and "patriarchal" are words used to describe gender inequality and sometimes, more literally, paternal authority. While their exact definitions remain contested, they generally label social arrangements that give mature heterosexual men power over others. The noun "patriarchy" (like "capitalism") describes an entity that stands alone or separate, like a sun circled by planets subject to its gravitational force. Instead, consider a social system consisting of many intersecting, interlocking institutional structures that circumscribe the opportunities available to members of distinct but overlapping groups—a galaxy of many suns.

The part is influenced by the whole, and the whole by its parts. A better picture of the larger social system constituted by multiple structures of collective power clarifies the significance of patriarchal institutions. By the same token, a closer look at patriarchal institutions can help explain the larger system, if links to forms of hierarchy based on race/ethnicity, citizenship, and class are closely analyzed. Attention to patriarchal structures of collective power provides a useful point of entry not because these are more central or more consequential than others, but because they have such a clear recent history of renegotiation and reform.

How do different institutions cohere into something that can be meaningfully called a structure of collective power? A rich body of feminist research describes rules, ideologies, and patterns of control over economic assets that put women at a disadvantage, what Bina

Agarwal refers to as "structures of social hierarchy."[1] Deniz Kandiyoti uses the term "patriarchal bargains" to explain how "women strategize within a set of concrete constraints" that present them with different "rules of the game."[2] Both individuals and groups engage in systematic efforts to defend or modify such constraints, to establish new rules.

This approach to structures of patriarchal power respects the importance of political, cultural, and economic forces and emphasizes articulations among social institutions that reflect and reinforce forms of collective identity and interests based on gender, age, and sexuality. It also reaches beyond feminist theory to provide a template for analysis of other structures of collective power based on dimensions of group identity such as race/ethnicity, nationality, citizenship, and class.

## Who Benefits?

Power is multidimensional, but its impact on policies (including laws), ideologies (including norms), and the ownership and control of resources (including people) can be assessed by a direct question: who benefits? Sometimes, only a small group, whose net benefits come entirely at the expense of others; sometimes, almost everyone benefits equally. More often, some benefit substantially more than others. Institutional consequences are seldom transparent; they often depend on hypotheticals. What would happen if this or that institution was reformed? Unfortunately, much social science and history offering answers to this question is biased by deployment of the very power that it purports to explain.

The history of resistance to feminist theory testifies to the impact of ideological power. Efforts to analyze patriarchal institutions have often been and are sometimes still derided by those in positions of authority.[3] Yet some of the sharpest edges of patriarchal power have been blunted in recent years, lending feminist theory new leverage and revealing linkages among political, cultural, and economic inequalities. Social structures are not easy to picture or explain, but their components can be distinguished, their buttresses revealed.

### The Psychological and the Institutional

Many feminist scholars reaching for a definition of the patriarchal have emphasized a behavioral or psychological trait—male dominance.[4]

However descriptive of the lived experience of many women, this emphasis is often problematic and at best incomplete. Dominance describes a behavioral trait rather than a social outcome. It is difficult to define, even when it leads to measurable consequences such as discrimination, domestic violence, or sexual harassment. The opposite of dominance is submission, yet many women never literally submit.

The dominance frame evokes discussions of hierarchies in other social species that are biologically hardwired. One need not dismiss the impact of physiological differences between women and men to observe that these cannot explain variations in gender relations over space and time. Evolutionary psychology cannot explain the rapid evolution and high variability of social institutions, and male dominance does not give fathers authority over sons or impose compulsory heterosexuality on men as well as women.

A definition of patriarchy based on male dominance implies that gender inequality is rooted primarily in psychology, encouraging a disciplinary division of labor in which class is rooted in economic exploitation, race and ethnicity in social discrimination, nationalism in political or military power. Yet the psychology of domination is terribly important to the reproduction of all forms of inequality, not just those based on gender, age, and sexuality. Dominance is not always male, and it is often accompanied by discrimination, exploitation, or appropriation. Both privilege and disadvantage typically have psychological, economic, political, and social dimensions, deeply coded in institutional structures that condition the ways they are expressed.

**Institutions and Institutional Structures**

The economist Douglass North defines "institutions" as "humanly devised constraints that structure political, economic and social interactions."[5] I have applied this definition in previous work because it effectively communicates the role of human agency in devising and modifying the social environment.[6] The term "constraint," however, is a bit misleading. Institutions do not merely constrain decisions; they also enable and facilitate collective action, promoting cooperation and minimizing the costs of coordination. In this respect, they can loosen as well as tighten constraints.

Institutionalist approaches to economic development and change are, almost by definition, less abstract than either Marxian or neoclassical economic theories, more attuned to specific historical and cultural circumstances. They can, however, go too far in the opposite direction, lapsing into purely descriptive accounts. The concept of a structure of collective power represents a methodological compromise, grouping political, cultural, and economic institutions together according to the distribution of the collective gains they generate. In economic history, references to capitalism and to slavery sometimes fit this characterization.[7]

Relatively few economic historians, however, acknowledge the relevance of patriarchal institutional structures. Most neoclassical and Marxian accounts of the emergence of capitalism presume a kind of stage-based transition from precapitalist to capitalist institutions without explicit consideration of collective conflicts that do not fit this sequence. Inequalities based on gender, race/ethnicity, nationality, or citizenship are often attributed to inherited attitudes, irrational preferences, sticky cultural norms, or capitalist class interests—absolving many historical agents of responsibility for them.

Conversely, much feminist social science focuses on the dynamics of gender inequality within families and firms, rather than a larger structure of patriarchal power, because the very concept of structure has fallen out of fashion. Postmodern theorists warn against overgeneralization and essentialism, and institutionalists sometimes seem reluctant to theorize. Sylvia Walby dislikes the very term patriarchal; Göran Therborn applies it primarily to outmoded family law.[8] Such hesitation can, perhaps, be overcome by the explicit effort to develop a broad, interdisciplinary analysis of collective conflict.

### The Capital Continuum

Triumvirates of political, cultural, and economic institutions are mutually reinforcing. Policies, laws, and rules seldom persist in the absence of ideological support, and they are often swayed by economic resources. Appreciation of their complex interactions is embedded in most nuanced analyses of capitalism as an institutional structure based on private ownership of capital—the means of production. Traditional Marxian analysis, however, defines both capital and production in very narrow terms. It says little about differences in human capabilities or about the costly processes of reproduction that create and maintain such capabilities.[9]

Control over women's bodies and their reproductive capabilities, like explicit ownership of other people, represents an economic asset. Membership in socially assigned groups, whatever the criteria for assignment, often provides access to opportunities that can be conceptualized as a form of social capital. The ability to pool risk and implicitly borrow from other group members is economically advantageous, as is the ability to restrict competition from nongroup members through discrimination. As the next chapter will elaborate, the ability to capitalize on collective allegiance helps explain the economic importance of group identity.

Most economic systems rely on forms of capital that are, in some sense, private, including the "self-ownership" of wage earners. All economic systems also rely on forms of capital that cannot easily be assigned a price and to which access cannot easily be restricted: they are public rather than private. Natural assets and ecological services fall into this category, as do the human knowledge and technology that reside in the public domain. Some human and social capabilities also fall into this category, because the benefits of investment in them spill over in unanticipated ways, including, for instance, greater productivity in nonmarket work, better governance, trust, and mutual aid.

The absence of a bright line separating ownership or control of financial capital from control over the capabilities and opportunities of other people highlights similarities among different structures of collective power. It widens the concept of economic institutions in ways that elucidate the structure of patriarchal power in particular. The evolution of direct and indirect property rights over people and the products of their paid and unpaid labor is central to the trajectory of patriarchal systems.

## Patriarchal Rights and Rules

Patriarchal political institutions fall into three somewhat overlapping categories: property rights over women and children; explicit restrictions on the individual rights of women, children, and sexually nonconforming individuals (often including limits on access to productive physical assets such as land or financial wealth); and rules of remuneration for time, effort, and resources devoted to the care of others, especially dependents.

Defined literally as "rule of the father," patriarchal law has more historical than contemporary relevance. Today, relatively few national societies are governed by laws that give men property rights over wives and children, and gender asymmetries in individual rights have been dramatically reduced.[10] This process of transformation testifies to the impact of institutional change driven by new forms of collective empowerment and mobilization. Social movements have played a particularly large part in global efforts to combat violence against women.[11]

Yet the crumbling of explicitly patriarchal law has offered men, as well as women, important benefits, including increased freedom from paternal control and reduced obligations for the support of dependents. Partly as the result of the expansion of market exchange, commitments to the care of others came to be seen as sources of personal satisfaction rather than as necessary contributions. It is easier to abolish old rules than to establish new ones: reluctance to acknowledge the economic value of the care services that women continue to provide has made it easy for both men and employers to free ride on voluntary contributions to the production and maintenance of human and social capital.

### Property Rights over Women and Children

Partly because so much feminist scholarship has defined the patriarchal in purely cultural and psychological terms, most economic analysis of property rights focuses on the contrast between private and collective ownership of physical or financial assets.[12] In a prescient exception, the institutionalist economist Steven Cheung published an article in 1972 detailing customary practices in prerevolutionary China that gave parents substantial control over the younger generation, particularly young women.[13] Cheung argued that daughters and daughters-in-law, many with bound feet that confined them to childbearing and family care, were easier to control than sons, whose productive contributions took them farther afield. While Cheung put more emphasis on parental power than on gender inequality, he explicitly recognized patriarchal property rights.

Such rights have a long history in most societies. Subjection to another person's authority tantamount to ownership extended well beyond the purview of formal slavery.[14] As a later chapter will argue, the enslavement of women probably preceded and provided a model for the enslavement of men. Yet patriarchal property rights often intersected with, and were sometimes entirely countervailed by, institutional structures based on other dimensions of collective conflict. For instance, most patriarchal slaveholding societies denied male slaves rights to marriage or family authority, as well as denying female slaves control over their own sexual and reproductive capabilities.[15]

Political approval of coercive and violent abuse of women by their own kin has been widespread. Foot-binding in China persisted for centuries, and genital mutilation remains pervasive in some areas of North Africa and the Middle East. Physical abuse of wives by husbands was legally tolerated in much of Europe until the late nineteenth century. Physical abuse was supplemented by many other forms of physical control. As August Bebel noted in his late nineteenth-century feminist classic, *Women and Socialism*, Prussian husbands had legal authority over whether and how long their wives could breastfeed.[16]

Patriarchal rules typically enforce a harsh sexual double standard, ostensibly in order to allow men to guarantee paternity. This double standard applies even to women long past menopause and remains influential even where access to modern DNA testing makes it possible to ascertain biological parentage. Whatever its motives, control over women's sexuality has long had the effect of limiting their mobility as well as constricting their choices. Fathers and brothers have often treated young female family members as property that could literally be devalued by sexual experience. At the opposite extreme, the institutionalization of prostitution—one of the earliest forms of paid employment for women—provided men with relatively inexpensive sexual gratification free of any responsibility for mutual pleasure or reproductive consequences.[17]

Patriarchal control over women's and children's activities has often been enforced by threat of physical punishment or incarceration. Roman law gave the male head of household the right of life and death over his children. In France, the Napoleonic Code stipulated husbands' authority over wives and gave fathers the right to incarcerate disobedient offspring.[18] In the early nineteenth century, many states within the United States passed laws stipulating wifely subordination, some of which remained legally enforceable until the 1970s.[19] Such laws often codified a husband's right to sexual access without his wife's consent.

Arranged marriages often involve economic exchanges that benefit the natal family of the bride or the groom, giving the older generation incentives to control marriage decisions.[20] Whether the exchange takes the form of bride price or dowry, brides are disadvantaged. In India, the threat of violence against wives is sometimes used to extract greater dowry payments from their families, especially in response to economic stress.[21] In some areas of Sub-Saharan Africa, women cannot leave their husbands unless they repay the transfer of cattle made by their husband to their father.

While explicit property rights over women and children are relatively uncommon today, implicit property rights remain in force. The coercive practices typical of organized prostitution and trafficking are tantamount to slavery.[22] Legal restrictions on women's rights to contraception and abortion tacitly assert public control over women's bodies. Even more common are abuses of omission, such as failure to effectively enforce laws against domestic violence or sexual harassment in the workplace. According to the World Health Organization, more than one-third of all global women have been victims of either physical or sexual violence.[23]

### Gendered and Sexed Restrictions on Individual Rights

Many aspects of traditional family law such as monogamy, restrictions on divorce, obligations for the support of family members, and sanctions against same-sex sexuality limit men's as well as women's choices. Gendered constraints, however, are typically more binding on women. Economists often describe marriage as a partnership in which both husbands and wives gain from trade.[24] Yet few marriage contracts have taken the same form as legal partnerships. Under English common law, for example, a wife relinquished her legal rights to separate property or income. Laws governing married white couples in the United States before 1850 gave husbands formal authority over the activities, earnings, and wealth of their wives and minor children in return for provision of financial support.[25] Financial support was stipulated as a minimal level of subsistence, not a specific share of family income.[26] Early nineteenth-century feminists in the United States campaigned unsuccessfully for legal reforms that would guarantee the rights of wives to one-half their husbands' earnings.[27]

Because marriage constrains the lives of women more narrowly than those of men, rights to divorce are more consequential for them. Patriarchal laws have traditionally made it easier for men to exit marriage than women, with asymmetric grounds for divorce (such as sexual infidelity of the wife but not the husband). Some societies gave only husbands the right to unilateral divorce; under some forms of traditional Islamic law still in force today, a husband can effectively banish a wife from his household by oral proclamation.[28] Such asymmetries have profound implications for health and happiness. Close analysis of the uneven process of divorce law liberalization that got underway in many US states about 1969 suggests that it decreased female suicide, domestic violence, and wife murder.[29]

Harsh laws against unconventional sexual practices, especially those unlikely to lead to conception, have a long and variegated history. Never completely ubiquitous, they were sometimes propagated by colonization. The British Empire famously changed the Indian Penal Code in the 1860s to make all forms of oral or anal sex punishable by life imprisonment, a law that remained on the books until 2018.[30] While the harshest sanctions have often been applied to gay men, women as well as men remain subject to punishment. In 2018 two women in Malaysia were caned for suspicion of attempting lesbian sex.[31]

The legal enforcement of compulsory heterosexuality has often been particularly stringent in societies prizing high birth rates. This historical association does not imply that pro-natalist societies are always homophobic or that homophobia always has pronatalist effects.[32] Rather, it illustrates parallels between the governance of gender and the governance of sexuality that remain significant today: strong adherence to traditional gender norms is often closely associated with disapproval of gay, lesbian, bisexual, and transsexual identities.[33]

Patriarchal family laws have typically given male household heads the power to prevent wives and minor children from engaging in activities outside the home, as well as control over their market earnings. Explicit restrictions on women's access to education and employment have been widespread and remain in effect in many countries. While international campaigns such as the Convention Against All Forms of Discrimination Against Women have steadily gained momentum over the past twenty years, enforcement has proved patchy and uneven.[34]

A number of large international databases detail the current legal and political dimensions of gender inequality, including the Gender, Institutions and Development database developed by the Organization for Economic Cooperation and Development, which scores and weights gender bias in four categories: family legal code, physical integrity, civil liberties, and ownership rights.[35] The design and analysis of a Social Institutions and Gender Index based on variables constructed from this database reveal regional and country-level variations correlated with measured economic outcomes.[36] Not surprisingly, women fare better economically when they have greater legal and political power. Research also shows that women's political empowerment promotes the provision of public goods, investments in education, and lower child mortality.[37]

Since 1995, the United Nations Human Development Report has constructed national indices of gendered economic outcomes. The Gender Development Index assesses women's life expectancy, educational attainment, and per capita income relative to men's; the Gender Empowerment Measure assesses political representation (number of parliamentary seats held), economic opportunity (employment in public office, managerial, and professional positions), and estimated earned income for women compared to men. Both these indices reveal significant progress over time that does not belie the persistence of significant inequalities linked to family law, rights to participate in activities outside the home, and private asset ownership.[38]

### Weak Rights to Remuneration for Family Care

The expansion of legal rights improving women's access to paid employment has distracted attention from the poor specification of women's rights to remuneration for family care from the fathers of their children, adult children themselves, and, more broadly, from the state. The distribution of income and leisure within married couples often benefits men, but coresidence ensures some commonality in living standards. Long-distance migration, separation, divorce, and nonmarriage all tend to reduce both coresidence and income pooling within households, rendering family caregivers, particularly mothers of young children, economically vulnerable.

In many traditional patriarchal systems, strong community sanctions and informal rules required a man to marry and provide support for a woman he impregnated, the so-called "shotgun marriage" rule. A variety of factors contributed to the breakdown of such informal rules, well-documented in the case of the United States.[39] In many areas of the world, nonmarital child-rearing remains uncommon; in others, its prevalence is growing. In Latin America, inequalities based on race/ethnicity and class aligned with gender in ways that left many mothers without legal means of enforcing paternal responsibility from a relatively early date.[40]

Information regarding specification and enforcement of the child support responsibilities of noncustodial parents is hard to come by, particularly outside Europe and the United States. The absence of systematic attention to the distribution of the costs of children between mothers and fathers reflects a general reluctance to quantify intrafamily transfers. An increased burden of supporting dependents, however, can easily outweigh the effects of increases in women's relative wages. (This is discussed in more detail in Chapter 9.)

Mothers and fathers generally receive some economic payback from their children in the form of support and assistance in old age. This expectation has often been formalized in family laws. In eighteenth-century France, for instance, adult children were legally obligated to support their parents, just as parents were obligated to bequeath a minimum share of their assets to children; in England, during the same period, adult children were held legally responsible only for the support of indigent parents, and all parents enjoyed testamentary freedom.[41] In affluent countries, laws dictating intergenerational responsibilities are seldom enforced today, although in some states within the United States adult children have been sued for the costs of nursing home care for their parents.[42]

In some Asian countries, legally stipulated responsibilities for elderly parents still bind. In India, China, and Korea, the expectation that sons would support elderly parents has created a continuing rationale for son preference.[43] Singapore's Maintenance of Parents Act of 1995 goes further than other national legislation, allowing parents to sue their children for failure to provide a specific monthly allowance.[44] The quantitative size of these transfers, however, remains unclear, as does their likely persistence over time. Many women live in countries where neither intrafamily transfers nor public pensions are a reliable source of income in old age.

Many modern pension systems (discussed in more detail in Chapter 8) have based retirement stipends on labor market earnings, penalizing those who take time out of paid employment to provide family care. European countries often provide family care credits and more generous support for single mothers than the United States, where family care does not fulfill the work requirement now imposed on most means-tested assistance. Even in Europe, however, single and widowed mothers remain economically disadvantaged.[45] Women in low-income families of the global South are probably the most vulnerable.[46]

Even in affluent capitalist countries that provide substantial public support for family care, public transfers represent only a small share of total expenditures of time and money on the care and maintenance of children and other dependents.[47] Women pay a disproportionate share of these costs, delivering significant benefits to children and other family members, future employers, and larger communities. Whether the product of their labor is termed human capabilities, human capital, or labor power, the work of producing and maintaining it is largely taken for granted.[48]

Simply reducing the legal authority of husbands and fathers does not necessarily lead to egalitarian gender outcomes. Traditional patriarchal rules offer women support for family care at the cost of subordination to patriarchal authority. Increased scope for individual choice, however, has a double edge: the absence of effective rules governing child support creates a high risk of poverty for many mothers and their children. The tally of patriarchal laws and policies that have been—or need to be— stricken from the books should be accompanied by a list of new ones necessary to encourage more equal distribution of the costs of care.

## Patriarchal Norms and Ideologies

All hierarchical institutional structures rely on normative principles that define both rights and obligations. The patriarchal construction of a binary distinction between appropriate masculine and feminine behavior is imposed on children at an early age. Strict gender bounda- ries are policed in many ways, including sometimes-violent punishment of those who violate them. These boundaries define a moral as well as economic division of labor and are so deeply embedded in language and culture that they often seem invisible until they are transgressed. Many women are conscripted into a permanent army of caregivers, pressed to serve selflessly on a daily basis and stigmatized if they fail to do so.

Moral double standards always accompany—and often outlast—legal double standards. Patriarchal norms of family obligation have economic consequences: men are expected to provide physical protection and financial support for family members; women, to provide emotional nurturance and care for dependents, especially children. Like the legal rules outlined above, however, these norms have asymmetric effects. Mothers raising children on their own are often viewed as failures, fathers in the same circumstances (and there are relatively few of them) as heroes.

Patriarchal norms stipulate, but do not strictly enforce, prescriptions for male virtue. A man who fails to support the child he has fathered may be labeled irresponsible; a mother who abandons a baby is generally considered heartless. A man who buys sex may be excused for succumbing to biological need; a woman who sells sex is generally considered morally bankrupt. Until recently, a man who beat his wife and children was considered more of an embarrassment than a criminal. Strict adherence to traditional gender roles often goes hand in hand with homophobic norms; while public disapproval of homosexuality has softened in recent decades, intolerance remains widespread.[49]

Conventional norms of femininity impose specific costs and risks on women. Defenders of gender segregation assert that it treats women and men as separate but equal. Yet, when legal and cultural borders become more permeable, women are generally more eager to cross into male territory than vice versa—not surprising, since femininity is costly. Female-dominated occupations seldom pay well, and the feminization of paid employment has proceeded far more rapidly than the masculinization of unpaid work.[50] Women have increased their share of financial support for dependents more rapidly than men have increased their share of direct family care. This divergence likely reflects male awareness of care penalties—the disadvantages of specialization in activities that benefit others but yield no immediate or certain economic payoff.

**Normative Power**

The intergenerational transmission of group advantage requires more than mere transfers of time and money. As sociologists have long emphasized, it requires the establishment and maintenance of social institutions that both organize and internalize norms of behavior.[51] Conformity to existing social norms generally favors those in already favored positions.[52] Once seized, rights to authority and property are often sanctified by ideology.[53] Norms of femininity and masculinity can reinforce gender inequality just as patriotic norms can justify aggression against countries, racist norms can fuel white supremacy, and elitist norms can legitimize class disparities. Cultural condemnation of gays, lesbians, bisexuals, transsexuals, and other sexual nonconformists often encourages violence against them.[54]

The effects of socialization reach beyond its effects on individual preferences, influencing the ways in which people perceive the world. Most people are predisposed to believe in a just world in which individuals deserve what they get and get what they deserve.[55] Well-designed experiments show that information regarding rewards trumps information regarding performance. Winners are perceived as significantly more competent than losers even in the presence of direct evidence to the contrary. These results are consistent with the sociological concept of "blaming the victim" and the economic analysis of framing effects.[56]

Belief in a just world can be economically advantageous for a group. It encourages good behavior and hard work and soothes the tensions of collective conflict, promoting cooperation and even docility.[57] Competition creates little ill will if losers are perceived as undeserving.[58] But belief in a just world also has a downside, leading winners to naïvely overestimate their own contributions and blatantly disrespect losers. When and if disparate outcomes are revealed as genuinely unfair, the ensuing conflicts may be vengeful.

The Marxian concept of false consciousness can be restated in terms consistent with modern behavioral economics: social norms affect cognitive perceptions as well as personal preferences. Individuals and groups lack accurate pictures of their social environment and can seldom clearly identify the causes or effects of social power.[59] Belief in the possibility of justice is indispensable to sustained efforts to achieve it; yet such efforts are often preempted by the assumption that people already get what they deserve.

Acknowledgement of conflicts over the social organization of care provision helps explain the ideological construction of gender roles. At the same time, it creates the opportunity to show how a systematic challenge to one particular belief in a just world—that gender inequality is natural—can spill over in subversive ways. Opposition to the feminist project often reveals fear of just such ideological spillovers.

**Compulsory Altruism**

Differences in men's and women's preferences and behavior may or may not be influenced by their biological endowments.[60] Resolution of this long-standing dispute matters less than attention to social institutions that amplify gender differences and mediate their economic consequences. The internalization of social expectations makes patriarchal norms particularly resistant to change.[61] Sociologists sometimes describe norms of gender-appropriate behavior as a literal script that human actors follow, instructions for "doing gender."[62] Much depends, obviously, on who has the power to write—and edit—the script. The economic consequences of the script also matter.

Some feminist theorists describe normative pressure on women as a gendered form of "compulsory altruism," a term that highlights the ways that female subordination tempers the pursuit of individual self-interest.[63] Many important episodes in the history of political economy illustrate how confidence in women's natural or God-given propensities for self-sacrifice enabled the masculine pursuit of economic self-interest. While this history shows that many nineteenth-century economists were anxious about the possibility that women might learn to act as selfishly as men, it also reveals a growing confidence in selfishness as an engine of capitalist economic development.[64]

Indeed, the growing influence of cultural norms derogating male altruism probably helps explain a resurgence of religious doctrines insisting that women should subordinate themselves to the common good defined by men. Many religious doctrines today hold women responsible for the success of a larger family defined by its obedience to a Father who will welcome them to heaven. As recently as twenty years ago, the convention of Southern Baptists, the largest Protestant denomination in the United States, declared that a wife should "submit herself graciously" to her husband's leadership.[65]

Women's own commitments to family care also reproduce gendered norms. In most societies, women devote significantly more time and energy to the care of dependents than men do, modeling personal responsibility in especially direct ways. Daughters often follow their mothers' examples.[66] UNICEF estimates that, globally, girls ages five to fourteen spend three times the hours that boys of the same age do in household chores.[67] Recent analysis of the American Time Use Survey from 2003-14 shows that young women between the ages of fifteen and nineteen spend about 50 percent more time on household chores than young men.[68]

For women, "doing gender" often means "doing care," an expression of the distinctively feminine form of compulsory altruism described above.[69] For instance, questions in the US General Social Survey ask whether respondents agree that "A preschool child will suffer if mother works" and "A working mother can have a good relationship with her children." These questions probe moral disapproval of maternal priorities. Their wording also presumes that caring for a child is not work, a nomenclatural convention that strengthens the presumption that such activities have moral but not economic valence. A longstanding item in both the General Social Survey and the World Values Survey asks whether respondents agree with the statement that "It is much better for everyone if the man is the achiever and the woman takes care of the home and family." This phrasing captures assumptions at the very heart of the traditional gender division of labor, implying that family care is not an achievement.

Social norms play a crucial role in the coordination of human actions, helping ensure altruistic commitments necessary for the sustainability of human society. Patriarchal norms lead to an unfair distribution of the costs of such commitments. Such norms can be and have been successfully renegotiated. This process of cultural bargaining, however, is still underway, and its future outcomes are far from certain.

### Normative Change

Some scientists claim that gender norms are so deeply embedded that they are unlikely to change in fundamental ways, while others warn that their very susceptibility to change threatens the future of human civilization.[70] Neither extreme is credible. Gender norms are somewhat flexible yet resistant to change. They evolved from processes of competition, conflict, and cooperation within families and among larger groups and have changed over time partly as the result of new layers of social division.

Such division helps explain uneven patterns of resistance to patriarchal norms. Steadily increasing levels of support for women's individual rights to education, employment, and leadership are apparent on a global level. Yet policymakers in affluent nations often express more concern about gender inequalities in poor developing countries than in their own, especially when trying to justify military or economic intervention in them. By the same token, efforts to impose gender equality from above or outside can elicit resistance, particularly if they threaten solidarities based on other dimensions of collective identity, such as those based on race/ethnicity or class.

Attitudinal surveys show trends toward greater embrace of basic principles of gender equality in affluent countries, in Asia as well as the West.[71] In the United States, surveys have shown increased support for more egalitarian roles since the 1970s. This trend briefly levelled out in the early 2000s, then resumed its upward trajectory, driven in large part by cohort change and growing support from young men.[72] Most common survey instruments, however, measure acceptance of women moving into masculine roles rather than vice versa. Nor has there been much exploration of attitudes toward public policies that could significantly reduce the costs of parenthood.

Survey wording often seems to offer women a choice between economic dependence on men who provide at least some support for family care or economic independence through wage employment that provides no support for family care. This is not much of a choice. It is hardly surprising that many women as well as men prefer norms of family commitment—however gendered and unequal—to norms of individual autonomy and selfish choice. Survey rhetoric itself impedes efforts to find a better, gender-neutral balance between autonomy and care.

Whenever economic success is determined largely by individual competition for paying jobs, caregivers will always operate at a disadvantage. Committed parents (and mothers, in particular) will pay an economic penalty in lifetime access to income and wealth. The tendency to view commitments to the care of others as optional lifestyle decisions rather than as socially necessary commitments reflects the ascendance of a market-centric individualism that defines productivity by private rates of return and measures gender equality solely by relative earnings.

Norms of feminine obligation are not merely ideological devices for oppressing women, and men are not the only beneficiaries. Employers and other members of society (including dependent children, the sick, and the frail elderly) also benefit from reliable low-cost care provision. The anger infusing many anti-feminist campaigns reflects the fear that, as women opt out of their traditional roles, the overall level of care for others with dwindle. This is not an entirely unrealistic fear: the renegotiation of gender roles requires a renegotiation of broader norms of obligation for the care of others, provoking resistance from all those hoping to avoid paying a larger share of the costs.

## Patriarchal Assets

Patriarchal political and cultural institutions are influenced by patterns of asset ownership and vice versa. This circular causality is also typical of other structures of collective power, including those traditionally defined by ownership of the primary means of production for exchange and capital accumulation. Capital, as conventionally defined, is a form of wealth that yields a future rate of return. It is often parsed into two categories: real assets such as land or machinery, and financial assets in the form of stocks, bonds, or cash. As modern accounting practices indicate, however, capital can also take intangible, less easily quantified forms: brand, reputation, software, or exclusive rights to particular forms of intellectual property.[73] This loosening of definitional boundaries is also reflected in the increasing usage of terms such as "human capital," "natural capital," and "social capital."

As hinted in the earlier discussion of patriarchal property rights, access to all these assets can be gendered. Patterns of ownership of real and financial assets by gender and age offer a particularly obvious parallel with traditional analyses of class inequality. Endowments of—and access to—other forms of capital are also relevant, because they help explain the persistence of many different kinds of group-based inequality over time.

### Real and Financial Assets

Historical restrictions on women's independent ownership of real and financial assets have been well documented, and they remain in effect in many countries today.[74] Institutional details vary: in some legal regimes (both formal and customary law) property acquired within marriage is subject to common ownership by both spouses; in others, husbands gain control of their wives' property ("coverture"). Historically, women's primary access to real and financial assets has come through inheritance of a portion of their fathers' or their husbands' estates, an economic arrangement rewarding obeisance to male authority.[75] The Married Women's Property Acts passed in the late nineteenth century in the United States and England led to a major redistribution of wealth.[76]

Most empirical studies of the distribution of wealth take households rather than individuals as their unit of analysis, often generating misleading results. For instance, the long-held belief that wealth was distributed more equally in colonial America than in the nineteenth and twentieth centuries is based on accounting that ignores legal institutions such as coverture, indentured servitude, and slavery.[77] Twentieth-century land reforms in Latin America, initially hailed as boons for low-income households, often concentrated private property ownership in male hands until later efforts were made to establish women's independent titles.[78] In many areas of the world, including Africa, privatization of previously common property has taken place at women's expense.[79] In South Asia, male resistance has limited the effectiveness of legal reforms designed to improve women's control over assets.[80]

Even in affluent countries such as the United States, the gender wealth gap exceeds the gender earnings gap.[81] Women with less wealth than their partners have less bargaining power within households and greater vulnerability to poverty on their own.[82] Policy design matters. One recent study of a housing reform in China that gave individual employees the opportunity to purchase the homes they had been renting from the state shows that male ownership altered patterns of consumption and housework in men's favor within married-couple households.[83] Gender differences in retirement assets (including pension benefits) often combine with women's tendency to outlive their older husbands to generate high rates of poverty among elderly women.

### Human Capital and Natural Capital

Neoclassical economists often use the term "human capital" in a very specific way that implies that everyone is, literally, a capitalist, making decisions to invest in their own future earning power. Yet human capital can be interpreted more broadly as what Marxian economists have referred to as "labor power." Both the distribution of productive capabilities and rates of return on such capabilities are shaped by social institutions and collective bargaining.[84] In a wage-based economy, restrictions on women's access to education and employment, like restrictions based on race/ethnicity or citizenship, reduce bargaining power and lower earnings.

Both the neoclassical and the classical Marxian traditions have largely ignored distributional conflict over the process of producing and maintaining the human beings that provide the substrate for the development of productive skills. This process of reproduction, indispensable to economic sustainability as well as evolutionary success, is a costly one, yielding benefits that are long in coming and difficult to commandeer. Future generations have the characteristic of a public good—they are not privately owned and they are not bought and sold in a competitive market. Children do not negotiate with parents over how and when they should be brought into the world or what kind of upbringing they should receive. In this respect, human capital has something in common with natural capital, the unpriced endowments of resources and ecological services on which all life on earth depends.[85]

Women and men are endowed with different physical assets. In general, women have a comparative advantage in the physical production of children. They also pay a greater physiological cost for them, face far stricter limits on their total number of offspring, and lose their reproductive capacity at a younger age than men. From an evolutionary perspective, mothers have more to lose than fathers do from the loss of a child.[86] Evolutionary biologists argue that natural selection rewards males for short-run success in mating, while it rewards females for a longer run objective: success in rearing offspring to maturity.[87] In most societies today women devote more resources to children—and to kin and communities that help care for children—than men do.[88]

Feminist social theorists have long been justifiably suspicious of overemphasis on biological differences between men and women, often aimed to justify the status quo.[89] The early misogyny of evolutionary psychology, however, has been superceded by more persuasive efforts at disciplinary synthesis.[90] Feminist evolutionary biologists emphasize the interplay of gender, sex, and collective conflict as influences on both individual and group selection.[91] Male specialization in risky and violent activities benefits their kin, but it also gives them potential to dominate and harass women; female specialization in family care benefits their kin but can also reduce their bargaining power and increase their economic vulnerability.

Women and men are endowed with different biological assets, but social institutions and economic environments largely determine the valuation of these assets. Unlike their precursors, capitalist institutions governing wage employment do not encourage population growth—they can take some credit for encouraging lower birth rates. At the same time, however, they have reduced economic incentives for individuals to invest in anyone else's productive capabilities. As labor market competition becomes increasingly based on human capital/labor power, collective efforts to restrict other people's access to education and skills can pay off.

Even where the "magic of the market" works as presumed, its effects are spotty, because markets are embedded in a much larger economic system in which both mothers and Mother Nature play a hugely important role. Patriarchal institutions facilitated the emergence of capitalist institutions through hierarchical control over reproduction. Not surprisingly, the weakening of patriarchal institutions has implications for capitalist institutions as well as for social relations based on gender, age, and sexuality.

Consider, for instance, the hypothetical impact of policies aimed to ensure that women have exactly the same probability of becoming successful capitalists as men. A gender-neutral distribution of real and financial assets would probably mitigate gender inequality, but not by much, unless the distribution of the costs of family and community care were also equalized. Patriarchal and capitalist institutions have this in common: they are both institutional structures that disempower those who invest in the capabilities of other people, putting women at a particular disadvantage. The impact of this disadvantage, however, is mediated by many other dimensions of collective identity.

### Social and Cultural Capital

When membership in a family or a larger group offers future benefits in the form of reciprocity and mutual aid, it represents a form of capital. Sometimes the term "social capital" is used to describe a generic level of trust in other people that is required for all forms of cooperation, including market exchange.[92] Trust often offers tangible economic payoffs and is also reinforced by such payoffs.[93] Levels of civic engagement and community solidarity, however, do not tell the whole story.

As sociologists have long emphasized, groups often create, accumulate, and hoard social capital as a way of advancing their collective interests.[94] Group membership, and often group allegiance, becomes a requirement of access to this form of capital. Membership may be defined by personal characteristics such as gender or race/ethnicity; it may also be signaled by subtle cues that indicate cultural capital, such as modes of dress or personal demeanor. For obvious reasons, social capital plays an important role in the formation of human capital.[95] The interaction between them, sometimes described in terms of neighborhood effects, can lead to the unintended reproduction of inequalities among groups.[96]

Social capital can also be used in more intentional ways to reinforce group advantage by enforcing discrimination against outsiders. Even libertarian strains of economic theory acknowledge that people may form clubs that enable them to restrict access to the public goods that they create.[97] Examples range from the mundane (private golf courses) to the economically consequential (private colleges, labor unions, business organizations). Many accounts of discrimination against women refer to the influence of the "old boys' network." One recent effort to quantify this influence in the United States finds that it directly affects employment prospects: people in white male networks receive twice as many job leads as those in female/minority networks.[98]

Ownership of real and financial assets shapes endowments of human and social capital, but it does not wholly determine them. In modern capitalist economies, college and postgraduate degrees represent an easily capitalized asset. Access to publicly financed education and health services reduces individual costs and potential indebtedness. Likewise, the legal right to immigrate to a high-wage economy, like the cultural advantage of networked access to information and employment, has quantifiable value. The coexistence of these different types of assets helps explain the complex interactions among different group inequalities that complicate the strategic environment for collective action.

## Structures of Collective Power

While some patriarchal institutions directly specify rights and obligations based on gender, age, and sexual orientation, others create disadvantage by failing to adequately reward the work of caring for others. Women lacking individual rights are easily pressed to specialize in care provision, which, in turn, reduces their ability to gain new rights. Caregivers require short-run support primarily because they provide long-run social benefits that are difficult to privately capture or capitalize. The notion that care does not represent a "productive" contribution legitimates the view that women depend on men more than men depend on women and makes women's relative lack of bargaining power in the home and in the labor market seem inevitable.

The patriarchal institutions outlined above dovetail to create a resilient structure of collective power that creates distinct—though variable— economic advantages for adult heterosexual men. Other structures of collective power based on aspects of group membership such as race/ethnicity, nationality, citizenship, and class can be explained in similar terms (and this list is not exhaustive). The political consequences hinge on interactions among the institutional structures that create the spaces where human agency comes into play. Many women, less confined than they once were, deeply appreciate the potential for structural change.

# 3

# Gender, Structure, and Collective Agency

If women can act on their common interests to reconfigure social institutions that put them at an economic disadvantage, so too can other groups. A general principle applies: tunnels and ceilings confine many people to the bottom of hierarchical structures unless and until they seize opportunities for alteration. The probability of success depends partly on which opportunities arise, whether as a result of structural weaknesses and/or external shocks. Even more crucial is the ability of heterogeneous groups to maintain solidarity and forge alliances based on political principle and architectural knowledge.

Intersectional political economy can build on important theoretical precedents even as it moves beyond them. Competing paradigms of economic inequality are typically based on competing claims regarding structure and agency. Those who hold individuals fully accountable for their own successes and failures typically ignore the impact of institutional structures, but those who blame institutional structures often fail to explain how or why these were constructed. Neither classical Marxian theory nor conventional neoclassical economics offer persuasive explanations of gender inequality, but scholars influenced by both traditions are developing a conceptual vocabulary that can illumine structures of collective power.

The visual metaphor of a pyramidal maze or labyrinth illustrates a social system that creates distinct entry points and obstacles for members of different groups, affecting the level of economic security they are likely to reach. Individuals and groups make strategic decisions in a dark, confusing environment in which the best path upward is seldom perfectly clear. Those who reach the pinnacle often gain the power to influence laws, ideologies, and asset distributions in ways that reproduce their own advantage. Yet the top of any pyramid depends upon the stability—the literal lack of movement—of its base.

## Structure Versus Agency

Different views of individual and social responsibility have stark political consequences. Most people, regardless of partisan allegiances, believe that bad social structures can undermine actors' good behavior. They typically disagree on which structures are good ones. From a conservative perspective, state interference in the economy threatens to undermine individual initiative; from a progressive perspective, capitalist institutions threaten to demoralize, disempower, or exploit members of disadvantaged groups.

Celebration of individual rather than collective action is a defining feature of conservative worldviews, memorably expressed by British prime minister Margaret Thatcher: "Who is society? There is no such thing! There are individual men and women and there are families and no government can do anything except through people and people look to themselves first."[1] Conservatives embrace markets as ideal structures of social organization because they afford ample scope for individual choice. They construe state participation in the economy, such as spending on social safety nets, as a form of interference with the market that discourages individuals from taking responsibility for themselves and their families.

This paradigmatic divide carries over to debates relevant to gender equality. Consider, for instance, the Paycheck Fairness Act proposed (but not enacted) in the United States, which would make it easier for women to determine whether they are paid less than men in their workplace and to join class action lawsuits to challenge discrimination. Support for this act has long been heavily divided along partisan lines: most Democrats favor it as a way of overcoming unfair practices. Most Republicans consider it unnecessary interference with the labor market, insisting that the gender pay gap simply reflects women's choices to enter less well-paying jobs. As one conservative commentator puts it,

Proponents of the wage-gap myth like to claim that the patriarchy pushes women into those less lucrative careers. That's a sad commentary on their way of thinking—their notion that women are simply too dumb or weak to think for themselves and choose the career they actually want.[2]

Contrasting views of structure and agency are also deeply embedded in most economic research on gender inequality. Traditional Marxists tend to attribute gender inequality to capitalism as a mode of production, neoclassical economists to factors that have less to do with collective power than with individual preferences and abilities.

### Classical Marxian Political Economy

Mode of production, defined by the way surplus is appropriated, is a central concept within Marxian political economy. From this perspective, a social structure labeled "capitalism"—a set of institutions including private property, production for profit, and wage employment—develops the forces of production. Modes of production succeed one another in a stylized sequence or some variation thereof: primitive communism, feudalism, capitalism, socialism, communism. Marx described capitalism as an advance over feudal and patriarchal social relations (and yes, he used the p-word), but he also emphasized internal tensions that would doom capitalism to periodic economic crises.[3]

The traditional theory of historical materialism treats ownership of productive assets as an economic foundation, with legal and normative institutions as superstructure or roof. Class structure represents a pyramid of oppression that exists independently of the motives, morals, or preferences of individual employers. Wage earners create a surplus because they are paid less than the value that they create. One iconic illustration, published in the 1911 edition of *Industrial Worker*, depicts royalty and state leaders at the summit, with clergy ("we fool you") and the military ("we shoot you") above capitalists themselves.

Class structures are generated by largely impersonal forces that people may not correctly perceive, much less fully understand. Ideological obfuscation or false consciousness creates the illusion that most individuals deserve what they get and get what they deserve.[4] Individual actions are far less likely to have a significant impact than one particular form of collective identity and action: class struggle. With some important exceptions, Marxian scholars treat both classes and families as entities that share common economic interests, even if they are divided as a result of misinformation or false consciousness.

This depiction of institutional structure explains why Marx and Engels treated gender inequality as the offspring of class inequality. Their hopes for a unified working-class struggle against capitalism jaundiced their views of the early women's rights movement, which they considered a distraction from anti-capitalist mobilization. Engels's treatise *Origins of the Family, Private Property and the State* aimed to counter *Woman and Socialism*, a socialist feminist tract by August Bebel that drew a direct analogy between the class interests of capitalists and the gender interests of men.[5] Most Marxian economists today consider Bebel an unimportant revisionist.

The conflation of class and economic interests carries over into later Marxist efforts to explain persistent gender inequality under capitalism. The first wave of Marxist-feminist attention to women's unpaid labor in the home insisted that it primarily benefited employers, enabling them to pay lower wages.[6] The International Wages for Housework Campaign successfully called attention to the value of unpaid work—and the degree to which capitalism as a system depends on it, but never clarified how such wages would be determined, or to whom, exactly, they would be paid. The possibility that gender inequality might be rooted in a distinct institutional structure or that men might act on their collective interests was widely considered a radical feminist diversion.[7]

In the *Communist Manifesto*, Marx and Engels characterized capitalist development as a process quickly undermining patriarchal—and, indeed, all non-class-based inequalities—a characterization that could explain their relative lack of interest in them. Some historians influenced by the Marxian tradition have persuasively argued that patriarchal institutions predated capitalism, serving, for instance, as a central pillar of the feudal mode of production.[8] Until recently, however, most focused primarily on the historical and political contingencies of class conflict without much attention to either gender or race/ethnicity.[9] Where gender inequality comes into the story, private property and capitalism take the blame: influential accounts of British history, for example, argue that women enjoyed substantive economic equality with men when both worked side-by-side to produce goods and services for family consumption.[10]

The emergence of a capitalist world system is sometimes considered the source of all economic evil. Immanuel Wallerstein, for instance, describes a flow of surplus from the semi-proletarianized workers of the global periphery to more affluent countries that is entirely driven by class dynamics.[11] No significant forms of intraclass conflict appear to come into play, except as a by-product of surplus extraction.[12] Even some efforts to bring gender inequality to center stage treat class conflict as the deus ex machina. Silvia Federici describes capitalists as the primary culprits of the witch hunts that convulsed Europe as early as the fourteenth century.[13] She relies on a rather loose definition of capitalists here (they closely resemble feudal lords). And what of the likelihood that many other men derived benefits from the systematic intimidation of women?

Some modern Marxian theorists note the similarities between women's family commitments and unpriced environmental assets, devalued and degraded by pressures to maximize short-run economic benefits.[14] This similarity complements a theory of economic crisis quite distinct from that originally articulated by Marx (and similar to that developed in later chapters of this book): a crisis of social and ecological sustainability. Yet it is by no means clear—except by a priori assumption—that capitalists are the only group eager to sacrifice long-term sustainability for short-run gains, or that capitalism is the only structure of collective power that is vulnerable to crisis.

**Conventional Neoclassical Theory**

While traditional Marxists see a world dominated by one pernicious mode of production, conventional neoclassical economists see a world that always has been (and always will be) inhabited by self-interested individual agents. The textbook version of microeconomics features Rational Economic Man maximizing his utility by buying and selling in competitive markets, responding to externally determined options. Herbert Simon offers a more general metaphor for emphasis on a problem-solving agent: a mouse in a maze, searching for cheese.[15] The maze, as structure, is taken as a given; the mice take no responsibility for its design. Whether mouse or man (or a family of either), the agents' preferences are also given, though perhaps influenced by previous rounds of competition for the cheese.

These theoretical priors yield a theory of discrimination based on preferences regarding characteristics such as race/ethnicity, gender, sexual orientation, citizenship, and so on. Employers' preferences influence their hiring decisions. As Gary Becker famously argued, such discrimination is potentially costly, because it is inefficient.[16] Discrimination by some employers lowers the demand for those discriminated against, lowering their wages. Employers with no desire to discriminate benefit because they can hire these workers at a lower wage, eventually driving their wages up. Rational self-interest gradually erodes irrational discrimination. If the metaphorical maze is a competitive market unencumbered by state regulation, then competition among employers should penalize those with discriminatory preferences. These employers will gradually disappear, and all those previously discriminated against, including women, will gain better access to the cheese.

Another preference-based explanation of inequality in earnings, more specific to gender, suggests that women simply care less about money—and more about fulfilling family commitments—than men do. They are willing to work for less pay in return for fewer responsibilities or shorter working hours, and they are also more willing to take responsibility for the financial support of children, despite the increased risks of falling into poverty.[17] Such preferences are treated as characteristics of the agents rather than as outcomes of institutional structure, and the possibility that the institutional structure might have formative influences on agents goes largely unexplored.

The convenient presumption that preferences (and the norms that shape them) can be taken as a given violates Simon's more holistic description of a maze in which agents engage in problem-solving behavior that could, in principle, include collective action to change the structure of the maze itself. Human beings are social creatures who come into the world through the bodies of others and learn a mother tongue. Imperfect but influential processes of socialization encourage children to conform and cooperate with those who raise them. Many preferences are inculcated through instruction, habit, and repetition.

Becker directly confronts the relationship between individuals and families, if only to simplify it. He posits an altruistic household head who acts as a benevolent dictator, using his power to induce others (including rotten kids) to also maximize household utility.[18] Oddly, Beckerian families operate much like miniature socialist societies, with leaders enforcing sharing principles: all for one and one for all. Institutional rules giving men greater bargaining power than women and children become irrelevant, because adults—while largely self-interested in the market—are largely altruistic in the home.[19]

In *Accounting for Tastes*, Becker notes that parents try to inculcate altruistic preferences in their children (especially those pertaining to the care of elderly parents) and that rich people try to inculcate docility in the poor. Yet he also insists that individuals choose to let themselves be influenced in this way.[20] Because their autonomy remains inviolable, they must take responsibility for every outcome. Because they are self-interested everywhere but within families, they seldom engage in collective action. Why would individuals choose to cooperate with others, given the risk that others will free ride on their efforts?

This agent-centered model enables magical optimism. In the competitive market, employers who discriminate against women will be punished by market forces; in the altruistic family, personal affection will neutralize the effect of any institutional rules that give adult men power over women and children. If social change occurs, it is attributed to the impact of external shocks, such as technological change, on the gender division of labor. For instance, Claudia Goldin attributes gradual increases in the ratio of female to male wages in the United States during the nineteenth century to the expansion of jobs requiring mental skills rather than physical strength.[21] Rick Geddes and Dean Lueck argue that the increasing value of human capital gave men incentives to relinquish power over women.[22] Jeremy Greenwood, Ananth Seshadi, and Mehmet Yorukoglu describe labor-saving household devices such as washing machines as "engines of women's liberation."[23]

Technology, however, is not destiny. Its effects are mediated by social institutions. Women had to struggle for access to education in order to move into white-collar employment. They had to organize for the right to vote alongside men, and they had to persuade husbands who controlled household income to invest in new consumer durables that would lighten their workload. We know that the "contraceptive revolution" in the United States during the twentieth century had positive economic consequences for women precisely because of significant variation across states in hard-won legal access to the new technology.[24] The importance of external factors such as technological change does not render institutionalized inequalities unimportant. From a feminist perspective, the progress of women's rights requires less explanation than the forceful resistance to such progress.

# Mediating Structure and Agency

While the paradigmatic pressure to choose either structure or agency as a starting point remains significant, many economists and sociologists offer a synthetic approach, describing institutions as places where agents both create structure and are contained by it.[25] Intersectional political economy can draw on new insights emerging from both the Marxian and the neoclassical traditions to develop a broader panorama of the interplay between structure and agency. More explicit attention to patriarchal institutions can enrich this theoretical landscape.

## Unpacking Modes of Production

Today, many scholars influenced by the Marxian tradition reject the notion that capitalism can be described as a unitary, hegemonic system. Historical experience has revealed that collective ownership and management of the means of production is more difficult than anticipated. A variety of explanations have been given for the perversions of state socialism (sometimes referred to as "state capitalism"); lack of attention to the institutional infrastructure necessary for democratic planning surely played a significant role.[26] The dramatic divergence of postsocialist trajectories in the former Soviet Union and China, as well as in smaller countries such as Cuba and Vietnam, also challenges any simplistic stage-based theory of history.

Many contemporary analyses of capitalism highlight variations and permutations. The social democracies of northwestern Europe are characterized by greater public provision of services and less earnings inequality than the so-called liberal regimes of the United States and Great Britain; countries that experienced colonial domination typically develop different class dynamics than others.[27] Some varieties of capitalism provide more centralized national direction and skill development than others, insuring workers to some extent against job loss.[28] While differences based on aspects of group identity such as gender or race/ethnicity seldom enter these discussions, attention to institutional dynamics enlarges consideration of them.[29]

The Marxian concept of social structures of accumulation also provides a broader frame, pointing to changes over time in historical and institutional specifics.[30] In both Western Europe and the United States, the decades after World War II were characterized by a steady growth of gross domestic product that delivered comfortable profit to capitalists and increased real wages to workers.[31] Gradually, however, increased global competition began to take its toll in these regions, reducing the power of workers and leading to the emergence of neoliberal policies aimed to reduce welfare state expenditures. While changes in the gender composition of wage employment over this period are treated largely as the outcome of purely capitalist dynamics, they do at least enter the story.[32]

Increased attention to divisions among workers has also created space for more nuanced approaches. Marxist sociologist Erik Olin Wright designates a professional-managerial class that inhabits a position intermediate between owners and workers. Like the petit-bourgeoisie in classical Marxism, this class has somewhat contradictory and contingent political interests.[33] Many institutional factors, including public policies, barriers to entry, and skill shortages, allow some workers to earn significantly higher wages than others. Institutional rules that disadvantage some workers on the basis of their gender, sexual orientation, race/ethnicity, or citizenship clearly fit this picture. While Wright reserves the term "exploitation" for class differences, he notes the significant impact of nonclass forms of oppression.[34]

In the wake of financial crisis in the United States, growing attention to inequality in wealth and income found political expression in the Occupy Movement's slogan "We are the 99 percent." This is a slogan that evokes structure—a rectangular building of rooms crowned by a tall spire representing the top 1 percent, a hypertrophied version of New York's Empire State Building. The slogan urges unified resistance against a tiny minority peering down at everyone else, suggesting that the inhabitants below are unified by their economic vulnerability. A spire that grows too tall can lose its stability, becoming more likely to topple or be toppled. Still, the big difference between those on the top floors and those on the bottom will remain.

Some Marxian theorists describe distinct modes of production linked together or articulated with one another in a larger metastructure or social formation.[35] The term "articulation" concedes the possibility of separate moving parts, more robot than edifice.[36] Feminists working within the Marxian tradition often embrace such hybrid forms. Antonella Picchio rejects romantic views of working-class family life along with assumptions that gender conflict results from capitalism alone.[37] Meg Luxton challenges the notion that capitalism is able to establish a "sex-gender system" that unambiguously serves its own interests.[38] Efforts to insert independent gender dynamics into analysis of an otherwise unitary system complement socialist feminist efforts to describe dual systems such as patriarchal capitalism.[39]

These more complex formulations have inspired new intersectional accounts of transitions to capitalism. Wally Seccombe provides a magisterial account of gendered conflicts and domestic violence within the working-class families of northwestern Europe, explicitly pointing to intersections between capitalist and patriarchal interests.[40] Cedric Robinson rewrites the history of the transition to capitalism in Western Europe, emphasizing racial and national conflicts and arguing that racial dynamics inflected capitalism long before the rise of colonial power.[41] Insisting on the need to move beyond dual structures, David McNally calls for a "historical materialist theory of multiple oppressions."[42]

These revisionists describe social structures with unpredictable contours and jagged edges rather than tidy shapes, acknowledging many different forms of domination and oppression. Still, they are reluctant to place nonclass conflicts on a par with those based on class, on the grounds that they have less economic basis. Perhaps this is because they define both "the economy" and "exploitation" too narrowly (an argument I make in subsequent chapters). They also seem oblivious to theoretical innovations emerging from the neoclassical tradition, perhaps considering them tainted by their family history.

**Beyond Constrained Optimization**

Models of decision-making that rely on stylized versions of rational choice subject to externally determined constraints are still enshrined in college-level textbooks. However, more creative and flexible approaches now make their way into mainstream economic journals, challenging the view that Rational Economic Person is either perfectly rational or entirely self-interested. Neoclassical confidence that market exchange is always efficient has been undermined by growing attention to its unintended consequences, including the horrific costs of global climate change and sharp increases in economic inequality.

New theories emerging from other disciplines—especially evolutionary biology and psychology—have also undercut neoclassical assumptions. For many decades, a popular interpretation of Darwinian theory emphasized individual-level competition, presuming that self-interest dominates all human interactions except those among close kin.[43] This theory has now been largely supplanted by the theory of multilevel selection, which holds that groups, as well as individuals, engage in competition with one another.[44] Groups are more likely to succeed if they develop a level of cooperation suited to their particular technical and strategic environment.[45] As a result, evolutionary pressures have almost certainly encouraged behavioral tendencies to strong reciprocity or conditional cooperation within groups.[46]

At the same time, the assumption that families can be treated as sites of complete solidarity has been shaken by attention to conflicts of interest between men and women, mothers and fathers, and parents and offspring.[47] Unitary models of household decision-making have been largely displaced by bargaining models that acknowledge the impact of differences in relative fallback positions.[48] While these models seldom ask how—or by whom—such differences in fallbacks were created, they inescapably raise such questions.[49]

The grip of conventional neoclassical assumptions has also been loosened by the emergence of behavioral economics, which explicitly incorporates insights from psychology. Humans may aspire to rationality, but cognitive limitations and visceral emotions limit their success.[50] Experimental evidence shows that the stress of poverty can impede cognitive functions, and people may internalize negative stereotypes that handicap their performance.[51] At the other end of the class spectrum, irrational exuberance among investors can lead to stock market crashes.[52] A bit of self-reflection has emerged: it seems that students who decide to study business and/or economics generally have more selfish attitudes than others do.[53]

Neoclassical economists have also grappled with the economic impact of force and violence. In the aftermath of World War II, the US government subsidized the development of conflict theory, combining principles of strategic optimization with game theory.[54] One pioneer in this area, economist Jack Hirshleifer, comes close to Marxism by another name when he argues that no group that anticipates significant economic benefits from forcible seizure of another group's property would be likely to engage in peaceful trade, tagging such opportunism "the dark side of the force."[55] While conflict theory has been applied primarily to military actions, it could also help explain the emergence of social institutions enshrined by the threat of violence.

When the term "externalities" first entered the vocabulary of neoclassical welfare economics, it was confined to bucolic, almost picturesque examples of unintended consequences, such as the benefits a beekeeper's pollinators might incidentally provide to neighboring farmers. Today, estimates of the market value of economic externalities loom larger than the size of the market economy itself.[56] Social externalities, such as the benefits of early childhood education and the costs of child poverty, have also begun to receive quantitative attention.[57] It is a short step from consideration of these specific public goods to a broader analysis of care provision as a source of valuable unpriced services crucial to the economic system as a whole.

Economists influenced by the Marxian tradition are sometimes skeptical of noncooperative game theory, which focuses on the strategic decisions of rational agents. But many of the classic payoff matrices central to this genre, such as the prisoner's dilemma, highlight the disastrous outcomes that can result from the unregulated pursuit of individual self-interest. A famous payoff matrix labeled "Battle of the Sexes" turns on a rather trivial coordination problem—whether a man and a woman desirous of one another's company, despite different preferences, will meet at an opera or at a prizefight. As later chapters will suggest, other coordination problems have rather more profound implications for gender inequality.

Some recent efforts to explore the interaction between technology and social norms go well beyond traditional neoclassical assumptions. Mukesh Eswaran summarizes a number of useful efforts to explain the emergence of patriarchal institutions in pre-capitalist societies.[58] Nathan Nunn, Alberto Alesina, and Paola Giuliano build on earlier research by Ester Boserup to explain why plough agriculture, more physically demanding than hoe agriculture, may have empowered men more than women.[59] Despite a hint of technological determinism, their emphasis on the long-run effects of an initial asymmetry in productive contributions relies heavily on the effect of social institutions that reproduce gender inequality. Once established, differences in institutional power are difficult to alter, exemplifying what is aptly termed "path dependence."

### Rethinking Structures

In Marxian thinking, structure is defined by ownership (or not) of the means of production, or—more broadly—financial wealth. In neoclassical thinking, structure takes the form of endowments and technologies that individuals bring to markets. In both cases, specific social institutions are also implied but not categorized in terms of their implications for diverse forms of collective aggrandizement. Not all social institutions lead to distributional inequality; some clearly enhance efficiency. Still, it often remains important to ask "efficient for whom"?

Consider a pyramidal maze within which prizes are produced and distributed, with most of them concentrated at the very top. This meta-structure or system could be constituted by many different structures that, while intersecting and overlapping, have distinct blueprints, shaping possible paths to the top. People are born into this maze at different levels, and their starting points affect the capabilities they develop and the obstacles they face—institutional arrangements that include glass ceilings, sticky spots, booby traps, and locked doors. Their likelihood of overcoming such obstacles depends in large part on their starting point.

The pyramidal maze is not merely the site of an intergenerational relay race. It is also a site for appropriation, production, reproduction, and the social reproduction of groups. Even those who are not making upward progress must keep moving, if only in circles, in order to adequately provide for themselves and their families. Individuals may set out on their own, following the route of least resistance. They are more likely to join with others, forming teams that try to get ahead. Teams can sometimes achieve the ability to modify the obstacles and alter the paths, compounding their advantage. Social institutions widen channels for some groups and narrow them for others.

Structure, as well as agency, is intersectional, sorting individuals by a variety of overlapping characteristics. Not all the obstacles and entry points are artifacts of class structure: some are based on exclusionary rules and discriminatory norms that limit chances of joining successful teams or forming effective alliances. Institutional structures of collective power constitute filters of advantage and disadvantage based on many different dimensions of group identity. Their effects are probabilistic, rather than deterministic: individuals are sometimes smart enough or lucky enough (or both) to outsmart them.

One could think of the pyramidal maze as the three-dimensional playing board of diverse overlapping games that create chutes and ladders, whirlpools and dead ends. The players can bargain with one another to modify the games, but they are also, in a sense, a product of the games, which influence their preferences, perceptions, and abilities as well as their strategic options. Many agents near the bottom adapt to the limited range of choices that they face; their energy feels better spent trying to advance rather than to alter the environment. By contrast, those starting near the top find it easy to defend their advantage by reinforcing or constructing obstacles.

This stylized image provides a way of picturing changes in patriarchal institutional structures built into larger complex systems. Women, sexual minorities, and youth tolerate such institutions until better options begin to seem feasible. In considering such options, they also recognize other dimensions of their collective identity such as race/ethnicity, class, and citizenship. Everyone operates in a confusing and risky strategic environment where gains in one corridor can be countervailed by losses in another. Nonetheless, women share a common interest in the development of social institutions that widen their opportunities. They also have something in common with other groups that face unfair obstacles, creating the potential for alliances based on principles of economic justice.

## Collective Agency

Class analysis focuses on the structure of the wealth pyramid, as well as individual locations within it; interest-group theory describes how individuals voluntarily join together to pursue common interests. Groups defined by gender, age, sexuality, race/ethnicity, and citizenship do not fit into either category; they are not reducible to wealth ownership (or type of employment) but are, for the most part, socially assigned. We are born into families, communities, and countries with distinctive names, and within them we are categorized by gender, age, sexual orientation, and many other descriptors. Some such categories have significant economic consequences.

Our allegiances, as well as our ability to define the groups to which we are assigned, are almost always limited. Yet we all enjoy some scope for strategic decisions as we create a portfolio of commitments to different types of collective identity and action. Does identification with a group enable the pursuit of group interests, or do opportunities for the pursuit of group interests enable group identification? The causality probably works both ways.[60] When people gain from cooperation with others, they often develop feelings of commitment to them; by the same token, feelings of commitment encourage mutually advantageous cooperation.

Competition can intensify allegiance to a group and hostility to those outside it, as in the famous Robbers' Cave experiment in which young boys similar in many respects were divided into teams and easily set against one another.[61] Opportunities for exploitation of others have similar consequences, leading to derogation of them. As Ta-Nehisi Coates explains in a different context, "race is the child of racism, not the father."[62] Patriarchal institutions that deliver economic benefits to men encourage sexist and sexually abusive attitudes toward women. While membership in a prosperous group delivers privileges that reward allegiance to it, membership in a less successful group may elicit less commitment, precisely because it is so costly.

### Class First?

Socialist activists have long recognized conflicting group interests as fault lines of political mobilization, but their visceral dislike of oppression has often been overshadowed by emphasis on the economic centrality of class. The Marxist geographer David Harvey notes, for instance, that capitalism is permeated with race and gender oppression but that the "logic of capital" is not affected by them.[63] He makes no mention of any "logic" of race or of gender. Some Marxist-feminist scholars, such as Lise Vogel, explicitly reject the notion that class, race, and gender are comparable categories of difference with potentially equal causal weight.[64] Nancy Fraser makes gentler distinctions, sometimes describing struggles around race/ethnicity and gender as struggles for recognition rather than redistribution and contrasting group identity with class interests.[65] But as Fraser notes, class consciousness also entails a struggle for recognition based on a common identities. Interests and identities often go together.

The classics of Marxian political economy acknowledge this issue in their treatment of "false consciousness." Marx himself described the ordinary English worker of his day as susceptible to cooptation:

> In relation to the Irish worker he feels himself a member of the ruling nation and so turns himself into a tool of the aristocrats and capitalist of his country against Ireland, thus strengthening their domination over himself . . . his attitude towards him is much the same as that of the 'poor whites' to the 'niggers' in the former slave states of the U.S.A.[66]

Vladimir Lenin further developed the concept of an aristocracy of labor which, he believed, shifted the epicenter of potential revolution toward less economically developed countries such as Russia.[67]

Cooptation does not necessarily result from misperception: it may rest on a calculation of relatively secure short-term versus rather risky long-term benefits. In the 1960s, a surge of interest in the aftereffects of colonialism and imperialism led to claims that trade with rich countries was impeding the economic development of the global periphery, making it easy for capitalists to collaborate with foreign capital rather than generate self-sustaining investments. Some Marxists argued that workers in the advanced capitalist countries were direct recipients of surplus extracted through a process of unequal exchange in which citizenship could trump class.[68] Such arguments influenced the political strategies of militant organizations in the United States, such as the Weather Underground in the 1970s, which discounted the likelihood that US workers could ever become a progressive force for change. Similarly, some feminist scholars have expressed concern that campaigns against sweatshop conditions of women's employment in the global South help protect workers in affluent countries from competition.[69]

The political economy of race/ethnicity has long emphasized conflicting group identities. In the early twentieth century, W. E. B. DuBois wrote eloquently of the "double consciousness" of people who identified themselves both as Americans and as Negroes.[70] B. R. Ambedkar applied Marxian reasoning when he lambasted Indian Marxists for their failure to recognize similarities between class and caste.[71] More recently, Charles Mills has described a "racial contract" as a coercive aspect of the larger social contract that encompasses racialized inequalities on the international and national levels.[72] William Darity and others have argued forcefully for parallels between class and race/ethnicity inequalities, explicitly bringing both group identity and interests into the picture.[73]

Many of these precedents maintain binary distinctions in which only class is repeated more than once: class and gender, class and nation, class and race/ethnicity, class and caste. The African-American Marxist Angela Davis, however, embraced what is now termed intersectionality when she noted that capitalists, men, and whites became codependent beneficiaries of the exploitation of disempowered groups. Her Marxism did not fit the conventional mold. While she sharply criticized the white feminist movement of the 1970s for its narrow focus on gender inequality, she also challenged those who focused on class alone (without attention to race/ethnicity and gender) or on race/ethnicity alone (without attention to gender and class).[74]

The importance of intersectionality has been more explicitly developed by African-American legal scholars and sociologists, including Kimberlé Williams Crenshaw and Patricia Hill Collins.[75] William Darity encourages intersectional political economy when he emphasizes "the competitive, and sometimes collaborative, interplay between members of social groups animated by their collective self-interest to attain or maintain relative group position in a social hierarchy."[76] Postcolonial and transnational feminist theories bring national allegiances into the picture.[77] National borders and immigration policies complicate the meanings of citizenship.[78] Self-described radical institutionalist economists, as well as many sociologists, describe parallels among inequalities based on race/ethnicity, gender, class, and nation.[79] This theoretical perspective reinforces a strategy often intuitively embraced by progressive activists: concerted efforts to ally disempowered groups around common long-run interests.

### Beyond Free Riders

Both history and everyday experience suggest that cooperation can be difficult to achieve. The costs of negotiating differences can be high, and groups often splinter into opposing factions. Yet cooperation sometimes coalesces in ways that deliver enormous benefits. Neoclassical economists, deeply rooted in methodological individualism, have long been skeptical of collective action. This skepticism finds particularly clear expression in the work of institutionalist economist Mancur Olson, who emphasizes the domino effects of temptations to free ride on the efforts of others.[80] Olson offers a pessimistic view of the potential for long-run cooperation, though he notes that small groups (and by implication, families) would find it easier to easily observe one another's efforts and punish shirking.

Other institutional economists, however, argue that social institutions can directly and indirectly foster group allegiances that reduce free rider problems.[81] The emerging field of identity economics emphasizes social norms that can encourage both conformity and solidarity. George Akerlof and Rachel Kranton describe a number of specific ways in which gender norms influence economic outcomes.[82] The relevance of identity economics extends well beyond gender: noncognitive processes and group identity may interact in ways that generate implicit bias (as well as explicit discrimination) against all people considered "outsiders."[83]

Conflict theory generally presumes that the benefits to collective military action either outweigh centripetal forces or can be used to overcome them. The military draft offers a specific example of institutional coercion. The democratic organization of eighteenth-century pirate enterprises, in which all sailors shared the spoils, provides a colorful example of positive incentives.[84] Michele Grossman explains the relative stability of large-scale alliances by turning Olson's reasoning around: the larger the number of members within these alliances, the more difficult the task of mobilizing opposition within them.[85]

While noncooperative game theory presumes that players act separately and alone on the basis of their knowledge of potential payoffs, cooperative game theory allows for the negotiation and enforcement of mutual agreements in shifting coalitions. Highly mathematical approaches typically presume homogenous, self-interested agents and take perfect information and initial endowments as a given.[86] They nonetheless provide some insights into political as well as military alliances. Some members of a coalition may be able to do better by leaving the group, and their departure potentially affects the distribution of the gains from cooperation among those who remain.[87]

While Olson's original treatment of free rider problems emphasized group size, other economists have emphasized heterogeneity or conflicting interests as a more serious obstacle to efficient collaboration.[88] A spate of empirical research suggests that both racial and ethnic diversity—especially when accompanied by economic disparities—reduces contributions to public goods.[89] In general, higher levels of social inequality are associated with greater degradation of the natural environment.[90] Significant differences between men and women's political preferences have also been well-documented: in both the United States and Europe, the expansion of female suffrage was associated with increased public spending on health and social welfare. [91] In the United States, persistent gender gaps in political preferences often bridge differences of class and race/ethnicity.[92] All of these patterns validate an intersectional view of collective action.

**Complex Identities**

One common objection to serious consideration of collective interests based on gender (as well as age or sexual orientation) is that women (like the young and the sexually nonconforming) are not a homogeneous group. From an intersectional perspective, however, no group is homogeneous. Scholars from subaltern groups see the cleavages particularly clearly. Not all groups can offer significant rewards for allegiance, and those that do may not deliver on their promises. Few people are motivated solely by potential rewards, but most are mindful of economic consequences for themselves and those they care for. They exert some agency over their social assignments, often seeking to renegotiate their cultural meanings and economic implications by choosing conformity or nonconformity and by engaging in acts of allegiance, transgression, or defection.

African-American and Latino feminists in affluent countries and feminists from the global South formed the vanguard of efforts to develop theories of intersectionality that encompass gender. Immigrant scholars have also been attuned to complex identities. As Amin Maalouf puts it: "Every individual is a meeting ground for many different allegiances, and sometimes the loyalties conflict with one another and confront the person who harbours them with difficult choices."[93] We all try to manage our identities and, sometimes, to renegotiate their cultural meanings and economic consequences.

Feminist theory in the United States in particular has historically focused on the circumstances of relatively affluent white women.[94] This vantage point was inevitably limited, and, in retrospect, is clearly revealed by language referring to "women and people of color" as though these categories were mutually exclusive.[95] This conceptual error validates the subterranean power of conflicting interests that can seldom be reconciled simply through moral exhortation.

# Economic Interests vs. Identity Politics?

Early socialist feminists never used the word "intersectionality," but they emphasized similarities in structures of collective power. The early Irish socialists Anna Wheeler and William Thompson put women's rights front and center.[96] In *The Subjection of Women*, published in

1869, John Stuart Mill and Harriet Taylor portrayed both patriarchal control over women and race-based slavery as expressions of collective self-interest: a "love of gain, unmixed and undisguised," combined with physical and military superiority.[97] They argued that both forms of inequality were institutionalized by the state and reinforced by cultural norms: "Was there ever any domination," they asked, "that did not appear natural to those who possessed it?"[98] Ten years later, in 1879, August Bebel argued in *Woman and Socialism* that all forms of oppression rested on seizure of independent property rights—including rights over women's bodies.

The term "identity politics" is often used to describe push-back against inequalities based on socially assigned categories such as gender, age, sexual orientation, race/ethnicity, and citizenship, which are often considered more subjective than inequalities based on class. When critics on the left worry that identity politics are divisive, they often seem to be shooting at the messenger rather than the underlying problem: if it were not for divisions based on other socially assigned categories, class consciousness and collective action would be far easier to achieve. Structures of collective power depend as heavily on political and cultural institutions as on ownership of wealth. Identity and interests go together. Subaltern groups demand both recognition and redistribution through structural change.

Intersectionality has always had uncomfortable strategic consequences for groups struggling to unify and consolidate their campaigns for institutional change. Theoretical blinders intended to minimize intragroup differences do not make these differences disappear. All forms of collective action are susceptible to potentially costly internal dissension and defection. Even when based on principles such as democracy, equal opportunity, collective ownership, and mutual aid, the empowerment of one group never guarantees the empowerment of all. This contingency helps explain the uneven successes of all efforts to challenge authoritarian hierarchies, including feminist movements. It also leads to an important conclusion: people's willingness to form alliances depends less on the level of their oppression than on their embrace of common ideals that can be realistically achieved in collaboration with others.

Competition among individuals and groups is central to our evolutionary history, but it does not block the development of more cooperative institutions any more than the force of gravity prevents us from leaving the ground. How do we lift off? To improve our capacity for institutional design, we need to understand ourselves better. By highlighting the complexity of collective conflict, intersectional political economy urges economists to develop a bigger picture of "the economic."

# 4

# Appropriation, Reproduction, and Production

The word "economic" derives from the Greek term for the household, "oikos." What, exactly, takes place in the oikos writ large? Marxian theory has traditionally focused on the extraction of surplus in commodity production; neoclassical economic theory on voluntary exchange, largely ignoring other types of transfers. A wider lens yields a more unified view: processes of reproduction entail distinctive forms of work and significant intergenerational transfers that take place within families and communities as well as firms, markets, and the state. All these activities are susceptible to the deployment of collective power.

Reproduction has particularly important implications for the evolution of patriarchal institutions. This activity, unlike the production of goods for one's own consumption—typified by Robinson Crusoe's initial survival on his desert island—can never be a purely individual endeavor.[1] Care for dependents cannot be organized entirely in terms of voluntary exchange, since dependents, by definition, have limited agency. Families and larger groups organize reproduction (defined here as the production and maintenance of human capabilities) in ways that help perpetuate themselves as groups (defined here as social reproduction), relying heavily on crosscutting institutional constraints.[2]

Reproduction, like production, can generate a surplus, realized through increases in the size or capabilities of a population, rather than accumulated material wealth. Reproduction includes but goes well beyond the self-investment emphasized in neoclassical economic theory, which often describes individuals as autonomous entrepreneurs of human capital. It also goes beyond the reproduction of labor power emphasized in some modern versions of Marxian theory as a process primarily benefiting a ruling class.

The production and maintenance of human capabilities is a necessary—and costly—aspect of all economic systems. Individuals and groups may bargain over the distribution of its costs, which are often unequally distributed. Like production, reproduction can create externalities or spillovers—the largely unpriced and often unanticipated side effects of individual decisions. In the long run, the social reproduction of any group is shaped not merely by its prowess in production but also by its ability to replenish and enhance its membership over time and its success in—or defense against—violent appropriation.

## Processes and Sites

People produce goods and services to directly meet their own needs and those of their families and friends, as well as for exchange in markets. People also produce other people: not just bodies, but also embodied physical, cognitive, emotional, and social capabilities.[3] Feminist economists sometimes use the term "social provisioning" or "social reproduction" to encompass all these processes.[4] This terminology requires more careful specification, but the terms themselves are less important than a holistic analysis of economic processes in which distributional conflicts and productive outcomes are closely intertwined.

Economists have proved especially reluctant to extend any analysis of collective conflict or institutional constraint to the process of reproduction. An influential precursor of both Marxian and neoclassical theory, Thomas Robert Malthus, assumed that population growth was driven by sexual passions that needed to be brought under moral control lest they lead to immiseration. This assumption remains deeply embedded in economic theory today, though it takes more sophisticated forms.[5]

Demographic history reveals a far more complex interaction between reproduction and production. Fertility (defined as births per woman, rather than potential births, or fecundity) came under social control in hunting and gathering societies, sometimes through explicit rules of abstinence, as well as through prolonged breastfeeding.[6] High fertility is by no means "natural." For obvious reasons, it is far more costly to women than to men, and there is little reason to believe that the preferences of men and women regarding family size are identical.[7] Most societies that have achieved high fertility rates have done so through the imposition of patriarchal institutions, and high fertility rates typically increase women's economic dependence on men, reducing their collective bargaining power and cementing patriarchal privilege.[8] Later chapters will show how this causal linkage weakened as families lost some of their importance as units of production, child-rearing became more costly, new reproductive technologies emerged, and—importantly—social institutions governing reproduction were collectively contested and renegotiated.

Now that birth rates have dropped below long-run replacement levels in many countries, demographic angst has reversed direction, fueling concerns about under- rather than overpopulation. Global population decline could help reduce environmental stress but is likely to cause considerable political and economic stress along the way. Not surprisingly, reproductive dynamics are now receiving wider attention. Early feminist research on links between patriarchal institutions and reproductive outcomes is now widely accepted.[9] Marxist-feminist scholars underscore the ways in which family caregivers subsidize capital accumulation.[10] Many social scientists measure the effects of motherhood on women's earnings and vulnerability to poverty.[11] Still, the androcentric assumption that reproduction takes place "outside" the economy remains hegemonic, partly because it is built into the subroutines of economic accounting.

### Defining Success

With relatively small exceptions, the internationally negotiated System of National Accounts defines "output" as the value of goods and services sold in markets.[12] Gross domestic product (GDP), long considered the arbiter of economic success, ignores the value of unpaid work, family investments in the care of dependents, and the unpriced contributions of what is commonly referred to as Mother Nature.[13] The putative goal of economic growth is increased consumption of commodities. The billionaire Malcolm Forbes testified to its childishness when he allegedly proclaimed, "He with the most toys at the end wins."[14]

Evolutionary logic suggests that this lighthearted joke could become an epitaph. The long-run success of human civilization requires efforts to minimize conflict, improve cooperation, and prioritize the development of human capabilities rather than the expansion of material consumption. The global economy relies heavily on unpriced goods and services that can easily be depleted or disrupted.[15] Their quantitative value can be estimated in a variety of ways, by asking what it would cost to purchase substitutes for them, what people would be willing to pay to protect them, or how their degradation will affect future generations. Increases in GDP are valuable only insofar as they capture net contributions to sustainable economic development.

Not everyone agrees that such estimates would be helpful. They carry the risk of capitulation to a money-centric analysis, another form of commodity fetishism. Yet the development of a broader economic accounting system would not necessarily divert attention from moral values or political priorities and could subvert the presumption that material living standards equate to money income. Both nonmarket work and natural assets and ecological services can be assigned an approximate market value.[16] While the methodologies behind such estimates require improvement, they yield startling results: a lower bound estimate of the replacement cost of nonmarket work in the United States in 2010, including time devoted to the supervision of young children, amounts to about 44 percent of conventionally measured GDP.[17]

### Love and Fear

An expanded measure of economic output enables an expanded picture of economic processes (and vice versa). Capital accumulation and market exchange take place hand in hand with more explicitly gendered activities, including appropriation and reproduction. Kenneth Boulding called attention to both when he described "economies of love and fear."[18] He pictured a triangle with exchange, love, and fear at its vertices, with points in its interior space representing a combination of all three.[19] Boulding deserves praise for bringing emotions into the picture, but he resorts to an out-of-date trope when he treats exchange alone as the domain of dispassionate rationality. Many male Enlightenment thinkers juxtaposed passions and interests, foreshadowing the modern, gendered distinction between identities and interests.[20] The contrast is overdrawn: appropriation and reproduction can involve rational calculation, and exchange can be motivated by visceral forms of love and fear.

Appropriation is often accomplished through strategic military decisions with long-lasting economic consequences. The Marxian theory of primitive accumulation explains how the seizure of productive assets such as land can institutionalize class inequality.[21] Some conflict theorists use economic models to illustrate how even costly wars can aggrandize their victors.[22] Appropriative processes also help explain gender differences. Feminist theorist Maria Mies argues that male control over weapons, the means of coercion in early human societies, provided a template for later forms of surplus extraction.[23]

Reproductive outcomes are shaped by rational calculations as well as strong emotions. People exercise at least some agency regarding sexual partnerships and commitments to the care of dependents. Passions and interests are not necessarily antithetical. Neoclassical theories of rational choice in exchange take preferences as a given; passions represent a particularly volatile preference, and their volatility challenges the notion that preferences are always stable or reliable guides to rational decisions.

Like sex, violence can be both passionate and calculating. Violent appropriation of economic resources can, in principle, be conducted by a single agent—a thief—but it is typically orchestrated through collective effort. The success of military ventures depends on institutional structures, including hierarchical discipline that streamlines decision-making, enforces obedience, and punishes desertion. Processes of reproduction also depend heavily on institutional structures, because those most dependent on others are those least able to provide for themselves. As Frank Knight put it in the 1920s, "We live in a world where individuals are born naked, destitute, helpless, ignorant, and untrained, and must spend a third of their lives acquiring the prerequisites of a free contractual existence."[24] Pedro Carneiro and James Heckman describe young children's lack of sufficient access to high-quality care and education as a market failure.[25]

All economic processes can go awry. Exchange in markets can fail. Military actions, like government in general, can fail. Families can also fail. Altruistic commitments are not always sustainable: domestic violence, sexual abuse, neglect, and emotional and economic abandonment are not uncommon. Family solidarity, like other forms of solidarity, cannot be taken as a given, and it is terribly misleading to describe all working-class families as havens in an otherwise heartless world, united in their efforts to resist capitalist exploitation.[26] It is also farfetched to assume that family members all want the same things (maximizing a joint utility function) or that they always achieve efficient outcomes in which no one could be made better off without making someone worse off (Pareto optimality).

Not all economic processes are the same, and emotions often run stronger in personal than impersonal interactions. On the other hand, competitive markets sometimes succumb to shortsightedness or panic, and advertising for consumer goods often brandishes the promise of social and sexual approval.[27] Love and fear, along with anger and greed, cross most boundaries. Likewise, the behavioral heuristics that most economists apply only to production and exchange—individual self-interest and collective aggrandizement—also pertain to appropriation and reproduction.

**Reproduction**

From John Locke to the present, liberal political theory has extolled the economic virtues of two private property rights: self-ownership and control over the products of one's labor. These two rights cannot, however, be easily applied to reproduction: parents "produce" children but cannot own them without violating children's self-ownership as adults. Reproductive commitments are sometimes described as meta-phorical investments (as in "investing in children"), but their future economic payoff is difficult for parents, as metaphorical investors, to claim. Nor is there a close relationship between the effort invested and the rate of return.

Caregivers derive some economic benefits from reciprocity and mutual aid, but the more diffuse public benefits they generate add up to a far greater sum.[28] Reproductive work pays forward more richly than it pays back, as when children grow up and rear children of their own. Caregivers often gain intrinsic satisfaction, or, in neoclassical terms, "psychic income," but this is less reliable and less fungible than mone-tary payback. In the vocabulary of game theory, caregivers suffer from a first-mover disadvantage: payback is difficult to ensure through volun-tary or contractual exchange. Neither tiny babies nor seriously wounded soldiers can bargain over the terms of their care.

Reproduction includes biological processes. So too does agricul-tural production: seed corn provided an early metaphor for economic surplus, and the multiplicative powers of rabbits and yeast have long been used to explain compound interest.[29] Growth in the size of a herd of animals produced for sale represents a form of wealth accu-mulation; money spent training dressage horses for sale represents investment. By contrast, population growth is not considered a contribution to national wealth, and neither public nor private money spent on education is entered in the investment column of the national accounts. Cross-country comparisons of per capita GDP place population in the denominator, as though people are nothing more than consumers.

GDP is merely one input into the health and well-being of a human population, but our very language obscures this reality. Only one specific and relatively brief episode of mothering—the painful passage of a baby through the birth canal—is commonly referred to as labor. In the United States, regular estimates of parental expenditures on children are published, for mysterious reasons, by the Department of Agriculture. They do not include a full valuation of parental time—either what its reallocation from potential income-earning activities would cost or how much money would be required to hire a substitute for parental supervision and care.[30] Likewise, public allowances set for foster parents are based almost entirely on the necessary cash expenditures, ignoring the value of parental time.

Reproductive labor should not be taken for granted in this way. Whether paid or unpaid, it is labor that should be valued in economic as well as moral terms. The production and maintenance of human capabilities require labor, capital, time, and energy, combined in ways influenced by technological change but often requiring close personal connection, or nurturant care.[31] Like production, reproduction can be an important source of intrinsic satisfaction and emotional connection and can also create significant social benefits and/or social costs.

So defined, reproduction is not confined to women or to families. It includes both paid and unpaid activities and responsibilities fulfilled in a variety of sites, including homes, communities, private firms, and the public sector. It includes self-care as well as the care of others, and it encompasses expenditures of money as well as time.

Not all the private or public benefits of reproduction can be easily capitalized. Human capabilities represent the activities available to people rather than their specific achievements.[32] They include education and job-related skills that offer a rate of return in the labor market, but also, more broadly, the potential to engage in other satisfying and socially valuable activities. Human capabilities are both a source of happiness and an economic resource for everyone who may be able to benefit from them, including employers, partners, and future generations. They are also valuable in and of themselves. As Amartya Sen puts it, "Human beings are not merely means of production (even though they excel in that capacity), but also the end of the exercise."[33]

Like many forms of production, reproduction requires a physical substrate: it is literally embodied. This does not imply that it can be measured in purely bodily terms. Measuring reproductive success in terms of number of descendants is a bit like measuring economic success in terms of calories consumed: not irrelevant, but incomplete and misleading. Personal maintenance overlaps with consumption; people need food, water, shelter and other basic amenities in order to survive. Many reproductive activities, however, reduce current consumption in favor of future consumption—either for one's self or for others. Such investments often represent personal commitments; they are seldom based on calculation of pecuniary payoffs, and they generally offer a higher social than private rate of return.[34]

Families and communities are especially important sites for the financial support and the care of dependents, especially young children.[35] They are not, however, the only sites. Reproduction also takes place in the public and the private sectors of capitalist economies. Much of the growth in women's labor force participation in countries like the United States represents a relocation of care services from households to paid employment in health, education, and social services.[36] In the United States and other affluent countries, public social spending supplements transfers once made largely within families and local communities, fulfilling responsibilities for intergenerational cooperation and mutual aid. As Chapter 8 elaborates, taxes paid by the employed population help finance the education of children and the retirement of the elderly. They also subsidize health care and provide insurance against a variety of economic hazards. Such forms of public spending represent a crucial—but under-recognized—input into market-based production.

The economic value of human capabilities cannot be reduced to the price that a hypothetical slave owner would pay to acquire control over them, or the wage that an employer would pay to rent them, because workers and their families also derive benefits from them. Future generations cannot fully reimburse their forebears for investments made on their behalf, just as they cannot gain full recompense for any harms to the natural environment bequeathed to them. Reproduction is based on socially organized transfers, not individual exchange. However strongly ingrained are human desires to engage in sexual intercourse and form partnerships with others, these desires alone cannot successfully perpetuate a social species.

If natural selection explains why individual desires evolve, social selection explains how institutional arrangements channel such desires into outcomes that can promote group success. Reproduction and production are both necessary for social reproduction, and vice versa. Much recent Marxist feminist analysis focuses on the social reproduction of capitalism as a unitary system, observing that employers benefit from women's unpaid work in the home because it allows them to pay lower wages.[37] True, but capitalists are not the only beneficiaries: struggles over the distribution of the costs of reproduction reach beyond class lines. They affect the relative well-being of men and women when exploitation comes home.[38] They also affect the well-being of some wage earners relative to others. On a global level, access to education and health is shaped by race/ethnicity and citizenship, not just class.

As Nancy Fraser observes, social reproduction represents a kind of glue that facilitates social cooperation.[39] The bonds it creates, however, are not necessarily universal ones; they can also be divisive. People are often glued into clusters, a point obscured by excessively broad definitions of social reproduction as everything "involved in the maintenance of life on a daily basis, and intergenerationally" or "the process by which all the main relations in the society are constantly recreated and perpetuated."[40] It is difficult to imagine anything that does not fall in this category, which seems to overcompensate for earlier reluctance to recognize the economic importance of women's unpaid work.[41]

I use the term "social reproduction" to describe the process by which socially assigned groups perpetuate themselves and their advantages over time—a process that encompasses both production and reproduction, accomplished through institutional structures that reinforce collective identities and interests. This usage accommodates Marxist feminist insights into the gendered interplay between production and reproduction in class relations.[42] However, it creates more conceptual space for analysis of inequalities based on other dimensions of collective identity. Most forms of privilege are socially reproduced.

# Who Pays for Care?

Because reproductive commitments primarily benefit future generations, institutional structures that distribute the costs of reproduction are indispensable. This does not imply that the most "efficient" institutional structure wins out. The winners emerge from multilayered processes of cooperation and conflict in which success is determined by contingent external circumstances as well as strategic decisions.

### Externalities

Because neoclassical economic theory defines "the economy" as a set of exchanges based on clear property rights in a competitive market, economic processes that violate this boundary are termed "spillovers" or "externalities." Whether they have positive or negative effects, such externalities interfere with the efficient allocation that should result from market processes. The prescribed solution is to internalize the externality by modifying prices. For instance, the negative economic externalities of carbon dioxide emissions can be internalized by taxing carbon emissions. Likewise, the positive economic externalities of child-rearing can be internalized by providing public support for parents.

Some social scientists have proposed more tailored financial rewards for parents. For instance, parents who raise exceptionally productive children could receive bonuses from the state or be given a legal claim to a share of their children's income.[43] These specific proposals are problematic not only because they commodify parental commitments, but also because they cannot accurately reward parental value-added. Parents are not the only ones who contribute to their children's capabilities, and these capabilities cannot be valued merely in terms of their lifetime earnings. As with many environmental problems, "getting prices right" is not necessarily enough, even if the right prices could magically be ascertained.[44]

No feminist schooled in the interdisciplinary critique of androcentric theory can ignore the phallic innuendoes of internalizing an externality, especially since childbirth can be described as the exact opposite of heterosexual intercourse—externalizing an internality. The application of market-centric reasoning to both mothers and Mother Nature seems intended to redeem the market by suggesting that it should simply be expanded further. It further obscures the economic importance of fundamentally nonmarket processes.[45]

Parents and other caregivers are seldom motivated by social benefits or costs; they often derive intrinsic satisfaction from their commitments. The externalities they create are not always positive, since children and other care recipients sometimes inflict harm on others. Nonetheless, the care of those who cannot care for themselves fits the textbook definition of a public good, generating gains that extend beyond bilateral exchange and are at least partly nonrival and nonexcludable in consumption.[46]

Children grow up to become taxpayers, helping repay public debt and directly or indirectly helping to support the older generation. They also perpetuate our species, our cultures, our communities, and our families. As the Covid-19 pandemic shows, healthy people unpredictably succumb to illness, often requiring assistance from family, friends, neighbors, and medical personnel. Eldercare is a form of reciprocity— the best we can all hope for is to grow old in a caring environment.

The risk of commitments that pay forward rather than pay back is substantial. Even in traditional noncapitalist patriarchal systems, parents typically devote more resources to their children than they receive in return. In most modern societies intergenerational transfers move through many different channels. Groups defined in terms of race/ethnicity and citizenship compete for access to reproductive resources. Capitalist firms benefit from public investments in education that save them the expense of educating workers who could take their acquired skills with them to another firm.[47] Modern welfare states tax the working-age population to provide benefits that flow to the older generation, whether or not they have helped raise that working-age population (see Chapter 8). In the absence of effective child support enforcement, noncustodial fathers can easily offload financial as well as direct care responsibilities for children onto mothers (see Chapter 9).

The distribution of reproductive costs is often contested in the public as well as the private sphere. Corporations or wealthy individuals taxed to help finance public spending on health and education typically invest in campaign contributions and lobbying designed to reduce their obligations. When state regulation requires firms directly to pay a share of reproductive costs by offering paid family leaves or providing childcare services, they often discriminate against mothers or women of childbearing age.[48] As with environmental regulation, evasion is often cost-effective. In this distributional contest, capitalist firms hold an increasingly valuable card: the threat to relocate to venues with lower taxes and less regulation.

## Offloading Costs

Yet tensions over the distribution of the costs of reproduction are not unique to systems that rely heavily on capitalist institutions. Raising children has always required significant investments of time and energy that almost inevitably reduce current consumption. While women's specialization in childbearing and child-rearing has often delivered great advantages to the reproduction of families and groups, it has always been costly. A daughter's potential economic contributions are more difficult to capture than those of a son even if she remains economically tied to her family of origin, because her comparative advantage lies in producing the next generation and extending the lineage, not in helping the family meet its immediate needs or in providing support for parents in old age.

Men, like women, experience gender-related economic risks. Their historical specialization in warfare has historically led to high rates of injury and death. This sacrifice on behalf of others, however, delivers significant benefits to those who survive, empowered by their prowess as fighters. A shortage of men relative to women also increases men's bargaining power in heterosexual dating and marriage markets. When reproductive success depends on economic circumstances, sons potentially offer more descendants than daughters, especially in relatively wealthy, high-status families where sons are likely to marry and become fathers themselves.[49]

In traditional patriarchal systems where parents bear most of the costs of raising children and depend on partial repayment in the form of insurance against illness and infirmity, son preference offers significant economic benefits.[50] As women's specialization in reproductive tasks diminishes, however, their potential contribution to short-run consumption goes up. Daughters can contribute more to parental income (and wives to household income) when their participation in directly remunerative work increases. Sons also become less crucial to the maintenance of elderly parents as new forms of life cycle insurance emerge—whether in the form of private savings or public transfers.

I argue in later chapters that the expansion of capitalist institutions has encouraged fertility decline and reduced son preference but has set other distributional conflicts into motion. Unlike slave owners or feudal lords, capitalist employers employ free labor with a double meaning: the laborer is free to choose, but the employer is under no obligation to cover the costs of producing or maintaining the laborer. The observation that the labor market does not necessarily yield wages high enough for workers to support a family has a long political history that finds expression in modern living wage campaigns.[51]

Science fiction provides a more pointed illustration. Consider an imaginary economy in which androids perform most tasks, requiring only periodic maintenance and battery recharge. In long-run competitive equilibrium, the purchase price for an android would equal the cost of producing it. But if some humans happened to love androids and find intrinsic satisfaction in producing them, the purchase price could go to zero. Androids could be put to work simply for the cost of keeping them fully charged and operational. That most humans prefer to produce other humans rather than androids helps explain why employers will probably continue for some time to find humans a cheaper work force.

Son preference has diminished but not disappeared in modern capitalist societies.[52] The differential valuation of men and women based on differences in their market earnings has proved more resistant to change. In the United States, for instance, public compensation for the families of victims of the 9/11 World Trade Towers attack followed precedents in tort law, placing heavy emphasis on the value of the victim's predicted future earnings. As a result, families who experienced the loss of a woman received significantly less public compensation, on average, than those who experienced the loss of a man.[53] Unpriced reproductive contributions seldom count for much.

### Reproduction and Bargaining Power

If responsibilities for dependent care were equally shared, they would not affect competitive outcomes in the labor market. In most countries today, however, women assume more care responsibilities than men, and mothers more care responsibilities than other women. In the 1990s childless women in the United States were earning almost as much as men with the same levels of education and experience.[54] Significant differences between the earnings of mothers and non-mothers, discussed in more detail in Chapter 9, could dissipate over time with the expansion of publicly subsidized high-quality childcare and greater paternal participation. On the other hand, reliance on the private purchase of substitutes for maternal care—often low-wage women disempowered by their race/ethnicity or immigration status—simply redistributes care costs along class lines. Care is a public good that should receive generous public support.

The uneven distribution of family care responsibilities has significant economic consequences. Differences in both social policies and cultural norms have measurable effects, revealed by variations in the motherhood penalty in earnings across countries.[55] The public good dimensions of reproductive commitments weaken women's collective bargaining power. Efforts to redistribute these reproductive costs meet opposition not only from many men and children, but also from many employers and taxpayers. Even older women may bridle at such cost-shifting, feeling that they have already paid their reproductive dues and that younger women should follow their example.

One could argue (and neoclassical economists often do) that those who offer care receive a compensating differential in the form of personal satisfaction or psychic income.[56] But individuals don't always choose their preferences, and caring preferences create vulnerability: in short-run competition, nice gals (as well as guys) finish last.[57] Women with few economic resources are often forced into care overloads; those in privileged positions often delegate the least remunerative tasks to others, regardless of their gender.[58] Neither preferences nor privileges nullify the links between gendered obligations and women's collective disempowerment.

## Socially Reproduced Inequalities

The distinctive features of appropriation and reproduction reveal major inconsistencies in liberal assumptions: markets do not deliver economic rewards commensurate with economic contributions, and equality of opportunity cannot be defined simply as absence of discrimination. Sometimes, individual competition rewards effort, commitment, and skill; more often, the rules of the game deliver significant advantages to members of empowered groups. Collective violence influences original endowments, and early winners can pass advantages on to their successors. Unequal outcomes in the first round can lead to unequal reproductive investments, unequal capabilities, and, therefore, unequal opportunities for following rounds. Such circles often go unbroken.

Social reproduction reaches far beyond the social reproduction of class. Financial capital is not the only source of group-based economic advantage. Opportunities to develop valuable skills and join supportive social networks facilitate accumulation of human and social capital, creating durable inequalities.[59] Families, communities, states, and firms are important sites for the production of human capabilities, the development of human knowledge, and the intergenerational transmission of many forms of economic advantage.

Social institutions convert durable inequalities into capitalized assets. Rights of citizenship in an affluent country are economically valuable and, in some important instances, can be purchased like other assets.[60] "Whiteness" can't easily be bought but nonetheless offers a significant payoff in countries like the United States.[61] "Maleness" can be acquired, albeit at a very high price, and it too offers distinct economic advantages. Heterosexuality also offers measurable economic benefits.[62] The list does not stop here.

While attention to social reproduction helps establish similarities between class and other dimensions of group membership, it also directs attention to inequalities reproduced in families and communities as well as the capitalist workplace.[63] Concerted cultivation by highly educated parents boosts their children's future earnings.[64] Increased inequality in family income in the United States has been accompanied by increased inequality in family spending on children.[65] Sons and daughters seldom inherit their parents' specific position on the economic ladder, but they typically end up close to it.[66] At the other extreme of the income distribution, extreme poverty suppresses the developmental trajectory of young children.[67] Childhood in an unstable or fractured family also contributes to poor developmental outcomes.[68]

Residential and educational segregation by race/ethnicity and class reproduce differences in human and social capital. Affluent families typically live in affluent communities, where many parents send their children to private schools and educational expenditures per student in public schools are richly funded by local property taxes. Recent research shows that sixth graders in the richest school districts in the United States today are four grade levels ahead of children in the poorest districts.[69] Simply living in a rich neighborhood increases exposure to information, supervision, networks, and role models.[70] Such socially constructed differences in economic opportunity are neither natural nor inevitable. They vary enormously within and across countries and are mediated by social institutions that can be—and often are—collectively contested.

# Beyond Production

Robinson Crusoe lived a relatively simple, but charmed life on his desert island. His means of subsistence were there for the taking, and he eventually gained a faithful servant. Karl Marx ridiculed Crusoe's story with good reason: the romantic tale of one man's ingenuity abstracted from the social relations of production and the harsh realities of exploitation. Yet despite his acknowledgement of aristocracies of labor, Marx himself defined social relations, production, and exploitation in narrow class-centric terms. His story, too, is overly simple.

The discipline of economics as a whole has largely ignored the economic consequences of the social organization of reproduction. Its failure to value reproductive commitments has distorted measures of consumption, production, and investment even as it has disguised inequalities based on gender, age, and sexual orientation. Continuing widespread reluctance to acknowledge tensions over the distribution of the costs of care for others has obscured important dimensions of collective conflict.

Reproduction and social reproduction are processes just as important as production, appropriation, and exchange; they are susceptible to institutional dynamics that can crystallize inherited inequalities even as they enhance some aspects of group success. Women are the group most directly affected, but families, larger groups, and society as a whole also have big stakes in reproductive outcomes, making social reproduction quintessentially intersectional. The complexity of resulting forms of collective conflict invites a more general theory of hierarchy, bargaining, and exploitation.

# 5
# Hierarchy and Exploitation

The many forms of hierarchical governance that reflect and advance collective interests often have contradictory effects. Clear lines of authority can help coordinate decisions in ways potentially advantageous to everyone. On the other hand, concentrated power typically leads to very unequal—and often unfair—distribution of the gains from coordination. It also creates rigidities that impede institutional adaptations to social and environmental change. Because powerful individuals and groups can advance their interests by increasing their share of the economic pie as well as by increasing its size, they tend to resist changes that might weaken their relative position.

Efforts to understand the tensions created by hierarchical institutions have a long history in political economy. From a classical Marxian perspective, class power provides an exploitative means of accumulating surplus that can promote technological change but, at some point, becomes susceptible to crisis and breakdown. From a traditional neoclassical perspective, hierarchical governance is efficient when it successfully aligns individual incentives with group benefits and lowers the cost of decision-making. This success, however, requires perfect markets, perfect prices, and perfect competition, which seldom prevail when consolidation of economic power offers huge advantages.

Intersectional political economy moves beyond capitalist firms and competitive markets to examine the dialectic of power and efficiency in social reproduction, picturing implicit gender bargains in terms that parallel other implicit bargains based on race/ethnicity, citizenship, and class and also emphasizing their mutual interaction. A new definition of exploitation as unfair division of the gains from coordination encompasses but goes beyond the extraction of surplus value in capitalist employment.

## Competition, Cooperation, and Coordination

From an evolutionary perspective, groups that develop forms of voluntary or involuntary coordination suited to their particular technical and strategic environment are likely to prevail over those that do not.[1] Altruism and trust enhance this process but seldom prove sufficient on their own. Nor do rich potential payoffs guarantee continued cooperation. The resulting coordination problems help explain why some groups devise hierarchical social institutions that offer a subset of group members powerful incentives for enforcing discipline.

Whether disempowered members of such groups can be said to benefit from such discipline or not depends partly on counterfactual alternatives—whether or not, with equal access to resources, they could do better on their own. While these counterfactual alternatives are shaped by external circumstances, they also depend on the capabilities of subaltern groups, including their ability to form sustainable alliances among themselves.

### The Costs of Competition

Even economists who regard competition as the tonic of success recognize its potentially toxic overdoses. Firms, like families, encourage long-term relationships rather than the constant turnover associated with a daily auction of competitive bids.[2] Intrafirm competition promotes efficient outcomes only if fly-by-night fraud and environmental harms are averted and no firm wields significant market power. In the absence of copyrights, patents, or similar protections, competition can undermine incentives for innovation. Most corporate personnel departments recognize that overzealous competition among employees can reduce effective teamwork.[3] Tournament-based or winner-take-all reward structures often encourage people to take excessive risks, obsess over their relative status, and attempt to undermine their peers.[4]

Many patriarchal institutions restrict competition for sexual or reproductive partners. Monogamy makes it difficult for powerful men to monopolize wives (though it hardly limits their sexual access to women) and aligns the reproductive interests of married mothers and fathers.[5] Rules of primogeniture discourage competition among adult children for a share of paternally controlled resources. Restrictions on women's access to wage employment increase the supply of potential wives. Sanctions against female promiscuity limit most women's ability to compare the sexual prowess of male partners, while prostitution provides a reliable reserve army of female sex workers to pleasure men.

Evolutionary biologists observe that excessive competition among members of the same species can undermine group survival.[6] Dominance hierarchies can reduce conflict because they discourage competition, creating protocols for leadership succession—an issue for corporate CEOs as well as stags.[7] In human societies, cooperation often breaks down in the absence of formally or informally binding agreements. The theory of noncooperative games, in which such agreements are ruled out, offers many telling examples of such breakdown. In the famous prisoner's dilemma, two entirely self-interested individuals fear mutual betrayal, leading them to the worst possible outcome: the guilty parties, interrogated in separate rooms, could escape without significant punishment if they insist on their innocence, but both confess because they fear being implicated by the other.

### Angels and Ants

Team competition provides a compelling metaphor for theories of multilevel selection that acknowledge both individual and group winners. Individual performance matters, but too much rivalry among team members can weaken collective chances of success. The balance between these two depends, often, on the characteristics of the sport. War offers the most chilling and bloody example: better to risk death fighting side-by-side with fellow soldiers than to stand alone against a hostile army. Yet the temptation to flee, the hope of escaping the conflict altogether, looms large. Armies punish their deserters.

Most groups develop hierarchical institutions that enforce a variety of different forms of cooperation. The likelihood that such institutions help ensure their collective success cannot be dismissed as mere functionalism; nor does it justify the forcible imposition of such institutions from above by individuals or subgroups who use them for their own ends. Rather, attention to the impact of hierarchical institutions provides an evolutionary explanation of the rise and decline of structures of collective power that distribute the costs and risks of cooperation in different ways.

Evolutionary biologists are not sufficiently attuned to social and economic complexity of this process within the human species. E. O. Wilson describes the force of group selection in morally loaded terms, as a source of altruism counterbalancing the pursuit of individual self-interest.[8] He writes that we are all

> suspended in unstable and constantly changing locations between the two extreme forces that created us. We are unlikely to yield completely to either force as an ideal solution to our social and political turmoil. To yield completely to the instinctual urgings born from individual selection would dissolve society. To surrender to the urgings from group selection would turn us into angelic robots—students of insects call them ants.[9]

Apparently, the two extremes represent individual self-interest versus robotic group control, almost a parody of capitalism versus socialism. In a variation on this theme, biologist Frans de Waal argues that moral systems provide much-needed (though not always success-ful) assistance in mediating the tensions between individual and collec-tive interests.[10]

These are partial truths. Group solidarity is not always moral or angelic. Groups are bound together by more than altruistic sentiments and often behave in callous ways. People are simultaneously assigned to many different groups within fractal hierarchies that create complex patterns of contingent advantage or disadvantage. Individual choices may be most consequential when they influence group loyalties.

Some economists propose that humans have inherited propensities for strong reciprocity that foster cooperation.[11] Experimental evidence suggests that many people are conditional cooperators, willing to punish opportunists even at some expense to themselves.[12] Such altruistic actions can lower the overall costs of altruism by discouraging oppor-tunism. It is easy to see how traits conducive to cooperation could prove advantageous for those under attack from less cohesive groups; on the other hand, these same traits facilitate cooperative aggression against less well-organized outsiders.[13]

Whether or not we are a "cooperative species," our cooperation is often socially engineered and institutionally enforced. Humans have likely evolved in ways that enhance receptivity to social influence, a trait that Herbert Simon labels "docility."[14] The history of political economy itself illustrates the gendered aspects of sacrifice for others, exemplified by terms such as "compulsory altruism."[15] Nineteenth-century scholars in the United Kingdom, the United States, and France praised men for seeking to better themselves, women for subordinating themselves to others as "angels in the house."[16] Men embodied competition, women cooperation: marriage represented an asymmetric bargain between the two. Even today, women are expected to "make nice," to resist the temptations of competitive individualism and temper its effects on men.[17]

This moral division of labor was not established by instinct or exhortation. It was imposed through the development of hierarchical institutions that limited women's rights to pursue their own self-interest and also created significant divisions among women. E. O. Wilson's metaphors are misleading: we are far more socially differentiated than any species of ants or angels.

### Free Riders vs. Top Riders

Voluntary cooperation is often difficult to sustain. Even a few opportunists—those who pursue their individual interests at the expense of a larger group—can undermine cooperation. They can steal from others, becoming bandits who specialize in appropriation.[18] They can shirk responsibilities to the group, becoming free riders.[19] Alternatively, they can seize authority to discipline bandits and free riders and then use that authority to skim off a surplus for themselves, becoming top riders or exploiters.

The idealized markets of neoclassical economics highlight voluntary cooperation—free exchange—by minimizing the implications of its preconditions. They don't explain how individuals obtain the resources or capabilities that they bring to markets. They don't conform to real-world conditions in which some participants gain market power. They don't fully acknowledge the extent to which the goods and services we rely on are public in the sense that they cannot be easily priced for individual exchange.

Natural endowments and environmental services (including a stable climate) offer the most obvious examples, but future generations of humans (and the groups they will constitute) are also public goods. They do not participate in today's markets or today's elections: they have no way of directly influencing the decisions that will bring them into existence. One way of addressing this problem, offered by the neoclassical strain of welfare economics, posits an imaginary, altruistic social planner whose aim is to maximize the welfare of society as a whole.

As inventors of this imaginary planner soon realized, the challenge of aggregating individual preferences in a society is exactly the same as the challenge of overcoming differences among close kin. Paul Samuelson observed, "What we have been calling a family is after all but a disguised version of society itself—i.e., a collection of more than one person."[20] The benevolent dictator of welfare economics resembles a good father who subordinates his own interests to those of his wife and children. Neither one necessarily lives up to expectations.

Some neoclassical economists, proudly skeptical of benevolence, have warned that social planners would likely become tyrants, engaging in rent-seeking behavior—a fancy term for trying to get something for nothing.[21] They have viewed government employees as the most threatening of opportunists, as though the public sector was the only venue for rent-seeking. Many socialists have seemingly taken the opposite tack, arguing that all capitalists are exploiters and that dictators like Mao or Fidel, whatever their flaws, had the best interests of their people at heart. In classical Marxian theory, the advent of a classless society theoretically makes cooperation easy, vitiating the need for realistic attention to the nuts and bolts of democratic governance.[22]

Whatever their vision of bad behavior, most economists continue to place unpaid work outside the "economy" partly because its altruistic elements jar with assumptions of selfish behavior on the part of classes or individuals. Metaphors of family solidarity have historically infused socialist rhetoric: brothers and sisters, rally together! Neoclassical faith in laissez-faire families has been formalized by Gary Becker's Rotten Kid Theorem, which explains how an altruistic household head can induce spoiled children to act in the interests of the household as a whole.[23] As Jack Hirshleifer quickly observed, this theorem boils down to the claim that selfish children can be bribed to behave.[24] Woe be it if the household head in question is selfish.[25] Obviously, rotten fathers, husbands, kings, dictators, and capitalists can do far more harm than rotten kids.

Many institutionalist economists, including Douglass North, John Joseph Wallis, Daron Acemoglu, and James Robinson, point beyond formal democratic processes to argue that inclusive institutions are more likely than extractive ones to foster economic development.[26]

However, they largely focus on political institutions, with little attention to other sites where "extraction" might take place, such as the capitalist firm, the patriarchal family, or the racist community. They never fully acknowledge the many ways that unearned bargaining power can give some groups easy claims to the services of others.

This institutionalist literature promotes a self-congratulatory history that holds the United States and Europe up as models for other countries and soft-pedals the global effects of colonial and imperial power. People in privileged positions tend to assume that top riders simply get what they deserve: as if serfs paying tribute to lords were merely paying for protection, as if slavery had a civilizing influence on slaves, as if colonial powers introduced innovations that compensated for violent subjugation, as if workers generating profits for employers were always paid the value of their work, as if women abused by men were nonetheless adored and well provided for.

Such ideological rationalizations are more far-fetched than most utopian socialist fantasies. Social institutions do not evolve in anything resembling an idealized market, and the most efficient institutions for increasing the production of goods and services do not always prevail. Institutional evolution is shaped by individual and collective bargaining power, including threats of organized violence in ruthless pursuit of economic interests.

### Hawks and Doves

The set of payoffs in the stylized game known as Hawk-Dove illustrates why individual choices can be less important than group characteristics. In this noncooperative game, the players cannot, by assumption, make binding agreements with each other. The evolutionary version focuses not on individual strategies, but on the outcome of a process in which one set of players designated as Hawks adopt a combative strategy, while the others, designated Doves, adopt a sharing strategy.

Whether the combative strategy pays off—allowing the population of Hawks to expand relative to that of Doves—depends on the outcomes of three type of encounters (Hawk/Hawk, Dove/Dove, and Hawk/Dove) and also on the composition of the population, which determines the relative probability that a Hawk will meet a Dove.

Players do not know in advance who they will encounter. If a Hawk encounters a Dove, Hawk gets a positive payoff and Dove a negative one. If a Hawk encounters another Hawk, it fights, with a substantial risk of losing the fight, being hurt, and suffering a negative payoff. If a Dove encounters another Dove, both share the available food, both receiving a positive payoff. A population consisting entirely of Doves enjoys a higher collective payoff than a population consisting entirely of Hawks, because no bird gets hurt. In this respect, Doves are more efficient. But it does not follow that Doves will prevail, unless they can keep all Hawks at bay.

Both Hawk and Dove do better in a population consisting largely of Doves, and a simple model of repeated encounters makes it possible to predict whether the relative population shares of Hawk and Dove will increase, decrease, or remain the same. Under different assumptions, different equilibrium shares will be reached.[27]

However, a small number of Hawks, invading a much larger population of Doves, will find plentiful sources of food and their population will expand (assuming that they can avoid fighting long enough to mate and raise their offspring, a detail that is typically—and tellingly—omitted). On the other hand, if their population expands so successfully that it renders Doves extinct, the Hawks will likely cannibalize each other. The last one will starve to death.

There is a hint of gender here: hawks are associated with masculinity, doves with femininity.[28] Yes, it's sweet—maybe the two actually need one another. But notice that the Hawks have the upper hand, or talon, as the case may be. Acknowledgement of pacifist vulnerability does not require game theory; Sun-Tzu and Machiavelli both made the point centuries ago that nice persons often finish last, even if bad persons depend on them for their existence.

What stylized noncooperative games leave out (as dictated by the technical definition of "noncooperative") are the various ways in which social institutions could alter the outcome: for instance, Hawks could forge a nonaggression pact with one another, Doves could hire some Hawks to protect them, or Hawks could disguise themselves as Doves. The main reason we play so many cooperative games with enforceable rules is that most noncooperative games leave everyone worse off. Even libertarians concede that free markets require rules.

Cooperation often confers significant benefits, and societies are particularly likely to gain from institutional efforts to minimize violence.[29] Even aggressors can gain more from the threat of violence than its actual exercise. Institutionalist reasoning suggests that, in early human history, roving bandits were replaced by stationary bandits (such as emperors and kings) who had incentives to increase the productivity of those they subjugated. As Mancur Olson puts it, they were less like wolves preying on elk than like ranchers protecting their cattle until they were ready for slaughter.[30] Domestication has proved more cost-effective than hunting.

Some Marxian economists describe capitalists as roving bandits, challenging the view that capitalist development fostered any positive forms of social or technological change. Stephen Marglin argues that capitalist development simply established new forms of class power that redistributed surplus and blocked potentially valuable forms of technological change.[31] Likewise, some feminist theorists argue that patriarchal institutions emerged simply as a result of men's desire to dominate women sexually or capitalists' desires to exploit working families.[32] An evolutionary perspective suggests that these explanations are too simple. Top riders have powerful incentives to increase the size and productivity—though not the strength—of those they ride upon.

### Democratic vs. Authoritarian Hierarchy

Hierarchical control does not necessarily lead to exploitation. Democratic institutions were designed to minimize this likelihood by combining leadership with accountability. Democracy, however, is no simple feat. Many versions of democratic decision-making—especially the "first-past-the-post" rules widely used in national elections—fall short of guaranteeing fair outcomes.[33] For most of its relatively short global history, democratic decision-making has been confined to a narrow range of political institutions within individual countries and left vulnerable to many varieties of corruption.

The economist Kenneth Arrow, famous for demonstrating the logical impossibility of a perfect democracy, qualified his results as follows. "Most systems are not going to work badly all of the time. All I proved is that all *can* work badly at times."[34] Winston Churchill made the same point in more memorable language: "Democracy is the worst form of government, except for all the others."[35] Both rueful assessments seem to assume that democracy has been clearly defined and put into practice. Yet the word itself is often used loosely. Many early nominal democracies initially excluded men without property, people of color, and women from the franchise. As Frederick Douglass put it in 1857, "power concedes nothing without a demand."[36]

All nominal democracies today leave children underrepresented, with neither direct votes nor parental votes on their behalf.[37] In the

United States, both prisoners and convicted felons are largely excluded from participation, and efforts to obstruct voter registration have become endemic.[38] Many forms of strategic manipulation, including gerrymandering, distort electoral outcomes.[39] Extreme inequalities in wealth and income lead to extreme inequalities in political influence and cultural voice.

Democracy has always progressed in stages. If it were improved and expanded in new directions, including economic self-governance, it could reduce both free riding and top riding, punish bandits, and reduce costly forms of collective conflict. It could also make the world safer for Doves. Needless to say, Hawks are not terribly enthusiastic about it.

## Efficiency and Inequality

Most of the games that people play involve both cooperation and conflict. Many contracts, including commitments to democracy, are difficult to specify and enforce. People who benefit from cooperation with one another on the international, national, community, or family level also negotiate over their share of benefits. Bargaining takes place explicitly or implicitly, sequentially or simultaneously, in a strategic environment structured by social institutions as well as technological and environmental parameters.

Social institutions are created by a process of collective nudging, pushing, and shoving. Once established, they in turn affect the fallback positions that define the spaces in which power can be exercised. This circular causality influences processes of production and reproduction in similar ways, and it explains why the neoclassical economic effort to separate efficiency from inequality is often futile. To define a social optimum as a situation in which no one can be made better off without making someone else worse off (in technical terms, Pareto optimality) is to ratify the existing distribution of bargaining power—which may well have been achieved by making someone worse off in a previous round.

### Principals and Agents

Economists have long studied the conceptual tug of war between equality and efficiency within capitalist firms. They have been less attentive to similar dynamics within patriarchal families. In both venues, principal-agent models illustrate the contradictory implications of hierarchical institutions. The term "principal" denotes "one with the power to specify the contract," and "agent" is "one who may agree to the contract but try to subvert it."[40] In most cases the principal is the leader or first mover, while the agent is the follower. This implies institutional context; in idealized forms of competitive market exchange, by contrast, buyers and sellers are on an equal footing and cannot influence one another's decisions.

Many neoclassical economists use principal-agent models to explain their confidence in the stylized capitalist firm as an efficient institutional form. Employers (principals) hire workers (agents) and agree to pay them for work performed over a specified period of time. Because employers are "residual claimants" with legal rights to whatever is left after all costs of production have been paid, they have a strong incentive to increase productivity in order to maximize profits.[41] From a neoclassical perspective, employers impose a form of discipline that may seem harsh (such as firing or laying off workers without compunction) but, in the long run, benefits everyone.

Of course, much depends on how the putative benefits of discipline are distributed. But the basic logic behind the claim of increased productivity is also flawed. When workers are paid according to hours on the job, rather than by a share of profits, they have an incentive to reduce their effort, or shirk. In production processes where piece work is impractical, teamwork is required, and pay-for-performance is difficult to administer, shirkers are difficult to identify.[42] Productivity is likely to suffer as a result. Profit sharing would likely align the incentives of owners and workers more efficiently.[43]

However, many economists remain skeptical of profit sharing because of vulnerability to free rider problems. If workers were co-owners, they might slack off in the expectation that other workers would make up the difference. Even one opportunist could undermine their efforts. This is true, and collective decision-making can be costly and difficult. On the other hand, workers have incentives to monitor and discipline one another and also to reduce other forms of free riding: they may be more willing to protect the environmental and social sustainability of their communities than a distant owner who cares only about the firm's bottom line.

Modern corporations do not fit the traditional picture of an owner-managed firm, because ownership is typically dispersed, with management delegated to salaried professionals (creating another layer of principal-agent problems). The logic of residual claimancy remains unchanged, however, with implications that reach beyond individual firms. Strategies for reducing shirking may include paying workers a premium that increases the cost of job loss in the event they are caught. This strategy, however, lowers overall employment and also increases inequalities between workers paid such an "efficiency wage" and others.[44] Other perverse outcomes can result. Owners and their deputized managers have a collective incentive to reduce the bargaining power of workers, by firing union organizers or merely threatening to relocate to lower wage communities. Such political investments can offer a higher rate of return than technological innovation or improved management.

Few economists recognize that the institutional structure of the capitalist firm was prefigured by the institutional structure of the traditional patriarchal family. For instance, until the latter half of the nineteenth century, English and US common law gave married men legal claim over both family property and the labor of their wives and minor children, including any wages they earned. Husbands and fathers were required only to provide for the basic subsistence of wives and children, not to fully share their income with them.[45] In other words, they were residual claimants who, like capitalists, legally controlled any surplus that remained after basic costs were covered.

Like workers in a capitalist firm, wives could shirk, a strategy sometimes dubbed "burnt toast." They also had recourse to more personal forms of bargaining, based on withdrawal of affection. Still, their options were limited; while they could not literally be fired, they could be beaten, confined, or economically neglected. That husbands could potentially resort to such options does not imply that they frequently did so. The mere threat of physical or sexual harassment exerted a disciplinary influence, making women more appreciative of (and dependent on) nonabusive men, just as horrendous treatment of many slaves in the American South enhanced the bargaining power of benevolent slaveholders. Many members of powerful groups choose to ignore or tolerate abuses of power that they would never directly perpetrate.

No matter how groups are defined, bargaining over distributional outcomes can create incentives for powerful groups to resist institutional changes that might increase overall output but reduce their share.[46] A large slice of a small pie can be more satisfying than a small slice of a larger one. Slaveholders in the United States outlawed the education of slaves because they believed that the resulting threat to their authority outweighed the potential economic benefits.[47] Individual employers may prefer technical innovations that preserve or increase their leverage over employees.[48] Capitalists as a class may prefer to keep unemployment high, reducing worker bargaining power, even if such policies reduce economic growth. Likewise, patriarchs may prefer to keep their wives at home under their control even at the cost of foregoing their potential earnings in the labor market.

The dynamics of level versus share—the absolute amount of surplus generated versus the share of that surplus that can be claimed—can also work the other way: sometimes a change in the potential size of the pie alters the way it is divvied up. Not that dispassionate cost-benefit analysis always drives decisions. People can become addicted to power, clinging to it even when costly or dysfunctional. Still, economic incentives can alter behavior, reshape negotiations, and weaken hierarchical institutions. Incentives for change are not always the byproduct of external events or technological innovation; sometimes they are created through imaginative forms of collective mobilization and institutional reform.

### Level and Share

The dialectic between efficiency and distribution is neatly illustrated by a diagram that highlights the distribution of collaboratively produced output. This diagram, featured in John Rawls's *Theory of Justice* and in many models of household bargaining, provides a way of visualizing both the causes and the effects of institutional power.[49] John Rawls, Amartya Sen, and others have referred to this process as "cooperative conflict," since it describes interactions between two parties who can benefit more from cooperation than from exiting the relationship.[50] Charles Mills correctly points out that this wording makes the process seem altogether benign and consensual.[51] Sometimes the more apt term is "coerced cooperation."

The altered wording highlights disparities created by structures of collective power that cannot be reduced to mere differences in wealth or income. Strategies of negotiation over institutional arrangements are shaped by fallback positions, next-best alternatives, or exit options that influence success in making distributional claims. Groups that gain institutional advantage—whether by legitimate or illegitimate means—can lock in claims to a larger share of the gains from cooperation, which, in turn, reinforce their collective power over social institutions.[52] This approach to collective conflict subsumes both the neoclassically influenced concept of rent-seeking and the Marxian theory of surplus extraction under a larger rubric of "gain-seeking."[53]

Picture two agents (be they individuals or groups) who are collaborating in ways that go beyond exchange in a competitive market. Imagine also that there are significant gains from cooperation, but it is difficult to measure individual contributions because they are contingent on synergies with others, unpriced resources, or public goods that cannot be neatly priced.[54] As emphasized in the earlier discussion of reproduction, human capabilities are themselves produced. Who, then, deserves the credit for what they create? In this context, the distribution of gains from cooperation is determined by a process of bargaining.[55]

Gains are defined here as economic output, but similar analysis could apply with other metrics, such as utility or leisure time. Figure 5.1 pictures a downwardly sloping line, labeled P, representing all possible allocations of a fixed resource between agents A and B—a kind of cooperative frontier that they have jointly achieved (technically dubbed a Pareto frontier). The vertical axis represents the resources available to A. If A receives all the gains from cooperation, its resources are represented by $A_1$. The resources available to B can be read off the horizontal axis. If B receives all the gains from cooperation, its resources are represented by $B_1$. All the points in the space between P and the axes represent allocations in which either agent could increase its resources without making the other worse off. All the points on P are efficient in the sense that no resources are "left on the table." On this line, the only way for either to increase its resources is to reduce those available to the other.

**Figure 5.1.** Bargaining over Shares When Fallback Positions Are Equal

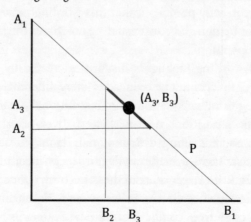

Both A and B have fallback positions that represent the resources available to them if they decline to cooperate or exit a cooperative agreement, labeled $A_2$ and $B_2$, respectively. Neither is likely to agree to an allocation of gains from cooperation that leaves them worse off than they would be on their own, so the range of feasible outcomes lies on the bold section of P between the two fallback positions, $A_2$ and $B_2$. That both can potentially gain from cooperation does not deter them from bargaining over the distribution of these gains. In Figure 5.1, their fallback positions are identical, which explains why the division represented by the point $(A_3, B_3)$ is an egalitarian one, and each player gets an equal share of the resources available.

A slight modification of Figure 5.1 illustrates the implications of unequal fallback positions. In Figure 5.2, player A has a much stronger fallback position than player B. As a result, the range of feasible outcomes (those which would leave both players better off) does not even include the possibility of equal division. Even if both players equally share the gains from cooperation—at point $A_3B_3$ on line P—player B receives a much smaller share. Indeed, player A is likely to do even better, claiming a share of the gains proportional to the difference in fallback positions.[56]

**Figure 5.2.** Bargaining over Shares When Fallback Positions Are Unequal

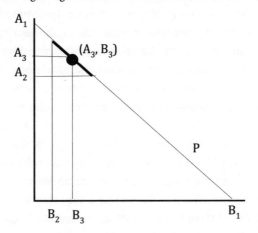

Figures 5.1 and 5.2 offer a static picture; in reality, bargaining is a dynamic process. The distribution of gains in an initial round can alter the position of P in a second round, by influencing either ability or incentives to cooperate to the fullest. Suppose that B's fallback is unknown or undetermined, and A offers B a specific distribution of the

gains from cooperation, including one that is quite unequal (such as a much higher level of $A_2$ and a much lower level of $B_2$). An authoritarian leader might be able to dictate shares at the point of a gun but would need to impose a penalty, or threat of punishment for exit in order for cooperation to continue, and this could be costly. If A is a first mover, he or she might also take subsistence constraints into consideration, ensuring that B receives a level of resources adequate to survival and continued voluntary or involuntary cooperation.

This incentive structure suggests a rough lower bound on the distribution of gains to the least empowered participant: a slaveholder has a vested interest in not beating or starving all his slaves to death; a capitalist must pay enough to ensure workers' long-run subsistence; a patriarch wants to ensure his sons' survival. However, forms of violence and neglect that are costly to individual power brokers may prove cost-effective for the dominant group because, as noted earlier, they exert a disciplinary effect.

### Democratic Hierarchy

Democracy is one of many social institutions that mediates these dynamics. Unlike an authoritarian leader, a democratically elected leader is subject to replacement. An elected authority is more easily held accountable than one who is not, even if perfect accountability lies out of reach. What determines the relative size of the total gains that an authoritarian and a democratically chosen leader are likely to deliver? If democracy is very time-consuming, if voters make poor decisions, or if voters block aggressive but potentially lucrative efforts to appropriate resources from other groups, the cooperative frontier could offer lower overall gains than that of an authoritarian regime. (In Figures 5.1 and 5.2, the P line would shift closer to the origin of both axes.)

On the other hand, authoritarian leadership generally requires greater investments in monitoring and punishment to shore up its distributional advantage, which could also lower total gains from cooperation. Further, an authoritarian leader is, by definition, less constrained than democratic leaders and so is likely to claim a larger share of the gains (like player A in Figure 5.2). As a result, people subject to authoritarian rule may fare worse than those subject to democratic rule even if democracy offers a lower overall level of total potential gains.[57]

The very existence of democratic institutions offering superior gains to most players can weaken authoritarian hierarchies in families and firms, as well as the polity. As a result, groups that benefit from authoritarian hierarchies based on gender, race/ethnicity, or class have less to gain from political democracy than others do. Likewise, citizens of rich countries have less to gain from global democracy than citizens of poor countries. Anyone in a position of privilege has an incentive to protect that privilege by denying its very existence.

The intersections of heavily entangled structures of collective power can have both stabilizing and destabilizing effects, with consequences for processes of social reproduction that may be unintended. For instance, potential gains from aggressive use of military power may increase along with a larger population, which can be achieved through appropriation of women from other groups and coercive pronatalism. No conspiracy is required: groups that adopt this strategy may simply prevail over those that do not. As I argue in Chapter 6, this possibility could help explain why authoritarian hierarchies often include patriarchal institutions.

On the other hand, the potential gains from accumulation of knowledge and creative innovation may outweigh those from other sources, creating economic pressures for more gender-egalitarian, low-fertility institutional regimes that discourage violent conflict and promote the development of human capabilities. While this scenario may sound like wishful thinking, it effectively illustrates possible shifts in collective payoffs that can alter bargaining outcomes. As Bob Dylan sang, when times are a-changin', "the first one now will later be last."

Once structures of collective power are well-established, they become inflexible and difficult to reform. On the other hand, they often develop a brittle quality that can shatter under pressure, leading to unpredictable consequences and, sometimes, collateral damage. Technological change is not the only catalyst of transformation. Much depends on the success of coalitional strategies that can enable disempowered groups to take advantage of their expanded bargaining space. Such strategies cannot be reduced to written agreements or official realignments. They can also find expression in principles of economic justice and mutual aid, enacted through cultural contestation, the threat of exit, and the development of alternative institutions.[58]

## Bargaining and Exploitation

Principles of economic justice and mutual aid are not easily agreed upon, for a rather obvious reason: they have implications for individual and collective redistribution. Neoclassical economic theory does not admit of the possibility of exploitation in voluntary exchange; classical Marxian theory typically locates it only in capitalist wage employment. Intersectional political economy requires a more general definition, which democratic principles can provide: exploitation can be defined as an unfair share of gains from cooperation resulting from the exercise of power gained by unfair means.

How is "unfair" to be defined? This is not a question to be answered by a college professor. It should, in principle, be democratically determined. In practice, we know that perceptions of fairness are themselves influenced by collective bargaining power, creating a circular problem similar to that which John Rawls proposed to solve by the imaginary thought experiment of putting decision-makers behind a "veil of ignorance" that blocked knowledge of their own identities and interests. Yet the definition of fairness is not entirely intractable, because it builds on the simple concept of a rule of law. We already negotiate binding definitions of legal and illegal that are based to some extent on definitions of fair and unfair, and this negotiation can and will continue, informed by a better understanding of the consequences for economic sustainability.

The principle of justice that Rawls espoused challenges unequal outcomes that do not leave the worst-off members of society better off. This principle connects quite clearly to the dialectic between the level of economic output and its distribution. Capitalist institutions historically derived much of their moral legitimacy from the promise of economic growth, as expressed in the saying "a rising tide lifts all boats." The Rawlsian challenge weakens, however, when the definition of "better off" extends beyond the metrics of income and wealth to include influence in shaping institutions of collective power. Even if and when disempowered groups enjoy increased levels of consumption, their potential for democratic participation and cultural clout may remain impaired, leaving them vulnerable to future exploitation.

One could interpret this concern for political and cultural as well as economic outcomes as an extension of the Rawlsian rule. But the concept of justice cannot be based entirely on consequences. History also matters. Some forms of collective and individual power are obtained by unfair means, such as violence, theft, fraud, and exclusion from political representation—violations conceded even by libertarian philosophers such as Robert Nozick. Marx described historical processes of expropriation as "written in the annals of mankind in letters of blood and fire."[59]

Both the direct and indirect effects of force and violence are often crystallized in the social institutions put into place by them. Expropriation of the means of production is only one such catalyst. Expropriation of people themselves through patriarchal rule, institutionalized slavery, and the imposition of colonial and imperial power, among other historical events, have equally momentous, long-lasting consequences. Systematic despoliation of common resources in the physical and social environment, including destabilization of the global climate, is only the latest addition to this list.

In the end, the definition of what is fair and what is not—like the legitimate rule of law—can only be established by democratic negotiation. Further, such negotiation is the only means to devise means and methods of redressing historical crimes through processes of reparation or reconciliation. Under what conditions could truly democratic negotiation take place? The answer to this question remains open. Whether it can be achieved or not depends largely on the potential for alliances among disparate groups that have experienced many different forms of disempowerment and exploitation. This potential, in turn, may depend on a clear picture of the ways in which fractured and overlapping forms of collective bargaining power influence economic outcomes.

### Cumulative Fallback Positions

The availability of visible, viable alternatives is a prerequisite of meaningful choices.[60] Weak fallback positions reduce bargaining power. Figure 5.2 illustrates parameters of empowerment that can lead to unfair allocation of gains from cooperation. Individuals sometimes overcome group-based disadvantage or squander group-based advantage, but this does not belie the effect of institutional structures of collective power on their likelihood of doing so.

A structure of patriarchal institutions reduces the fallback position of women. Likewise, a structure of racist institutions reduces the fallback position of groups based on race/ethnicity, and so on. Since individuals belong to many groups simultaneously, their individual bargaining power is a function of all their group memberships as well as their individual capabilities and effort. Their relative advantages or disadvantages do not necessarily cumulate in an additive or linear way, but it is usually possible to ascertain the sign of the effect: all else being equal, memberships in socially disadvantaged groups contribute to individual economic disadvantage.[61]

Such disadvantage means that members of such groups are less able to develop their capabilities or those of their children. It also implies that individual effort is rewarded less generously for some than for others, potentially reducing overall effort or diverting it toward activities that create social costs rather than benefits. In other words, it probably shifts the production frontier pictured in Figure 5.2 downward, toward the origin, even as it increases the share of output available to advantaged groups.

Efforts to increase the share of output, rather than its overall size, are sometimes referred to as "rent-seeking," because rents are largely a return to ownership rather than to effort. A more apt and less confusing term is "gain-seeking." An increase in total output represents what economists call "value creation," whereas an increase in bargaining share, or gain seeking, represents value extraction—in ordinary language, "making" creates value and "taking" redistributes it.[62] These terms are ideologically contested: conservatives argue that rich people are makers and poor people, takers, just as they once argued that men were workers and women, dependents.

Unfair bargaining power is a form of value extraction that encompasses what Marx described as exploitation. This terminology challenges the distinction that Erik Olin Wright and most other modern Marxist thinkers make between oppression and exploitation. Wright argues that the welfare of the oppressor (unlike that of the exploiter) "depends simply on the exclusion of the oppressed from access to certain resources, but not on their effort."[63] But the mutual dependency of groups—their voluntary or coerced cooperation—need not take the form of direct control of labor; it can take more indirect forms such as contributions to public goods, willingness to help others, or respect for the rule of law. The social distancing that helped buffer the effects of the Covid-19 pandemic, for example, required substantial effort on the part of some to help others. Yet in the United States, the gains from such actions were unequally felt; racial/ethnic minorities typically suffered much higher levels of mortality.[64]

Wright's distinction between exploitation and oppression remains meaningful, and discrimination can affect both. Not all economic inter-actions can be reduced to bargaining, be it fair or unfair. Some of the most consequential economic interactions take the form of outright theft, expropriation, injury, murder, or genocide. At the other extreme, some take the form of gifts. In between, however, lie many forms of gain-seeking behavior shaped by social institutions established by profoundly undemocratic means. When exploitation is defined as unfair advantage, even apparently innocent and impersonal choices made by those with no evil intent can lead to exploitative outcomes.[65]

Patriarchal institutions that increase men's bargaining power relative to women in both the family and the labor market lower women's life-time incomes, increase their vulnerability to poverty, and lengthen their total work day. Men benefit. Racist institutions that increase the bargain-ing power of whites diminish the relative access of other racial/ethnic groups to both private wealth and public services.[66] Whites benefit. Partly as a result of imperial legacies, citizens of affluent countries enjoy more purchasing power and political power than citizens of the global South; they are also, as a result, buffered from many of the costs and risks of extreme climate change. And so on. However difficult it may be to locate different forms of institutional power on horizontal and verti-cal axes, it is easy to understand how collective disadvantages reduce available options.

### Exploitations

Attention to structures of collective power expands Marxian accounts of dispossession as a form of primitive accumulation by highlighting the ways in which coercion can be capitalized into a steady stream of economic benefits.[67] The notion that history matters stands in sharp contrast to libertarian insistence that voluntary exchange—that is, exchange that does not take place literally at the point of a gun—is both equitable and efficient.[68] It rejects the view that people can inherit privi-lege without any responsibility for the ways in which it was obtained.

Structures of collective power create long-lasting economic legacies, effectively dramatized by debates over reparations for slavery in the United States.[69] To ask what slavery cost Black Americans as a group is to ask how much better off they would be if it had never existed or if earlier political promises to compensate for it had been kept. Such coun-terfactual thought experiments offer another way of assessing fairness.

Marxian economist John Roemer argues that workers are exploited if they would be better off withdrawing from a capitalist economy with their per capita share of total productive assets.[70]

Roemer defines exploitation exclusively in terms of asset ownership, which has limited application to gender inequality. But his counterfactual reasoning could easily be extended to include a broader set of social institutions. What if men had never established property rights over women themselves? What if women had always had equal access to education, skilled employment, or the franchise? The list of questions could go on. Building on Roemer, Robert Goodin aptly proposes a "feminist withdrawal rule" that pertains especially to the division of labor within partnered households: women are exploited if they work longer hours than they would if they exited the partnership taking with them an equal share of all the value created by it, including valuation of time devoted to family care.[71] Such a rule would be difficult to implement in practice, but it dramatizes the disadvantage resulting from the difficulty of capturing economic benefits from family care.

Counterfactual reasoning can also be applied to possible future outcomes. Erik Wright argues that "capitalism systematically generates unnecessary human suffering—unnecessary in the specific sense that with an appropriate change in socioeconomic relations these deficits could be eliminated."[72] One could substitute "patriarchal institutions" or "racist institutions" (or other coercive institutions) for "capitalism" in this claim. Economists who purport to study trade-offs seldom ask if and when the well-being of the many outweighs the luxuries of the few.

Not all oppression leads to exploitation. Nor is exploitation necessarily the more evil of the two. Indeed, sometimes people gain economically by entering into an exploitative relationship because it represents a better alternative to what they would otherwise fall back upon. This is exactly why fallbacks—and the processes by which they are institutionally constructed—are so important.

### Fallbacks, Power, and Complexity

The very term "fallback" has a military feel, connoting the best option for retreat. Socially constructed fortresses of advantage are often built from the prizes of a prior round of bargaining. Just as large firms can gain market share and then take advantage of economies of scale to ward off new entrants, groups can direct their collective winnings toward investments in their own long-run hegemony, whether by influencing laws and ideologies or simply by accumulating wealth. Perhaps this is just another way of saying that bargaining power has many different dimensions, including the power to obfuscate or habituate its deployment.[73]

The notion that social institutions have intersectional effects on the bargaining power of entire groups of people builds on feminist models of bargaining between husbands and wives in married households. Whether described as "extra-environmental parameters," "gender-specific environmental parameters," or as weights placed on individual preferences in a joint utility function, the effect of social institutions on the allocation of household resources is now widely recognized.[74] Yet attention to household/family dynamics also warns against overemphasis on purely individual interests: love and affection for others both mediates individual bargaining and increases the total gains from cooperation. If I love you, your gain is my gain, at least in part.

Altruism doesn't eliminate bargaining, but it certainly complicates it. We are all faced with uncertain and uncomfortable strategic choices: how much do we really care about people other than ourselves, and how much do others care about us? How much time and effort should we devote to improving our individual trajectories, how much to challenging—or reinforcing—exploitative institutions that constrain those trajectories? The difficulty of answering these questions demonstrates the limits of formal bargaining models, inviting more qualitative considerations.

As advertisements for a prominent business training consultant put it, "You don't get what you deserve. You get what you negotiate."[75] Even this slogan is too narrow. Not all bargaining is based on negotiation, and not all games end with contractual agreements. Threats and promises, fakes and feints, persuasion and coercion, coalition and compromise can take place without participants ever sitting down together at a table. Even market exchange is often contested.[76]

The process of negotiation probably matters as much as the structure of payoffs.[77] Effective bargaining may benefit from rational calculation but is easily undermined by inadequate information, poor communication, and emotional dysfunction. (Military strategists refer to these problems as the "fog of war.") Explicit bargaining is costly and time-consuming; it can also create resentment and ill will. Economists typically assume that outcomes are efficient in the narrow sense that agents always reach the bargaining frontier—that is, they won't block a move that improves another's outcome if it comes at no cost to them.[78] In the real world, however, spite often trumps reason, invites retaliation, and leaves both bargainers worse off than they were before: domestic murders are sometimes followed by the perpetrator's suicide. On the global level, the threat of mutually assured destruction—whether as a result of all-out nuclear conflict or irreversible environmental damage— continues to loom large.

These difficulties explain why social norms are so important: they offer implicit rules and sometimes explicit solutions to costly forms of disagreement. How best to divide a pie? "You slice, and I'll choose." Want to avoid a fight? "Let's flip a coin." Yet conformity to existing social norms generally favors those in already favored positions.[79] Once seized, rights to authority and property are often sanctified by ideology. As Edna Ullmann-Margalit writes, a norm may "be conceived of as a sophisticated tool of coercion, used by the favored party in a status quo of inequality to promote its interest in the maintenance of this status quo."[80] Just as norms of appropriate femininity can reinforce gender inequality, patriotic norms can justify aggression against countries, racial pride can fuel white supremacy, and elitist values can legitimate class disparities.

Norms are often internalized in ways that affect individual prefer- ences and perceptions. If one bargainer cares more about the other (or about third parties who may be affected), bargaining outcomes will be skewed in favor of the less altruistic or more assertive member. In a generalization of the "hidden injuries" of class, confinement to the bottom of a hierarchy weakens individual and group agency.[81] Reminders of inferior social position (known as "stereotype threat") can hamper the performance of those who are stigmatized.[82] Heteronormative values as well as homophobic attitudes undermine the confidence of those labeled deviant. Patriarchal power and colonial power can be poison- ously internalized in remarkably similar ways.[83] The view from the top, by contrast, is empowering—often dangerously so.

## Modes of Production vs. Hierarchical Systems

Individuals make strategic decisions constrained by institutional struc- tures of collective power. These structures do not result purely from class conflict, and they cannot be reduced to a single mode of production such as capitalism. They can best be understood as interlocking hierarchies based on many different dimensions of assigned group membership, including gender. None of these dimensions is intrinsically more consequential than the others; their relative importance depends not just on specific economic circumstances, but also on strategies for building effective coalitions.

The magnitude of top rider problems puts free rider problems in perspective, and the similarities among different forms of authoritarian hierarchy provide some clues to their coevolution. The deep legacy of collective conflict in human history cannot easily be overcome, but rotten dads, rotten employers, and rotten leaders can be deposed. Ideals of democratic cooperation, equal opportunity, and mutual aid have sustained successful challenges to many authoritarian hierarchies, including those that can be described as patriarchal. Moreover, the empowerment of women prefigures other possible advances toward democratic governance on a larger scale.

# II

# Reconstructed Narratives

# 6

# Patriarchal Ascents

Although structures of collective power constitute much of the scaffolding of human history, our understanding of their institutional construction remains seriously incomplete. Evolutionary reasoning suggests that hierarchies may emerge because they provide some advantages to the groups that create them, allowing them to eliminate, disable, out-compete, or gradually displace other groups. Speculative accounts of the origin of hierarchy typically dwell on the implications of productive technologies, comparing gatherer/hunter, pastoral, agricultural, and industrial societies. These distinctions elide important variations within these technological categories, minimizing the significance of the social institutions that govern collective violence, production, and reproduction.

Early research on the possible origins of patriarchal institutions initially had little impact outside feminist scholarship but has gradually gained traction.[1] Some revisionist applications of Marxian historical materialism bring sexuality and reproduction front and center.[2] Likewise, some forays into the time spans of "big history" incorporate conflicts based on gender and age, noting their implications for social transitions over vast periods of time from the prehistoric to the present.[3] None of these approaches, however, provide a consistent theoretical framework for analysis of intersectional conflicts.

The historical record reveals multiple interactions among structures of collective power based on gender and other forms of socially assigned group membership. In the early stages of human history, patriarchal and other authoritarian institutions appear to have coevolved under the pressure of conflict and competition among groups. Despotism, slavery, feudalism, capitalism, and colonialism did not represent new stages of history or even new pages replacing old ones. Rather, they created new layers of hierarchy that overlaid and sometimes altered preexisting inequalities.

## Histories of the Patriarchal

Speculation on the links between social evolution and gender inequality has long animated feminist theorists eager to believe that history was on their side. The notion that traditional gender roles were anachronistic relics of an earlier era—a byproduct of economic circumstances and social institutions rather than divine design—found expression in nineteenth-century social science and historical research. The more specific argument that patriarchal institutions were linked to war and other forms of collective conflict has particularly deep antecedents in the cultural history of Western Europe.

### Gender and Evolution

Some early feminists welcomed Darwinian theory as a powerful rebuttal of religious doctrines of feminine responsibility for original sin and expulsion from the Garden of Eden.[4] Charlotte Perkins Gilman, author of the widely read *Women and Economics,* published in 1898, argued that social norms encouraging women to specialize completely in family care were both unnatural and maladaptive.[5] While Darwin was no advocate of women's rights, his ideas regarding group selection provided an opening for feminist reasoning. The sociologist Leta Hollingworth anticipated some of the arguments in this chapter when she wrote, in 1916:

> The fact is that child-bearing is in many respects analogous to the work of soldiers: it is necessary for tribal or national existence; it means great sacrifice of personal advantage; it involves danger and suffering, and, in a certain percentage of cases, the actual loss of life. Thus we should expect that there would be a continuous social effort to insure the group-interest in respect to population, just as there is a continuous social effort to insure the defense of the nation in time of war. It is clear, indeed, that the social devices employed to get children born, and to get soldiers slain, are in many respects similar.[6]

Thinkers influenced by Friedrich Engels's *Origins of Family, Private Property and The State* have generally attributed gender inequality to the rise of private property in early class societies.[7] August Bebel's earlier work, *Woman and Socialism*, however, treated inequalities based on class and gender as parallel, rather than sequential phenomena, attributing both to the violent imposition of coercive laws and norms.[8] Engels's view may have prevailed because it was the more optimistic one. It had become apparent that hunting and gathering societies occupied a large span of human prehistory. If such societies were entirely cooperative and egalitarian, they set a powerful precedent for future socialism.

Some gatherer/hunter societies seem to fit this idealized picture, and the transition to private property may well have consolidated inequalities based on class and gender.[9] On the other hand, the claim that gatherer/hunter technology and the absence of private property and a state automatically guaranteed egalitarian outcomes seems far-fetched. Patriarchal institutions may well have preceded the emergence of private property in either land or livestock. Maria Mies argues that a "predatory mode of production" allowed men to seize surplus in the form of young women from other groups.[10] Riane Eisler describes neolithic European societies based on partnership between the sexes that were overrun and overwhelmed by violent authoritarian marauders.[11]

All such arguments are handicapped by the difficulty of historically reconstructing what were essentially prehistoric events. Yet evolutionary reasoning linking hierarchy to organized violence resonates with iconic episodes drawn from the ancient history of profoundly patriarchal cultures.

### The Spoils of War

The much-studied history of Western Europe reveals potent associations between war and control over women. The *Iliad* begins with the theft of a wife and features a general who hopes to gain divine assistance by cutting his daughter Iphigenia's throat. The warriors who besiege and ultimately destroy Troy compete with one another for concubines. The Amazon Penthesilea wins Achilles' respect in hand-to-hand combat, but her defeat relegates women warriors to the past. In Aeschylus's classic drama, Iphigenia's mother kills her husband in revenge for her daughter's sacrifice, only to be killed in turn by her own son.

Roman history also tells a gendered story of collective conflict. As Plutarch tells it, the men who founded the city of Rome were unable to find wives without resorting to trickery. They invited the neighboring Sabines to bring their families to a festival, ambushed them, drove the men away, seized the young women, and impregnated them. By the time the Sabine men regrouped and returned with allies to reclaim their kin, many of the women had given birth.[12] The mothers threw themselves between the armies, begging their fathers and brothers not to fight the fathers of their newborn children. Their collective gesture was immortalized by some of the greatest artists in Europe, including Nicolas Poussin, Jacques-Louis David, and Pablo Picasso.

The abduction of the Sabine women illustrates how maternal commitment could make rape an effective strategy for individual men (enhancing their reproductive success) and for groups (effectively increasing their numbers). It also reveals how allegiances based on kinship could complicate or even reinforce group inequalities. Control over women's marriage decisions offered groups a means of building some alliances and effectively blocking others—a dynamic that later became central to caste systems, racial boundaries, and national identities.[13]

The Hebrew Bible, or Old Testament, often placed rape and war under the same rubric as in "You may enjoy the spoil of your enemies."[14] Under the leadership of Moses, the Hebrew tribes vanquished the Midianites, seizing their goods and livestock and killing all but the young women who had never had sexual intercourse (32,000 in all).[15] The text of Deuteronomy 21 specifies that women taken captive during war could be taken as wives after one month.[16] In the late nineteenth century Friedrich Nietzsche reiterated this ethos in terms that would later saturate Nazi ideology: "Man shall be trained for war, and woman for the recreation of the warrior."[17] In this context, recreation carries a double meaning.

## Social Evolutions

Productive efficiency, reproductive fitness, and military power may all contribute to group success in a variety of ways. Evolutionary psychologists and neoclassical economists tend to emphasize inherited behavioral propensities or preferences; feminist psychologists and economists are more likely to emphasize social institutions.[18] These two approaches are not mutually exclusive, a point emphasized in human behavioral ecology, which points to the dual inheritances of genes and culture.[19]

Social institutions mediate the expression of biological differences as well as their economic consequences.

Evolutionary success does not necessarily imply superior efficiency; it may result from opportunistic violence rather than from productive or reproductive capabilities. Murder and theft can lower overall output but benefit their perpetrators. Human groups have grown rich not only by increasing their own productive capacity, but also by extracting resources from other groups, two strategies that have often proved complementary. Moreover, as Tyrannosaurus rex and other fossilized relics of extinction attest, evolutionary success often proves temporary.[20]

### The Behavioral Ecology of Gender

The behavioral ecology of primates and monkeys reveals links between characteristics of the natural environment, group competition, social organization, and differences based on sex. For instance, among baboons, ground dwellers that often stand and fight, males are much larger and stronger than females; among arboreal monkeys, tree dwellers specialized in evasion and flight, males and females are physically similar. Behavioral variations are vast. Differences in dynamics between females and males are significant even among primates that inhabit only slightly different ecological niches, such as chimpanzees and bonobos.[21]

Evolutionary biology has traditionally emphasized the selection pressures at work on males, emphasizing their competition for females. A growing literature, however, emphasizes the selection pressures directly at work on females. Among species in which offspring are dependent on maternal nurturance and protection for a prolonged period, maternal intelligence, resourcefulness, and strategic thinking enhance reproductive success.[22] If male success is affected by ability to manipulate and control females, the opposite is also true: female success is affected by ability to minimize the adverse effects of such manipulation on their own reproductive fitness.[23] Female primates, for instance, often form coalitions designed to protect themselves and their offspring from male violence.[24]

Attention to sex-based forms of collective action among primates supports the claim that social institutions mediate the effects of gendered behavioral propensities. In human societies, memes are especially important relative to genes: the biological coevolution of male and female strategies is overlaid by the cultural coevolution of social institutions that can improve both reproductive success and economic advantage.

## Before Sedentary Agriculture

In the gatherer/hunter societies long considered representative of the least hierarchical stage of human history, women tend to specialize in gathering or foraging, men in hunting. Most research on their social evolution focuses on the implications of these technologies of production, lumping all gatherer/hunter societies together. Recent research, however, shows considerable variation within this category.

Both gathering and hunting activities can contribute to caloric intake, complementing one another in terms of nutritional value and seasonality. Gains to cooperative hunting are often greater with large game (whether stags or whales) than with small game. Likewise, gains to cooperative gathering may be greater when forage possibilities are concentrated rather than scattered and diffuse.[25] The relative payoffs to cooperation in a Fruit Hunt game may parallel those in the stylized game known as Stag Hunt, with a payoff matrix that conveys the trade-offs between collaboration and going it alone.

Reproductive priorities also come into play. Gathering and foraging are more complementary with care for dependents than are most hunting activities. When women work together collecting and preparing food, they can easily share responsibility for the supervision of young children or the care of sick or frail adults. The relative costs of caring for dependents are affected by many factors, including the age at which children can begin to care for themselves (or one another) and contribute to their own subsistence. For instance, hunting is a skill that requires years to develop, which implies that male children do not begin to contribute to adult consumption until a relatively late age.[26]

The demographic dynamics of gathering and hunting groups were probably distinct from those of groups that settled in place. The need to keep on the move without the assistance of domesticated animals probably made high dependency ratios costly. Young children must be carried, and an adult cannot easily carry more than one at a time. As a result, highly mobile groups were likely to limit their birth rates, encouraging lengthy breastfeeding (which reduces the probability of conception) and imposing restrictions on forms of sexual intercourse likely to lead to conception.[27] They may also have resorted to infanticide. Norms that encouraged the disabled or frail to leave the group—or be abandoned by it—could also have limited care burdens.[28]

## Fighting and Stealing

The economic organization of many gatherer/hunter societies may have contributed to relatively egalitarian gender relations, but variations in weaponry and social institutions could lead to distinct outcomes, particularly in areas where intense intergroup conflict emerged. Fighting and stealing, rape and subjugation could affect both productive and reproductive success.

Marxian scholars such as Eleanor Leacock have often romanticized gatherer/hunter societies, arguing that their failure to generate a surplus meant they had little to quarrel over.[29] But the archaeological record of early gatherer/hunter economies reveals a variegated pattern of altruism within groups combined with considerable fighting among groups, efforts to capture women, and many violent deaths.[30] Egalitarian groups hoping to avoid conflict may have proved vulnerable to invasion by aggressors who could both expand their territory and increase their own numbers by seizing women and children.[31] As the Hawk-Dove Game outlined in Chapter 5 suggests, aggressive groups are most successful when surrounded by groups who are conflict-averse. Jared Diamond's riveting account of the Maori extermination of the Moriori provides a memorable example.[32] The Moroiori islanders, with no experience or expectation of armed conflict, proved easy prey.

Male specialization in hunting and warfare could have had spillover effects on gender relations, increasing men's ability to dominate and physically abuse women. The most successful warriors are also the most able to threaten and dominate other group members, and they may parlay that advantage into the establishment of authoritarian institutions such as hereditary leadership.[33] Intergroup conflict indirectly promotes hierarchical institutions by making it difficult for individuals to survive on their own, reducing their exit options.

Early examples of warfare technology include archery and the use of domesticated animals, technologies that reached far beyond the neolithic era.[34] In the Great Plains of the United States, the expert management of horses by some Native American tribes such as the Comanche allowed them to vanquish their sedentary neighbors.[35] Greek tales of Amazons were likely based on female Scythian warriors who rode side-by-side with men; a woman on a horse armed with a bow is deadlier than a man standing with sword alone.[36] Perhaps in this respect

Amazons foreshadowed the gendered implications of drone warfare today—women can click on virtual triggers just as fast as men.

The costs and benefits of war in prehistoric times were probably measured largely in demographic terms: the high mortality of young adult males versus the increased fertility that could be achieved through the capture of young adult females.[37] In such circumstances, young men faced a terrible trade-off: the risk of injury or death was almost certainly greater than the likelihood of individual rewards. At the same time, the logic of group selection could have delivered significant advantages to groups in which young men were socialized to fight—whether or not they had a behavioral propensity to do so.[38]

The costs of war were also high for women. They were subject to murder, capture, and rape as well as economic vulnerability resulting from the death of their partners.[39] A high incidence of warfare may also have reduced their collective bargaining power relative to men's. In addition to the reproductive costs from the loss of sons (higher for mothers than for fathers who could potentially sire more), both high male mortality and the capture of young fertile girls would have increased the overall supply of women relative to men, reducing their bargaining power and making it difficult for them to form monogamous partnerships. Once established, patriarchal control over women could contribute to demographic flexibility rather than expansion, enforcing female infanticide as a kind of safety valve.[40]

Pastoral economies based on privately owned domesticated animals may also have facilitated the subordination of women. The economic incentives to organized theft were magnified by wealth on the hoof. Many pastoral societies engaged in constant raids, particularly during periods of economic stress such as drought.[41] Theft of large animals could easily have been extended to theft of young women, and seclusion of these women could have made it easier to control them. Domestication is a word easily applied to both animals and people.[42] Indeed, in some pastoral societies men obtain wives by paying a bride price in livestock.[43]

Frederick Engels noted that private property increased men's desire to ensure paternity of their children, motivating control over women's sexuality.[44] Modern evolutionary theory offers a more specific theory of male mate-guarding, based on levels of paternal investment that affect the patriarchal bargain. If fathers do not devote many resources to their biological children—whether as a result of rape, casual sexual encounters resulting in pregnancy and paternal abandonment, or community-level support for child-rearing—female partner fidelity may not significantly affect their reproductive success. If fathers devote substantial resources to children, however, they seek to ensure that those children are their own. Male control over private property ensures that the resulting terms of trade (support in return for fidelity) are favorable to them.

Both gatherer/hunter and pastoral societies that developed patriarchal control over women could have become more likely to fight, steal, and raid than other groups.[45] They could also have achieved greater regulation of their population size. The most successful warriors could obtain more women, benefit from their productive and reproductive services, and further consolidate their authority.[46] If women and men ever lived in a Garden of Eden, it was not Eve's disobedience that forced them from it. Nor is there sufficient evidence to conclude that private property was the original sin.

### Not Just Surplus

Sedentary agriculture increased the potential for generating surplus that could easily be stored and accumulated, providing a greater basis for wealth accumulation. Many institutionalist economists, as well as some directly influenced by the Marxian tradition, have emphasized causal links between agriculture and the emergence of extractive institutions.[47] Archaeological research suggests a more mixed picture, with variable levels of wealth inequality among gatherer/hunter societies.[48] Some early agricultural societies, such as the neolithic community of Çatalhöyük in what is now Turkey, were apparently quite egalitarian.[49] The Çatalhöyük site also reveals relatively little economic differentiation between women and men.[50]

The potential to generate an agricultural surplus almost certainly promoted hierarchical institutions, but centralized systems of political control—"states"—probably emerged from military victories when defeated groups unable to flee or relocate could not avoid subjugation.[51] Sedentary societies were often vulnerable to external attack. Recorded history provides some clues to prehistoric dynamics: the thirteenth-century Mongol leader Genghis Khan allegedly claimed that he knew no greater pleasure than to vanquish his enemies, steal their possessions, and impregnate their wives and daughters. A recent summary of his conquests describes genetic evidence that more than thirty-two million people in the world today are descended from him.[52] It did not take long for this roving bandit to discover the advantages of settling down. When the Mongol army conquered northern China in the thirteenth century, one Khan proposed extermination of the native population until a minister pointed out that taxing them all would be more profitable.[53]

Both economic productivity and military success were influenced by the organization of reproduction, with possible economies of scale for large populations in both domains. High birth rates may also have proved advantageous to groups as an impetus to both technological change and to territorial expansion.[54] Many economists still assume that population growth in the past was driven largely by changes in mortality, with a constant level of "natural" or unrestricted fertility, but this Malthusian assumption has been undermined by evidence of variability in the birth rates of pre-industrial populations.[55]

The economic transition to sedentary agriculture probably encouraged increased fertility for a number of reasons: infant mortality rates remained high (and may even have increased) because the advantages of increased caloric intake were counterbalanced by greater exposure to vectors of contagious disease. The need for mobility was reduced, and care of children could be combined with directly productive activities close to home, including hoe cultivation and care of small animals. Children could contribute to agricultural work such as watering and weeding at a relatively young age.

The microeconomic incentives built into agricultural technology were reinforced by patriarchal institutions. Property rights over land gave men economic leverage over their wives and children, increasing the likelihood of receiving substantial support in old age.[56] At the same time, restrictions on the economic alternatives available to women outside of marriage limited their agency within it. While both parents could benefit from increased control over children, mothers literally bore most of the costs of raising large families.

Coercive pronatalism and compulsory heterosexuality pressured both men and women to raise as many children as possible.[57] The Book of Genesis in the Old Testament or Hebrew Bible exhorts all to "be fruitful and multiply." Other major world religions, including Christianity and Islam, uphold high fertility and homophobia, promising rewards in the afterlife in return for adherence to their doctrines. Such promises, encouraging submission to secular as well as religious authority, have proved especially costly for women.

# Hybrid Hierarchies

Could systematic forms of control over women have emerged in the absence of other forms of collective conflict? Simple hierarchies based on gender and age alone would likely have proved unstable, susceptible to continuous conflict and bargaining. More complex, intersecting hierarchies could not eliminate such costs, but they could reduce them, creating overlapping incentives for acquiescence. Despotic rulers with the greatest levels of political power typically enjoyed the greatest access to women's sexual and reproductive capabilities; women might comply for the sake of their future children.[58] Men subject to the authority of other men were, perhaps, partially consoled by their authority over women and children. Structures of collective power impose subtle and enduring forms of subordination.

## Slavery and Patriarchy

As Gerda Lerner and others have observed, it seems likely that the enslavement of women both preceded and informed the enslavement of men.[59] Slavery, defined as institutionalized control over another person's body and labor power, initially emerged in the aftermath of war as an alternative to extermination of the defeated. Most of the slaves referred to in the *Iliad* and the *Odyssey* are women. In ancient Greece and Rome, enslavement of both women and men—often foreigners—was relatively widespread.

Though the extent of physical authority over slaves in Greece, Rome, and elsewhere varied, its abusive and exploitative character was never limited to mere forced labor on farms or in mines. Slave owners typically demanded sexual and reproductive services as well. In some areas, infibulation of female slaves—installation of a metal ring closing the labia majora to prevent intercourse—was not uncommon.[60] Historical evidence suggests that female genital cutting in northern Africa was originally devised to expedite an extensive slave trade in concubines whose virginity (and nonpregnancy) had to be guaranteed until their final sale. Descendants of groups involved in this early trade appear more likely than others to engage in such cutting today.[61] In his comparative study of sixty-six societies, Orlando Patterson argues that a distinctive feature of slavery was forced abnegation of family ties, resulting in "social death."[62] Couples could not form lasting relationships, and children were often separated from their parents.

In Western Europe during the Middle Ages, religious doctrine discouraged the enslavement of Christians but often justified the enslavement of infidels. As international trade expanded along with colonization, slaves came to be harvested, like other raw materials, from vulnerable societies. The demand for slave labor was fueled by the development of labor-intensive plantation-style agriculture in new European colonies, where workers could be closely supervised and disciplined by overseers. In this context, slave ownership became a source of significant capital accumulation, contributing to the emergence of new class differences as well as intense race-based exploitation.[63]

The enslavement of "others" reduced the threat that intense exploitation might otherwise pose to group solidarity. In the eighteenth century, the German naturalist Johann Blumenbach devised an influential racial classification system codifying a hierarchy of worth with Caucasians, named after his favorite European mountain range, at the top.[64] In the United States, race was legally determined by genealogy; evidence of any Black ancestor or, in more colloquial terms, a single drop of African blood, defined a person as Negro.[65] National origin and race were often conflated, as in the derogatory designation of Irish immigrants to the United States as "blacks."[66]

The bounty that slavery offered a landed elite engaged in global commodity trade spawned a particularly vicious and enduring form of racism based on exploitation in reproduction and production. In French and English colonies, slave owners wielded virtually complete control over their human chattel, guaranteeing a cheap supply of sexual services for their owners and demographic accumulation of labor power/human capital. In the US South, slave children became a cash crop that became particularly lucrative after the international slave trade was banned, boosting domestic demand.[67]

White slave owners in the United States could sell their own progeny. Interviews with ex-slaves indicate that whites fathered children in about one out of every six mother-headed families.[68] Elsewhere, slave owners were subject to stricter regulation. In Spanish colonies, royal decrees influenced by Catholic doctrine stipulated that slaves could marry, that married couples could not be separated, and that individuals had the right to purchase their freedom. These costly legal constraints may have contributed to the relatively early decline of slavery there.[69]

Slave-based systems were often stabilized by a complex overlay of hierarchies. White women tolerated patriarchal institutions not only because they perceived no alternatives, but also because class differences pitted them against one another in competition for alliances with powerful men. Racial privileges increased their stake in the status quo. Southerners defended slavery as a familylike institution, but whatever affective bonds developed between the masters and mistresses of the plantation and their chattel were tenuous at best. Ideological justifications took elaborate forms, often based on assumptions of natural inferiority.

Still, wherever slavery existed, collective resistance was sometimes fortified by intersectional dynamics. Ancient Greek history offers a parable of sorts. In the late eighth century B.C.E., the Spartans conquered their neighbors, the Messenians, taking control over their land and their labor. Because Messenian slaves were prone to revolt, control over them required the virtually permanent military mobilization of Spartan men. Spartan women, left largely on their own, took considerable responsibility for the administration and management of agricultural estates. Perhaps as a result, they gained far greater rights to property ownership than their counterparts elsewhere in Greece.[70]

Spatial segregation affected the organization of reproduction, as well as production. Often separated from their husbands, Spartan wives typically bore fewer children than other Greek women, reducing the growth rate of a population already lowered by war-related mortality. Over a period of more than two centuries, the relative decline of the Spartan population reduced the relative size of the Spartan fighting force, and the Messenians finally overthrew their masters. In the wake of the resulting military demobilization, the property rights of Spartan women were restricted and gradually reverted to the Greek norm.[71]

The end of slavery in the United States was also inflected by intersectional dynamics. The Civil War broke out as a dispute over states' rights as well as the legitimacy of slavery itself. Economic differences between the North and the South pitted two very different wealth-owning classes against one another. In the North, popular outrage against the institution of slavery was fueled by Harriet Beecher Stowe's popular book, *Uncle Tom's Cabin*, a tale of the forced separation of slave mothers and fathers from their children. The conduct of the war itself pushed President Lincoln to the then-controversial signing of an Emancipation Proclamation that resulted in a huge redistribution of wealth from slave owners to slaves themselves.

## Patriarchal Feudalism

European historians have long used the term "feudalism" to describe Western European hierarchies that relied heavily on forms of coercion that fell short of slavery but restricted the mobility of a rural peasantry.[72] Inherited property rights in land, forced labor, and military conscription allowed lords and ladies alike to prosper at the expense of those who grew their food and served their tables. Yet ladies had far less scope for individual choice than their lords, and peasant women, despite their important economic contributions, remained subject to male authority, violence, and harassment.[73]

Class hierarchy sometimes overrode gender hierarchy, as when lords laid sexual claim to the brides of their subordinates. Many variations were evident. The English monarchy (unlike the French) allowed women to rule as queens in the absence of a male heir. In general, however, monarchs reinforced the authority of most men over most women and children in return for obeisance to their own power as head of a metaphorical household—a patriarchal quid pro quo.

Until the late seventeenth century, patriarchalism was a largely unchallenged tenet of European political thought.[74] The French philosopher Jean Bodin described fathers and kings in parallel terms.[75] Sir Robert Filmer's *Patriarcha*, published in 1680, eloquently defended the divine right of inherited male authority.[76] It described men as children of a heavenly father ruled by his representatives in the flesh. Filmer purported to trace the lineage of the King of England to the first Adam and attributed men's dominion over women and children to Adam's birthright.[77]

Patriarchal feudalism created strong pronatalist pressures that almost certainly contributed to high birth rates and, when mortality subsided, population growth. In a labor-intensive economy based largely on cooperation among kin, more children meant more workers, and more workers meant more surplus. Religious doctrines restricted women's opportunities outside marriage, sanctified their subordination within it, and prohibited sexual practices unlikely to result in conception. Contrary to Malthusian reasoning, the resulting population growth did not always lead to immiseration. On the contrary, it often stimulated technological change, including improvements in agriculture such as draining of swamp land and terracing of fields.[78]

High fertility also helped guarantee a large supply of labor, reducing the bargaining power of workers as a group. External demographic shocks tended to undermine hierarchical institutions. The devastating effects of the Black Death plague in fourteenth-century Europe empowered peasants and weakened the grip of feudal elites.[79] Orphaned daughters and widows, in particular, gained new access to property. Silvia Federici argues convincingly that the intensified persecution of witches—primarily women—during this period represented a ruling class effort to reassert patriarchal—and pronatalist—control over women.

Oddly, however, Federici absolves men of any agency in this process, explaining their collusion as the result of "propaganda and terror."[80] She never explains why capitalism itself "demanded a genocidal attack on women" or which capitalists, exactly, she is referring to in a society dominated by feudal and semi-feudal relations of production.[81] Her riveting account of organized violence against women is more consistent with an intersectional approach in which the class interests of landholders and the gender interests of men overlapped in lethal ways.

It seems likely that the quantitative impact of plagues overshadowed the demographic impact of witch hunts and weakened patriarchal institutions in Europe relative to those in other regions of the world. Still, these institutions remained in force, and as population growth gradually regained its momentum, opportunities for expanding cultivation narrowed. In some areas, families found it difficult to provide adequate land to support the next generation, and fragmentation of land holdings contributed to the immiseration of the rural population.

Under these circumstances, the very institutions that allowed the elderly to recoup some of their investments in the younger generation by relying on them for support proved adaptive. By discouraging early marriage (and withholding the transfer of property or use-rights required to make it feasible), fathers increased the gap between generations and improved chances of future prosperity.[82] The Catholic Church provided a place for unmarried sons and daughters, enforcing their celibacy as monks and nuns, while institutionalized prostitution provided a carnal safety valve for men.

The very imbrications of patriarchal feudalism in Europe lent it resilience. Control over women's sexual and reproductive lives, never absolute, nonetheless reinforced class-based forms of economic and political power based on inheritance of property. The opposite was also true: class power, for the most part, enforced gender power. Yet despite these forms of exploitation—and perhaps partly because of the particular forms they took—Western Europe achieved gradual improvements in its collective military and economic capabilities that positioned it for later capitalist development and imperial domination.

### Patriarchal Hybrids Outside Europe

The class-based hierarchies that emerged in many areas of the world outside Europe also perpetrated patriarchal authority over women and children, taking a variety of overlapping forms. While egalitarian arrangements sometimes survived in their interstices, large-scale states imposed centralized cultural, as well as political control. The emergence of major world religions testified to homogenizing forces that often took a patriarchal form.

In China, Confucian principles dictated women's Three Subordinations: as daughters, to their fathers; as wives, to their husbands; as widows, to their eldest sons.[83] Male household heads enjoyed property rights over their children.[84] Rapid demographic expansion in China between the seventeenth and nineteenth centuries (as in some other regions of the world) was curbed by female infanticide. A detailed study of demographic trends in one province between 1774 and 1873 reveals consistently tilted sex ratios that could not have been achieved by any other means.[85]

Confined to social roles that offered them no other path to prosperity, women sometimes took action that perpetuated their own collective subordination. The history of foot-binding in China provides a case in point. A crippling practice initially encouraged by the nobility sometime between the tenth and thirteenth centuries, it gradually spread to other classes and other regions; by the early nineteenth century more than half of all Chinese women had suffered a permanent mutilation that caused excruciating pain, endangered their health, and restricted their mobility. The resulting disability limited their ability to work outside the home and helped enforce their seclusion and fidelity.

Only the poorest families, most reliant on women's participation in agricultural labor, seemed willing to spare their daughters' feet. The custom of foot-binding persisted for centuries, only to be abruptly undone in the early twentieth century when a group of influential men publicly announced that they would never marry a woman with bound feet. Their actions tipped mothers toward the hope their daughters might actually fare better if they defied tradition.[86]

In India, the elaborate caste system of Brahminic Hinduism relied heavily on family control over marriages and female sexual behavior as a way of simultaneously enforcing subgroup identities and bolstering male authority. In the early twentieth century, B. R. Ambedkar insisted that patriarchal institutions such as sati (self-immolation of widows) and denial of property rights to women served the interests of privileged castes. Female compliance was achieved through a "combination of consent and coercion."[87] That caste rules regarding both endogamy and the division of labor have varied considerably over space and time is hardly surprising: these were institutions whose economic rewards were often contingent on specific circumstances.[88]

In the Middle East, Islamic doctrines with less explicit rules regarding gender helped unify otherwise disparate groups. The actual letter of religious texts such as the Quran had far less impact on family law than interpretations proffered by political and religious authorities.[89] While some economists argue that Islamic family law impeded economic development, hegemonic patriarchal institutions in other regions of the world did not cause long-term blockages.[90] Intersectional forces in the Middle East were distinctive: economies based largely on extraction of highly monopolized oil resources, combined with multiple forms of international interference, channeled a defensive ideological response into patriarchal practices that discouraged productive investment.[91]

The terms of patriarchal bargains vary enormously over time, but the basic parameters for women are remarkably similar: submission to men and specialization in family care in return for a modicum of economic support. The stability of this bargain depends in large part on the viability of other options. While these options are circumscribed by the physical and technological environment, they are also influenced by the formation of coalitions capable of modifying interlocking structures of collective power.

## Patriarchal Colonialisms

Between the sixteenth and nineteenth centuries, European countries converted their geographic and economic advantages into military capabilities that often, in turn, reinforced their economic success.[92] The record of collective aggrandizement by force and violence, including enslavement, belies cheerful accounts of the "rise of the West" based largely on entrepreneurial innovation.[93] Historical accounts of the impact of the slave trade on European capital accumulation prefigured the emergence of postcolonial scholarship that documents both the material and ideological legacies of colonialism.[94]

It is difficult to determine what portion of the extracted surplus fed the process of capital accumulation. Colonization sometimes poisoned its perpetrators, as when vast appropriations of silver and gold from the Incas led to crippling inflation in Spain.[95] Imperial power also funneled vast riches into the maws of corrupt monarchs.[96] Yet in many instances, colonization empowered an emerging class of traders, investors, and entrepreneurs capable of generating significant ongoing economic gains. Colonial powers often brandished the potential benefits of global power to their subaltern populations, promising them ample compensation for their subordination. Their marketing of the putative benefits of modernity enhanced their ability to divide, conquer, and control entire countries.[97]

### Colonial Fatherhood

Conquest alone was never sufficient to establish institutional control over vast new geographies. Colonization required strategic political administration and ideological justification as well as military power. European gender ideologies were often grafted onto preexisting roots and cultivated on a trellis of intersectional tensions. Colonists sometimes sought to destabilize the patriarchal institutions they encountered in order to assert their moral authority and impose their own favored forms of hierarchical control.

In a profound illustration of divide-and-conquer strategy, the Spanish conquest of Mexico was advanced by alliances with ethnic groups chafing under Aztec imperial domination and by female defection. After one of his early military victories, Hernan Cortes received a tribute of twenty female slaves, including a woman who became his lover, the mother of his son, his interpreter, and his advisor. Known as La Malinche, she became a symbol, to Mexicans, of treason against her own people. The definition of "her own people," in this instance, apparently refers to those who sold her into slavery for use as military tribute.

While colonization typically generated disproportionate benefits for those at the top of intersecting hierarchies of nation, race/ethnicity, and class (including many wives and daughters), it was typically regulated in ways that reinforced patriarchal authority over women. For instance, the ruling elites of Spain and Portugal, fearing a loss of population, severely restricted female immigration to the New World. As a result, in sixteenth-century Latin America, European men outnumbered European women by more than ten to one.[98] Native populations were devastated by the combined effect of military subordination and immunological vulnerability; European men enjoyed virtually unrestricted access to the women who survived, resulting in the rapid growth of a mestizo population.

The explicit rules of Catholic marriage, however, were held in abeyance. As early as 1549, the Spanish Crown passed a law excluding persons with any Indian ancestry from inheritance of land grants, or *encomiendas*, regardless of the legitimacy of their birth.[99] In one historian's words, the mestizo race was born of the "intercourse of white men and Indian women outside the pale of matrimony."[100] The term "mestizo" itself came to be virtually synonymous with "illegitimate." Paternal contributions to the support of their children were entirely voluntary and seldom reliable.

In similarly sexualized colonial encounters, some European companies in charge of overseas enterprises in the Pacific, such as the Dutch East Indies Company, hired only single men. While encouraging concubinage, they discouraged marriage by prohibiting European men with native wives and children from return to Holland.[101] By one estimate, unmarried men living with Asian women represented almost half of the European male population of the Indies in the 1880s. Children born of these unions had no legal claims on their fathers' income, and European feminists expressed both outrage and concern over their plight.[102] Giacomo Puccini's famous opera, *Madame Butterfly*, which premiered in Europe in 1904, dramatized the vulnerability of Japanese women deceived by false promises of commitment.

The so-called Eurasian population became a problem in India in the late eighteenth century, when posts within the East India Company became increasingly attractive to British applicants. A policy adopted in 1791 discouraged ethnic mixing by banning Eurasians from higher grades of the army and civil service, claiming that Indians themselves looked down on those of mixed blood and would not take orders from them.[103] Even when such official obstacles were lowered, the British managed to keep Eurasians, not to mention Indians themselves, on the lowest levels of the occupational hierarchy.

In 1810 the colonial government's Medical Board recommended giving soldiers easy access to prostitutes and encouraging them to "attach themselves individually to individual women."[104] High-level company administrators and major landowners, on the other hand, conformed to British upper-class conventions. They could consort with whom they pleased, but they avoided both attachments with and commitments to those beneath them.

Colonizers may have deceived themselves, as well as their subject populations, by racist doctrines and religious allegiances that disguised the realpolitik known as "might makes right." Patriarchal ideology proved remarkably malleable, suggesting, for instance, that native populations, like children, needed calm and capable elders to rescue them from paganism and barbarism.[105] The English political economist James Mill famously argued that English women did not need the vote because their fathers, brothers, and husbands would represent their interests. He offered a perfectly parallel explanation of paternalistic British rule in India.[106] The French added maternal solicitude to the picture, carried to laughable extremes in William Adolphe Bouguereau's 1883 painting, *Motherland*, in which Marianne, the symbol of France, embraces an assortment of children with skin and hair of different shades.

### Dispossession and Segregation

The gendered consequences of colonization differed when European migration was family-based. Settler colonialism created distinctive structures of collective power.[107] In South Africa, Kenya, Rhodesia, and Zambia, class differences among white settlers were less pronounced than elsewhere, and sanctions against intermarriage with Africans were severe. As a result, little racial mixing took place. Government policies such as poll taxes were designed to drive African men into wage employment, providing a cheap source of agricultural labor.[108] African women were largely limited to employment in domestic service or prostitution.[109]

Ethnographic accounts of the relative position of women among indigenous African tribes have often proved unreliable, based on observations over a period of rapid adjustment to new conditions, including, obviously, external threat.[110] In general, European authorities in the colonial era seemed willing to challenge aspects of traditional tribal authority that gave elder men control over the marriages of their children, but were reluctant to encourage actions that might otherwise empower women.[111] In early Tanganyika, colonial policies toward the Maasai, based on the presumption that only men owned cattle, almost certainly diminished women's economic opportunities.[112] Like settler governments in South Africa, the Rhodesian government in what is now Zimbabwe adopted policies that made it difficult for women to migrate to urban areas, leaving many confined to native reserves.[113] Such policies of spatial gender segregation had long-lasting and disruptive effects on African family life.[114]

In Australia, the ratio of available land to people was quite high, and aboriginal populations were commonly driven into the periphery where they engaged in sporadic employment combined with subsistence foraging. In the United States and Canada, the process of dispossessing Native Americans (or First Peoples, as the Canadians put it) was more complex, involving military mobilization and state policies designed for relocation and confinement. The threat of war forced tribes into a weak negotiating position, leading to their confinement and immiseration on reservations.[115]

With the exception of Palestine, politically dismantled by the creation and territorial expansion of Israel, many countries of the Middle East experienced a form of colonization motivated primarily by strategic military concerns and access to a wealth of fossil fuels. For the most part, colonial powers focused on the cooptation and manipulation of existing elites, often taking advantage of tribal and religious divisions and reinforcing patriarchal and feudal institutions. Economic development, based primarily on rents for natural resources, did little to encourage changes in the social relations of production.

Description of these circumstances motivated Deniz Kandiyoti's concept of a patriarchal bargain, or what Suad Joseph terms a gentleman's agreement to convert religious laws into state laws, reinforcing traditional forms of authority.[116] Women's participation in this bargain was shaped not only by their lack of viable alternatives, but also by a larger sense of vulnerability to external control and outside attack. The political and cultural condescension of the West helps explain a political slogan that embeds intersectionality in metaphors of kinship: "My Arab brother before my Western sister."[117]

Challenges to male authority were seldom strategically viable when entire groups were under attack. As a result, female resistance to colonization itself has been interpreted as a "kind of subterranean, unrecognized form of feminism," because it represented a form of collective resistance to external control.[118]

## Expansion and Globalization

As evolutionary biologists have observed, isolated ecosystems buffered from outside competition often develop in divergent but similar ways. Many of the famous literary utopias of the West, including Plato's *Atlantis* and Francis Bacon's *New Atlantis*, flourished on islands.[119] The shipwrecks of two great heroes of early eighteenth-century English literature, Robinson Crusoe and Lemuel Gulliver, thrust them into environments entirely different from their own. One man became an icon of rational economic man, easily able to survive on his own. The other became an icon of ethnographic curiosity, comparing the morals of Lilliputians to Brobdingnagians.

Both these fictional characters distracted attention from the larger drama. Colonization was an extension of earlier processes of intergroup competition and conflict in which gender played a central part. As the many literal and figurative islands of the world came into greater contact with each other through trade, many began to bargain over the terms of their engagement. The biggest share of the gains was not captured by the most rational or the most productive, but by the most powerful. Their power derived not only from military prowess and accumulated wealth, but also from interlocking structures of collective power that relied heavily on patriarchal institutions.

Colonization delivered economic advantages that were as much cause as consequence of capitalist development.[120] The resulting fruits were distributed quite unequally, but often in effectively cooptive ways, trickling down from top to bottom in ways that dampened resistance to authority. The promise of just-enough prosperity, even if only intermittently fulfilled, often seemed to justify subordination. If the resulting tensions remained in check, however, they also remained poorly understood and largely unresolved.

# 7

# Capitalist Trajectories

The transition to economic systems heavily reliant on capitalist institutions proved variable, complex, and incomplete. Some outcomes were happy ones, offering potential benefits to everyone. Technological change shifted the frontiers of production, expanding potential output and increasing the returns to education and innovation. Reproductive results also improved, with a lengthening of life expectancy and enhanced ability to control reproductive outcomes. Many women found new avenues for empowerment.

Some outcomes of capitalist development, however, were devastating for a large percentage of the global population. Divergent patterns of economic success gave some countries the ability to prey on others and fueled the expansion of the Transatlantic slave trade. A disproportionate share of the payoffs to increased investment were channeled to groups that already had a firm grasp on collective power, intensifying differences in wealth ownership. Meanwhile, nineteenth-century political economists celebrated the male pursuit of individual self-interest but insisted that married women should remain angels of the home.

The cumulative effects fit Joseph Schumpeter's vision of "creative destruction," the "process of industrial mutation that incessantly revolutionizes the economic structure from within, incessantly destroying the old one, incessantly creating a new one."[1] Schumpeter's concept of economic structure, however, was a simplistic and narrow one, constituted only by capitalist firms. Even more profound changes took place in the institutional structures governing the interface between production and reproduction. Class conflicts were interlaced with many other forms of collective contention.

When traditional patriarchal ideologies reigned supreme in Western Europe, rationales for discrimination against women in the labor market were stated as seemingly obvious truths. As Andrew Ure put it in 1835, the low level of wages offered women in factory employment was entirely desirable because it "tends to make household duties their most profitable as well as agreeable occupation, and prevents them being tempted by the mill to abandon the care of their offspring at home."[2] In 1890, the English economist Alfred Marshall argued that women's participation in wage employment would make them unfit for motherhood.[3] Economists like him urged men to seek their fortune in the emerging marketplace but reiterated women's moral obligation to dedicate themselves to the care of others. Even today, economists sometimes rationalize gender inequality as a soulful manifestation of women's altruistic preferences.

## Synergies

If all societies are capitalist, then capitalist imperatives tell us little about the hugely important variations among them. Over the last two hundred years, many now-affluent capitalist countries expanded democratic governance, outlawed slavery, reformed patriarchal law, implemented social insurance, and enjoyed economic growth. Some moved in these directions more successfully and more equitably than others. Variation has also been pronounced in what Chandra Mohanty refers to as "the Two-Thirds World" inhabited by the majority of the world's population.[4] Countries that evaded or minimized colonial control prospered sooner and more easily than others. Some Asian countries developed state-managed but market-driven economies that defy standard definitions of either capitalism or socialism.

Whatever labels are attached to them, most economic systems are characterized by significant group-based differences in bargaining power, and members of groups with the least bargaining power are generally the cheapest source of paid and unpaid labor. Wage earners are typically paid far less than they could have garnered as co-owners or co-managers but more than those left behind or excluded from employment. Competition for jobs, exacerbated by the threat of unemployment, has often given workers pecuniary incentives to exclude or restrict entire categories of potential fellow workers. Early growth in wage employment in Europe and the United States yielded better jobs and higher wages for white men than for other groups.

In traditional Marxian theory, the reserve army of labor weakens the power of the working class by reducing its bargaining power. A more intersectional approach outlined by Rhonda Williams in 1987 foreshadows modern stratification economics, insisting that reserve-army effects are compounded by nonclass differences.[5] Even workers who believe their employers exploit them may find it strategically advantageous to exclude other workers willing to work for lower pay. Unless labor markets are tight, employers have little to lose in the short run and much to gain in the long run from divide-and-conquer strategies that stratify the labor force. Intersectional conflicts among workers are compounded by intersectional complementarities among employers and managers, typically more homogeneous in gender, race/ethnicity, and citizenship.

### Overlaps

Capitalism can be, and has been, defined in a number of ways: as a system based on a drive for profits, on private ownership of the means of production, on market exchange, or on wage labor.[6] The definition chosen largely determines the chronology of the putative transition to capitalism. The first, broadest definition, based on motives of the "greed is good" variety, locates the transition at a very early date, spreading like some cultural virus that infects everything it touches. The last definition, based on a particular way of organizing work, implies a transition that takes place much later in time, remains incomplete even in affluent countries, and shows signs of faltering in much of the world as wage employment stagnates.

Both the definition and the timing matter. If all actions aimed at individual and collective aggrandizement are defined as capitalist, then capitalists obviously take the blame for all forms of exploitation. Yet, as indicated in the previous chapter, collective dispossession by warfare reaches far back in human history. Many of the predations that Marxian scholars have described as primitive accumulation did not immediately precede a transition to capitalism, and they continued to take place long after that transition was supposedly achieved.[7] Early patriarchal and slave-holding societies may not have maximized something they called profits, but they delivered lucrative flows of surplus to privileged subgroups.

Much postcolonial scholarship reaches beyond traditional Marxian accounts of the transition to capitalism by emphasizing the confounding effects of imperial domination. Yet even this scholarship seems to credit capitalism with the very invention of exploitation.[8] Similarly, some Marxist feminists inserting "patriarchy, racism, colonization and imperialism" into their narratives describe capitalism as the larger category that contains all these.[9] By making it the larger category, they imply that it is the more important target. Tithi Bhattacharya eloquently insists that social reproduction theory shows the "organic totality of capitalism as a system."[10] Yes, it shows an organic totality, but one in which institutions that long predated capitalism enjoy some partial autonomy within it.

Intersectional political economy, by contrast, treats capitalist exploitation as a particularly potent form of wealth accumulation that emerges within multilayered structures of collective power, often with contradictory effects. Profit maximization that leads to the accumulation of financial capital is a powerful force, but it is not the only historical force at work. Indeed, it typically relies on the concentration of institutional authority in the hands of an alliance of relatively privileged groups able to gain and maintain power. Fractal forms of inequality make it difficult for disempowered groups to overcome their differences and challenge authoritarian exploitation.

Reconsideration of the historical process of proletarianization—the rise of wage employment—lends support to this view. Even in the now-affluent capitalist countries, this process took place slowly and unevenly. With some exceptions, such as soldiers, domestic servants, and farm workers, wage earners remained relatively uncommon until the sixteenth century in Great Britain. In many other parts of Europe, wage employment began to grow substantially only in the nineteenth century; even so, family-based farming and artisanal production remained significant, particularly in France.[11]

Debates over living standards in Great Britain and the United States during the heyday of proletarianization have focused almost entirely on trends in real wages. Yet detailed historical research shows that women's nonwage (and often nonmarket) work made important contributions to family consumption.[12] Then, as now, the conceptual vocabulary of political economy overstated the predominance of wage employment: census-takers and statisticians were urged to regard the nonmarket work of housewives and mothers as unproductive, deflecting attention from their contributions and justifying their subordination as dependents.[13]

The officially designated "labor force" excludes those providing unpaid services to family and friends. The quantitative dimensions of proletarianization are usually traced by considering the percentage of wage earners (compared to small proprietors and the self-employed) in paid employment. The share of wage earners in the total working-age population would be a more relevant measure, yet it has seldom, if ever, been officially calculated. Even when limited to men alone, the wage-earner share shows surprising trends in an era usually described as mature capitalism. In the United States, the percentage of men between the ages of eighteen and sixty-four who were employed for wages peaked at 75 percent in 1970 and had declined by 2013 to 64 percent, a result of expanding educational enrollments, early retirement, and declining real wages.[14]

Women moving into paid employment have long been described as new entrants into the labor force, as though they were doing nothing before. The reallocation of their time from uncounted to "counted" work helped artificially boost gross domestic product (GDP). Estimates of the market value of women's nonmarket work in the United States from the nineteenth century onward show that the rate of growth of total output was significantly lower than that of "counted" output.[15] Married women poured into wage employment in the second half of the twentieth century, boosting measured growth and making the golden age of US capitalism seem more golden than it actually was. The surge slowed in the 1990s and peaked in 2000 at about 60 percent of prime-age women.[16] Not incidentally, the GDP growth rate slowed about that time as well.

That proletarianization itself is less important than its diverse forms and consequences is confirmed by the experience of most countries of the global South. Increases in formal employment have proved quite uneven, heavily influenced by particular circumstances as well as by globalization and trade.[17] Many workers languish in subsistence agricultural production or precarious livelihoods in the urban informal sector. Most workers in low-income countries who are self-employed have no other way to feed themselves and their families.[18] The slow (even nonexistent) pace of job creation undermines the cheerful view that economic growth will automatically empower women. In India, for instance, the paid labor force participation of women in urban areas has remained about 18 percent since the 1980s, despite relatively rapid growth in both women's education and GDP per capita.[19] In China, married women's paid labor force participation has declined since the early 1990s.[20]

Some Marxian scholars have argued that capitalist accumulation requires women's unpaid work and manages to draw surplus from all noncapitalist spaces.[21] But a global labor surplus vitiates the need for workers, much less unpaid work, even as it reduces workers' bargaining power. One could as easily argue that capitalism, as traditionally conceived, has proved both less successful and less hegemonic than anticipated and is proving unable to generate the overall gains in output it once promised in return for obeisance to its rules. Wage employment accounts for 86 percent of all official employment in high-income countries, but only 54 percent of total global employment. The global remainder is comprised of employers (3 percent), own-account workers (32 percent), and contributing family workers (10 percent).[22] Unemployment and underemployment are particularly serious global problems for youth between the ages of fifteen and twenty-four.[23]

Even today, unpaid work plays a crucial role, dramatized by the global return to home-based care and provisioning occasioned by the Covid-19 pandemic. A colossal decline in market demand for restaurant services and gasoline took place as people began cooking more of their own meals and travelling less. Even before the pandemic struck, estimates from many affluent countries showed that the total amount of time devoted to nonmarket work (or, in Marxian parlance, the production of use values) was approximately equal or slightly greater than the amount of time devoted to market work.[24] Indeed, as per capita income increases, the share of unpaid work in total work does not generally decline: in poor countries the need to grow sufficient food or earn sufficient income necessary for subsistence often takes precedence over unpaid childcare activities.[25]

The surprisingly tenacious role of households as units of production and reproduction explains why patriarchal property rights over land and housing continue to exert significant influence in many regions. Even in countries of South Asia where legal reforms have improved rights of female inheritance and co-ownership, men enjoy far greater de facto control over land than women.[26] The process of extending actual rather than merely theoretical ownership rights to women in Latin America remains incomplete, and gendered patterns of land ownership and control characterize much of rural Africa.[27]

Wage earners without access to substantial human or financial capital inhabit an economic system that constrains their choices and leaves them vulnerable to exploitation. Yet wage employment often benefits from economies of scale and scope that make it more remunerative than any other form of work, even when workers are paid less than the value of their contributions. Wage earners themselves often hire domestic servants (often members of groups disadvantaged by race/ethnicity or citizenship), and they depend heavily on the unpaid work of others to convert their wages into the services they need. These tangled social relations suggest that many different forms of exploitation can—and often do—coexist with variable forms of solidarity and mutual aid.

**Convergent Class and Gender Interests**

A closer look at one particular episode in the classical transition-to-capitalism literature is telling. Economic historians have dwelt at length on the experience of Great Britain in the late eighteenth and early nineteenth centuries. The early advent of factory production led to heated conflict between employers and workers over wages and working conditions. Yet male employers and male workers shared a common interest in patriarchal institutions that were already well in place.[28] The early piecework system provided married women with income-earning opportunities that neither interfered with their domestic contributions nor threatened the authority of male household heads. The first recruits to wage employment were youngsters who handed much of their earnings over to their parents, reducing pressures on parents to cover the costs of their subsistence.[29]

With increased enclosure of common land and declines in the viability of home-based production, more adult men were forced into factory employment, and the downsides of reliance on wages intensified. Public policies and technological changes helped create a large reserve army of labor that weakened the bargaining power of wage earners as a class. Factory employment made it difficult for women to effectively combine productive and reproductive work; adult children became more likely to leave their homes and communities of origin; speed-up on the factory floor, restrictions on child labor, and new educational requirements made it difficult for young children to contribute to family income. Many working-class families struggled to adjust, and women were indirectly affected. Still, men, whether single or married, continued to enjoy greater access to skilled occupations and a male wage premium.[30]

Capitalist employers could have hired women for traditionally male jobs at little more than traditionally female wages. They had several possible reasons not to do so, and, instead, to partition their labor force by gender. As men, they had a personal stake in patriarchal institutions that privileged them within their own families and communities. As employers and citizens, they had a stake in the quantity and quality of their country's future labor force, to which wives and mothers contributed. (Some employers also recognized the potential benefits of child labor laws and public education.)[31] As employers, they anticipated anger from male workers should they attempt to replace them by women, and they preferred to keep workers divided.

Other intersectional motives reinforced occupational segregation and pay discrimination. Male-dominated trade unions organized around the concept of a breadwinner wage that helped buttress patriarchal authority.[32] Even though such wages remained out of reach for most men, they resonated with the imperfectly realized ideal of working-class family life as a heroic source of resistance to capitalist exploitation.[33] The notion that their own sisters, wives, and daughters might be disadvantaged by such a bargaining strategy remained literally unfamiliar: those women belonged at home, cooking meals and doing laundry.

Outright discrimination limited the economic independence that women could achieve. Their occasional refusal to exit wage employment upon marriage, often dictated by economic desperation, occasioned moral outrage and cultural panic. In his *Condition of the Working Class in England*, Friedrich Engels warned of increased child mortality, the destruction of family life, and the "unsexing" of unemployed husbands by their breadwinning wives.[34] Similar concerns were vividly expressed by William Stanley Jevons and Alfred Marshall, two founding fathers of the neoclassical economic paradigm.[35]

Capitalist and patriarchal interests also overlapped in contestations over reproduction. Despite his call for delayed marriage to slow population growth, Thomas Robert Malthus considered use of contraceptive devices such as the vaginal sponge an "improper art." Some critics of this view, such as Francis Place, believed this art could reduce the size of the reserve army of labor and increase wages, but early trade unionists (like later Marxists) warned against any diversion from direct class struggle. Nor was there much support from working-class men, later in the century, when feminists challenged the regulated medical inspection of prostitutes as an infringement on women's rights and an encouragement to sexual commodification.[36]

Experiences obviously varied across countries, but it is difficult to find examples of employers who failed to maintain a gender segmented and, wherever feasible, a racially and ethnically segmented labor market. In countries with an ample supply of labor relative to demand, women and members of disadvantaged groups typically made little headway in formal employment. Even when export-oriented economic development in East Asia pulled large numbers of women into manufacturing jobs, they typically remained concentrated in highly competitive industries paying relatively low wages. Both their employers and their national economies profited.[37]

Cause and effect are difficult to distinguish. Did patriarchal norms enforce a preference for discrimination against women even when they lowered profits, or did such norms prove economically advantageous for at least some employers? Did such norms deliver significant benefits to men as a group? While these questions are difficult to answer, they raise possibilities that are not mutually exclusive.

### Convergent Class and Other Interests

Convergent interests based on class, nation, and race/ethnicity conditioned capitalist institutions in a variety of ways. Both David Ricardo and Karl Marx were certain that British capitalists and landlords were at odds. And so they were, especially with respect to the Corn Laws, restrictions on imports that pitted landlords (who benefited from high grain prices) against capitalists (who did not). In other respects, however, the interests of landlords and capitalists were aligned. Families with inherited wealth had money to invest, and profits were convertible into status. Intermarriage between families with distinguished pedigrees and those with newfound wealth is a central theme of nineteenth-century English literature.

The racism and nationalism built into the European imperial project encouraged cross-class alliances. Racism permeated Western European feudal society in its earliest stages. The German concept of a master race, the Herrenvolk, long predated Hitler's application of it.[38] Both intranational and international conflicts within Western Europe were soothed, though obviously not fully assuaged, by common animosities toward barbarians, infidels, Jews, and Slavs. Like kings and queens, capitalists could draw on deep reservoirs of racialized solidarity to legitimate their economic authority. Tiffs between landlords and capitalists never hampered the expansion of the British East India Company or the larger colonial enterprise: "Rule Britannia, rule the waves. Britons never shall be slaves."[39] As noted earlier, Marx himself suggested that English workers were vulnerable to cooptation.

In the United States, faith in the manifest destiny of white Americans to claim the continent drove a process of territorial expansion that could not have been achieved without the deployment of armed forces that expropriated and forcibly relocated Native Americans.[40] Although tensions between a rapidly growing industrial economy in the North and a slave-based plantation system in the South led to a horrific Civil War, major property owners in both regions were reconciled once the war came to an end. The emancipation of slaves was not accompanied by any significant redistribution of other forms of wealth. Contrary to the Union Army's promises of "40 acres and a mule" to emancipated slaves, land ownership remained in primarily white hands, creating long-lasting intergenerational disadvantage.[41]

Much of the debate over racial segregation in the US labor market poses an either/or question: was it the result of employers' desires to divide and conquer, or of native-born white workers' efforts to restrict low-wage competition?[42] Both explanations are relevant, and class interests were not the only collective interests at stake. As long as a reserve army of labor remained deep and wide, both white men and employers (who were, after all, predominantly white men) gained from institutional arrangements that created barriers to low-wage competition—including strict immigration restrictions that remained in place well past the halfway mark of the twentieth century.[43]

Other convergent interests between white employers and their white employees were apparent outside the capitalist workplace. In the US South before 1950, a large percentage of employed African-American women cooked meals, cleaned house, and supervised children in white homes.[44] Even white families with modest incomes benefited from a relatively cheap supply of Black and Latino domestic servants to reduce the burden of housework, childcare, and gardening.[45] State policies exerted enormous influence: the organization and finance of educational institutions both reproduced racial/ethnic inequalities and diverted attention from less visible but nonetheless influential inequalities based on class.[46]

Even as industrial investment became an engine of economic expansion in the United States, land remained an important asset, generating significant rents to those who acquired or inherited it. Whether put to agricultural use or parlayed into speculative urban development, land ownership, as Henry George famously argued, could determine the difference between prosperity and poverty. Both farmers and real estate developers had collective interests distinct in some respects from those of industrial capitalists, but they also constituted part of a larger, predominantly white, propertied class.

Owners, like workers, were factionalized, but they remained a smaller, more homogeneous group. Their common interest in minimizing taxation proved easier to orchestrate than any redistributive plan that pitted potential beneficiaries against one another. Indeed, capitalist industrialization seemed to proceed especially quickly when propertied groups were able to reconcile their differences in ways that strengthened their collective hand. In countries yoked by colonial or imperial domination, wealth-owners were often at odds; those riding the coattails of foreign capital were less reluctant than others to invest in national economic development.[47]

Specific class configurations and institutional arrangements shaped trajectories of growth in goods and services produced for sale.[48] South Korean industrialization was boosted by land reforms that put capitalists in a strong political position that enabled them to orchestrate industrial investment.[49] At the opposite extreme, many countries rich in mineral resources simply extracted national wealth from the ground rather than trying to produce more. Extractive strategies reinforced patriarchal power far more effectively than entrepreneurial ones. The weak bargaining position of women in many oil-based Middle Eastern economies may be more attributable to slow employment growth than to Islamic orthodoxy.[50] Saudi Arabia and the Emirates may play a central role in global capitalist transactions, but they are primarily patriarchal regimes.

Collective economic interests tend to converge more strongly at the top than at the bottom. Powerful men of the same race/ethnicity and nationality can coordinate their efforts to reinforce all forms of inherited privilege, including dominion over women. Members of much larger, more heterogeneous groups, on the other hand, face more complex strategic choices. Women often find themselves in particularly contradictory positions when pursuit of their gender interests threatens to weaken forms of solidarity that offer potential benefits to brothers, husbands, fathers, and sons. It is often hard to say which collective commitments take precedence.

# Dislocations

While hierarchical systems create stabilizing synergies, they remain vulnerable to both internal tensions and external shocks. The principles of liberal individualism, initially reserved for white men, were stubbornly claimed by others. In at least some countries, the gradual expansion of democratic rights enhanced both the bargaining power of workers and the efficacy of other coalitions of the disempowered. When labor was relatively scarce and competition for workers intense, capitalist expansion helped corrode at least some structures of collective power.

Such corrosion became evident in most English-speaking countries and much of Western Europe in the nineteenth and early twentieth centuries. Technological change, opportunities for international migration, the growth of wage employment, and fertility decline altered many group fallbacks. Anti-slavery and feminist movements gained a foothold. The expansion of the franchise had positive—though often painfully delayed and indirect—effects. Still, the hope that capitalist growth would have inevitably liberating effects on women proved completely unrealistic.

## The Anglo-European Experience

Nineteenth-century economic growth in many now-affluent countries took place under unique conditions, including imperially enforced opportunities for migration to newly accessible resource-rich areas. High levels of outmigration from Europe and the eastern United States weakened both intergenerational ties and gendered constraints. Early industrializers enjoyed a tremendous advantage in access to global raw materials and new markets that allowed them to pull men and women into wage employment. The expansion of commodity production created cheap substitutes for goods and services once produced at home and encouraged efforts to limit family size.

While both patriarchal and feudal institutions rendered workers largely immobile, capitalist institutions favored mobility and competition. The growth of factory employment could provide alternatives to family-based production that were particularly attractive to the younger generation, especially those unlikely to inherit viable farms or businesses. Mere receipt of wages was never liberating, as many domestic servants, paid a pittance for household drudgery, could attest. But increases in the productivity of paid employment, when combined with labor shortages, enabled workers to garner a share of the surplus they helped create.

Opportunities for sustainable work outside the family economy, however partial and uneven, encouraged flexibility within families—creative renegotiation rather than creative destruction. The surge of largely unrestricted international immigration that began in the 1820s continued until World War I.[51] The massive relocation of population to land-rich areas often separated adult children from their parents, tilted sex ratios, decreased marriage rates, and increased the percentage of the elderly within the sending population. This disruption, however, painful, created space for women to take on new roles.[52]

Internal migration within large countries could have similar effects. In the northern United States, the westward migration of young men left many young women with poor marriage prospects, encouraging their participation in paid employment. Proud spinsters like Susan B. Anthony helped energize the early feminist movement. The Homestead Act of 1862, designed to attract more women to the frontier, allowed women to claim land on the same basis as men. Women's greater opportunities for both marriage and independent livelihood in the West enhanced their political bargaining power; western territories and states were among the first to establish female suffrage.[53]

The rapid expansion of commodity production yielded significant gains that were distributed unevenly and unpredictably. Business cycles put many families at the mercy of market forces that were difficult to understand, much less control, and the emergence of socialist and social democratic parties testified to a growing awareness of class dynamics. In the early twentieth century, socialist revolutions in the Soviet Union and China, promising more egalitarian economic arrangements, created new ideological pressures. Still, imperial power, racial/ethnic conflict, and gender dissension dampened class solidarity. Major wars involving Europe, Japan, and the United States reinforced patriotic allegiances, temporarily muting other distributional tensions.

While the Great Depression of the 1930s shook faith in capitalist institutions, the outbreak of World War II altered coalitional logic. In the United States, the financial demands of the war effort sparked new demands on the very rich: income tax rates in the United States became more sharply progressive than ever before or since.[54] The women who entered factories to replace men who had gone to fight often enjoyed access to childcare services, altering perceptions of policy possibilities along with gender roles. The mobilization of Black soldiers in the US army did little to directly weaken practices of strict racial segregation, but won at least some new respect for fellow citizens. A new cultural narrative included elements of what is now termed "shared prosperity."[55] In Europe, war-related mortality tilted sex ratios, encouraged women's entrance into wage employment, intensified concerns about national health and welfare, and motivated some of the welfare state policies described in the following chapter.

Military mobilization and its aftermath of European reconstruction helped pull the global economy out of recession. The relatively sustained economic expansion that began soon after, sometimes considered the Golden Age of US capitalism, had some equalizing effects, nudging employers to reach into new pools of previously underutilized labor power.[56] Real wages increased steadily for a time, and collective efforts to challenge discrimination based on race/ethnicity and gender gained momentum, leading to passage of the Civil Rights Act of 1964 and new paths for educational and occupational mobility. Economic growth itself was less catalytic than shifts in the relative bargaining power of workers, women, and racial/ethnic minorities.

Yet even at the height of the boom, shadows loomed. Increasing concerns regarding water and air pollution prompted a declaration of Earth Day in 1970, a watershed in environmental activism. Initially derogated as a kind of luxury good that only rich countries could afford, environmental protection gradually came to the fore as an issue of economic sustainability. Economists began to challenge the concept of GDP as a measure of success and to develop alternatives that factored in both declines in unpaid work and the degradation of natural assets. The Genuine Progress Indicator (GPI), for instance, suggests alchemical reversal: the Golden Age of economic growth in the United States began turning to lead in 1978.[57] Accurate or not, the invention of the GPI prefigured what is increasingly recognized as an inconvenient truth: as a measure of total output, GDP is largely fictional.

**Uneven Global Development**

Even a brief consideration of capitalist trajectories outside Great Britain and the United States reveals an uneven process of collective contestation. Postcolonial feminist scholarship challenges any characterization of European invaders as modernizers rescuing indigenous women from oppression by their fathers and husbands. Colonization itself was often cloaked in patriarchal imagery, including descriptions of childlike natives in need of firm paternal authority and chivalrous protection. Even where colonizers outlawed—or tried to outlaw—some patriarchal practices, they colluded with and reinforced others.[58]

Most women experienced multiple forms of disadvantage.[59] Whether or not nascent feminist movements existed before colonization (as they did in India), their participants often chose to prioritize national liberation movements, even where nationalism was expressed in patriarchal terms such as "regaining manhood."[60] Inequalities of class and caste were intertwined with gender, often taking the form of proscriptions against intermarriage or concubinage. Not surprisingly, the feminisms of the global South are intrinsically intersectional, levering the vocabulary of gender justice into the ideological loopholes of neoliberalism.[61]

Incentives for employers to breach patriarchal norms are weak when the supply of labor far exceeds the demand, as in many countries subjected to colonial control. After India achieved its independence in 1948, many believed that economic growth would undermine traditional caste distinctions and gender inequality, but these expectations were not met.[62] In many Latin American countries, racial/ethnic inequalities have also proved relatively impervious to increases in GDP per capita, a pattern particularly well-documented in Brazil.[63]

Intense competition for jobs and markets can intensify preexisting inequalities, whatever form they take. In countries where a relatively small ethnic minority is economically dominant, ethnic and class conflict often merge, as in the Philippines, Indonesia, Burma, Thailand, Laos, Malaysia, and South Africa.[64] Ethnic conflicts fueled extreme violence between Serbs and Croats in Bosnia and between Tutsi and Hutu in Rwanda in the 1990s. Backlash against the formidable economic and military power of the United States and Israel has encouraged the efflorescence of Islamic identity and jihad in much of the Middle East.

International comparisons suggest that feminist mobilization proved most successful where economic growth delivered higher living standards and racial/ethnic and class differences were relatively muted. Under these conditions, strong social democratic alliances could build elements of family support, gender equity, and shared prosperity into public policy, as in the Nordic countries. Both there and elsewhere in Western Europe, such alliances have been weakened by the combined threat of intensified global competition and backlash at an influx of economic and political refugees from low-income countries.[65] While it is more difficult to reverse feminist policies than to block them, their future progress remains unclear.

Economic growth and ethnic homogeneity do not necessarily combine to empower women. In Japan, the determination to recover from military defeat in the 1940s bolstered patriarchal and nationalist institutions. Both outmigration and in-migration were strictly limited. While relocation from rural to urban areas was extensive, the distances involved were relatively short. Strong filial obligations remained in force, and explicit public policies, combined with employer discrimination, retarded the paid labor force participation of married women. Japanese feminists made little headway until declining birth rates began to threaten the demographic future of their country and their culture.[66]

## Demographic Shocks and Transitions

Whether gradual or abrupt, demographic changes influence both economic trajectories and political alignments. Mortality rates have the most dramatic impact: the Black Plagues of fourteenth-century Europe reduced the size of the agricultural labor force and destabilized both feudal and patriarchal institutions. The infectious diseases that Europeans carried to the Americas cleared the way for colonization. Two major wars of the twentieth century cut a cruel swath through the working-age male population of Europe. The ultimate effects of the unprecedentedly global Covid-19 pandemic remain unclear, but they will likely be momentous.

Fertility trends move more slowly than mortality but can have powerful cumulative consequences. As Francis Place observed in the early nineteenth century, efforts to limit family size could benefit working-class families both directly and indirectly, by reducing the number of future workers. Similar reasoning has led some feminist activists to argue that capitalist interests are driving efforts to roll back reproductive rights in the United States.[67] This seems unlikely. Marx himself persuasively argued that the number of unemployed was determined more by technological change and public policy than by population growth.

For most of the twenty-first century, the global economy has suffered more from an oversupply than an undersupply of workers. This may change as a result of the resurgence of nationalism and the closing of borders resulting from the pandemic. Regardless of current political trends, the historical record shows that capitalist expansion has generally encouraged fertility decline. The growth of wage employment and decline of family-based production for the market increased the relative cost, to parents, of raising children. The demographic transition to lower fertility encouraged investment in both human and financial capital. In nineteenth-century Europe and in most of its Anglophone offshoots, increases in life expectancy associated with innovations in public health and, in some areas, higher wages, improved the productivity of reproductive work.[68]

In most so-called Western nations, average births per woman declined considerably between 1900 and 2000, the result of various strategies for reducing births, which, while seldom reliable on the individual level, had a significant aggregate effect.[69] In the early twentieth century, the development of new technologies, including the rubber condom and the diaphragm, made birth control easier. The later development of surgical sterilization techniques, pharmaceutical contraceptives, intrauterine devices, and abortifacients offered women the ability to avoid pregnancy without the cooperation, or even the knowledge, of a male sexual partner.

Women's ability to limit births was recognized as a form of empowerment with potential consequences for many dimensions of collective negotiation. German Social Democrats called for a birth strike in 1913 to reduce the reserve army of labor, a strategy vigorously opposed by some Marxists, including Rosa Luxemburg.[70] In 1938, an article in the *North American Review* described parents in the United States as engaged in a sit-down strike against "unsatisfactory procreative conditions."[71] Even more loudly expressed were concerns about the future of "the race" (implying the white race) manifest in the rhetoric of eugenics. Legal restrictions, economic constraints, and cultural norms initially limited access to contraceptive use, but as these were contested, take-up rates gradually increased. In the United States, policy variations across states after 1960 provided a natural experiment that has been retrospectively assessed: statistical analysis demonstrates that legal access to contraception enabled many women to improve their opportunities for education and employment and, in the long run, to increase both their family income and their children's college completion rates.[72]

Like most technological innovations, contraceptive technologies proved susceptible to misuse. Their safety and reliability were often overstated, and sterilization was sometimes coercively imposed on poor or otherwise vulnerable women and men. In some countries, ultrasound

technology facilitated sex-selective abortions that significantly diminished the ratio of female to male births. National interests came into
play: international investments in family planning were sometimes
motivated by Malthusian fears of rapid population growth in the global
South.[73]

Yet fertility decline proceeded apace, gaining a momentum of its
own. It was not confined to countries enjoying imperial affluence, and it
proceeded rapidly in countries that industrialized at a fast clip after the
mid-twentieth century, such as Japan and Korea. China implemented
coercive policies such as the "two-child" rule introduced in 1969 and the
"one-child" rule of 1979, but fertility decline preceded these interven-
tions, and there is little expectation that it will reverse now that these
rules have been dropped.[74] The one area of the world where family size
remains relatively high is Sub-Saharan Africa, where household-based
agricultural production continues to predominate.

The widespread goal of maximizing per capita GDP makes any
decrease in the ratio of dependents to producers of market income
appear spuriously advantageous. However, the large ecological benefits
of lower population growth stand out. High levels of per capita consumption of fossil fuels in affluent countries—if they continue in the wake of
pandemic economic shocks—pose far larger immediate threats to the
global environment than population growth in poor countries. Still, the
size of the global population also matters—especially for those who
hope to reduce its widespread poverty and privation.

The institutional effects of fertility decline are particularly profound
for women. Motherhood is physically demanding, increases economic
dependence, and encourages specialization in activities that offer relatively little bargaining power. Fertility decline alters gender dynamics in
ways that tend to weaken patriarchal institutions. The trend toward
fewer children encourages maternal emphasis on socialization and
teaching rather than physical care. Competition among women for
partners becomes less influenced by perceptions of potential fecundity
and norms of compulsory heterosexuality.

The very notion of family planning gave women more agency and
decision-making power. By separating heterosexual intercourse from
biological reproduction, effective contraception altered the meaning of
sexual intimacy and, in the process, weakened homophobic norms. On
the other hand, the reduced economic importance of children weakened incentives for paternal support. When women gained new rights

to choose pregnancy, men gained new ways to opt out of responsibilities for fatherhood.[75]

### Pressures on the Patriarchal Bargain

Capitalist development can undermine patriarchal bargains, but much depends on how rapidly it takes place and how its potential benefits are distributed. A rapid expansion of commodity production, driven in part by heightened demand for goods and services once provided by wives and mothers, can render some historically important aspects of household production (baking bread, sewing clothes, and preparing meals from scratch) economically obsolete. The care and supervision of children becomes costlier when it can no longer be complemented by other forms of domestic work. Likewise, with fewer children at home, female specialization in domestic work production becomes less efficient—women's time is better spent earning market income.

When wives can contribute more to family income by departing from traditional gender roles and entering wage employment, their husbands too will benefit. On the other hand, women gain bargaining power from access to independent income. Husbands are faced with the prospect of receiving a smaller share of a larger (and not necessarily home-baked) pie, and the relative costs and benefits are not always obvious. A patriarch's bargaining power over any surplus produced by the household can give him an incentive to resist change, even at the expense of some reduction in potential family income.

Patriarchs, like any group that enjoys institutional advantage, sometimes face trade-offs between efficiency and power. A wife's market income would increase total family income if (holding her total hours of work constant) her market earnings per hour are greater than the value of her domestic work. On the other hand, increases in his wife's bargaining power could reduce her husband's share of household income or leisure. The economic impact on him of her market earnings depends on the relative magnitudes of the increase in total income and the reduction in his share of total household consumption.[76]

Significant improvements in women's property rights—including married women's rights over their own earnings—were correlated with indicators of capitalist development across states within the United States.[77] Some economists argue that changing economic incentives led men to voluntarily renounce their institutional power.[78] Some men surely did. But only a very few became outspoken advocates of feminist reforms. Economic opportunities matter, but it was women's personal and political bargaining that eventually persuaded men of the benefits of change.

The empowerment of women requires collective action, which, in turn depends on opportunities to increase political power, influence cultural discourse, and increase access to economic resources. Political democracy of the one adult-one vote variety is a very rough proxy for such opportunities, but comparative research shows that it has a positive effect on women's empowerment.[79] One study of measures to address violence against women in seventy countries found the level of feminist activism to be more important than left-wing parties, numbers of women legislators, or national wealth.[80] The level of transnational activism is more difficult to measure, but surely, it too has a significant effect, promoting ideals of gender justice and publicizing the policy measures needed to achieve them.

## Reconfigurations

Paths shaped by intersecting hierarchies take many twists and turns. New openings for the empowerment of women sometimes led to long detours and dead ends. Women's ability to capitalize on new economic opportunities was constrained by deep normative commitments to family care, higher standards of child-rearing, and institutional inertias. Within the labor market, occupational segregation channeled them into roles consistent with patriarchal ideals of femininity. Even as women's bargaining power increased relative to that of men, class and racial/ethnic dynamics intensified differences among them, weakening their ability to mobilize as a group. International socialist movements embraced the cause of women's liberation, but regimes based on authoritarian central planning revealed a distinctly patriarchal bent.

### Occupational Segregation

Occupational segregation emerges from circular dynamics. Overt restrictions on the ability of some groups to gain access to financial or human capital relegate them to the bottom tier of the labor market, limiting their ability to invest in their children's economic future. The ideological stereotypes used to justify such restrictions prove more difficult to change than explicit rules, in part because they are internalized.

The common assumption that legal rules are the only social institutions that constrain individual choices—itself an ideological construction—implies that no further change is necessary, because people are "free to choose."

Occupational segregation of women crowds them into certain segments of the labor force, lowering their wages, limiting their bargaining power in the home, and increasing their specialization in family care.[81] Historical patterns of increased female participation in paid work were steered by gendered obligations: women entered before they married or became mothers, withdrew when their first child was born, then rejoined the paid labor force after their children matured. Only in recent decades have mothers of young children in affluent countries become highly likely to combine wage work and family work. The need to remain available for family care has pushed them into part-time or intermittent employment, often in jobs emotionally—as well as temporally—complementary to family care.

Explicit efforts to limit women's access to highly paid occupations are part of the historical record in the advanced capitalist countries.[82] Such efforts protected men from economic competition, ensured a low-cost supply of family care, and helped employers keep a lid on labor costs. Initially, women had little individual or collective power to challenge discrimination precisely because of their responsibility for dependents. Mothers raising children on their own were often forced to take whatever jobs they could get.

Women married to high earners enjoyed comfortable living standards but were narrowly confined to pursuits considered culturally appropriate, including interior decoration, gourmet meals, and dinner parties. Increasing emphasis on children's educational outcomes led to higher standards for maternal engagement with developmental activities, including homework, sports, and social events. Institutional rigidities established in earlier eras proved resistant to change: employers' work schedules typically conflict with public school schedules, a mismatch of little concern to the men typically in charge of both. Increased competition for professional and managerial jobs created new, distinctly male-biased criteria for measuring success, such as willingness to work long hours, including evenings and weekends, and travel on short notice.

Normative pressures on women remained powerful, often channeling them into jobs compatible with ideals of femininity. In the United

States—and most likely, elsewhere—the growth of the service sector over the course of the twentieth century largely represented a relocation of domestic services from the family to the market.[83] Women often expressed preferences for jobs that entailed care for others and a desire to do good, in part because any perceived lack of femininity could hurt their chances to find a male partner. They were not always aware of how costly such preferences could be, nor the extent to which their altruistic commitments subsidized selfish enterprise. By inserting feminine values of care for others into wage employment, many women softened the impact of commodification on consumers of care services. They also paid a considerable price in reduced economic autonomy and bargaining power.

Today, women in wage employment remain globally concentrated in traditionally feminine jobs and often overrepresented in public employment.[84] This pattern is sometimes described as continued allegiance to traditional gender norms, or gender essentialism.[85] Some argue that such allegiance reflects innate propensities.[86] Whether propensities to care for others are influenced by biology or not, the economic penalties they entail are institutionally determined: gender essentialism is both costly for women and advantageous for capitalist development. If all women abruptly adopted current masculine priorities, global processes of social reproduction would become significantly more costly.

### The Increasing Significance of Class

Class-based processes can effectively reinforce, even incorporate, a variety of inequalities derived from very different dimensions of collective membership. The intergenerational transmission of both financial and human capital puts disadvantaged groups in a weak starting position. Capitalist institutions deliver rich rewards to those who have capital to invest, allowing them to accumulate financial assets and remunerative skills that consolidate their bargaining power. The concentration of wealth, income, and market power has become a prominent feature of twenty-first-century capitalist development in many countries.[87] Some people are able to climb from the bottom to the top of the pyramidal maze; their success does not belie the low probability of upward mobility for those at the bottom.[88]

The growing disjuncture between the promises and the realities of employment opportunity has potent consequences for intersectional alliance. Legal proscriptions of discrimination against racial minorities

cannot easily counteract legacies of exploitation or patterns of segregation that reproduce inequality in access to financial wealth, safe neighborhoods, and high-quality education.[89] Despite the emergence of a
small Black and Hispanic middle class in the United States—a legacy of
earlier decades of expanding employment opportunities—poverty has
proved persistent, particularly among families with children raised by
mothers on their own. What William J. Wilson describes as the declining significance of race could better be termed the increasing significance of class.[90]

Heightened class inequality can intensify racial/ethnic animus. In the
US South, the economic expansion of the 1960s and 1970s boosted the
earnings of both Black and white workers, allowing both groups to enjoy
benefits in the wake of the Civil Rights Act of 1964.[91] By the 1990s,
however, employment opportunities for non–college-educated workers
began to contract in many areas of the United States reliant on manufacturing employment. The resulting economic stress, combined with a
steady influx of migrants competing for low-wage jobs, fostered latent
resentments that revivified white supremacy.

Divergent economic trajectories also divided women in the United
States, leading some social scientists to adopt Wilson's phrase and point
to the declining significance of gender.[92] Between 1970 and 1990, disparities between men's and women's earnings declined, then stabilized.[93]
Reduction of institutional barriers for educational credentials and
professional-managerial jobs increased opportunities that not all women
could take advantage of. While some were able to climb the corporate
ladder, and even to crack the glass ceiling, most women born to disadvantaged class and racial/ethnic positions remained on the sidelines. In
recent years, the gap between the median earnings of high-school and
college graduates has widened among women as well as men.[94]

Alternating currents of collective identity and action have driven the
ups and downs of feminist mobilization, which was initially strongest
where class and racial/ethnic differences were muted, then dampened
by its own partial successes. If only small subgroups of women and
people of color achieve success, they are easily coopted by inclusion:
class differences within subaltern groups weaken their collective ability
to further challenge hierarchical institutions based on gender and race/
ethnicity. Sometimes, however, intersections can become overlaps,
fostering broader allegiances; much depends on how social divisions are
perceived, interpreted, and acted upon.

## Patriarchal Socialism

Revolutions culminating in political control over the means of commodity production have never been completely driven by conflicts between capitalists and workers and have often been motivated by resistance to feudal, colonial, or imperial control. Regimes such as the Soviet Union and the People's Republic of China initially delivered some new rights to women but institutionalized gender inequality in their own ways despite greater public investment in health, education, and social services. Their resistance to democratic governance seriously impeded feminist mobilization.

Putative commitments to gender equality were often more ideological than substantive. The Russian case is particularly instructive. The Bolshevik revolutionaries who took over the Soviet government in 1917 transformed traditional family law, guaranteeing access to divorce and abortion and eliminating the legal category of illegitimacy. In the process, however, they weakened mothers' claims on any assistance from the fathers of their children, leaving many women and children economically vulnerable. Legal changes in 1926 designed to deal with this problem stipulated family responsibilities in the form of alimony or support payments, but these were poorly enforced.

In 1936, fear of declining birth rates motivated the elimination of abortion rights and the creation of new legal obstacles to divorce. Under Stalinist rule, coercive pronatalism intensified, with family allowance, tax policies, and medals such as the Order of Maternal Glory designed to encourage high fertility.[95] The actual level of support delivered—including the number of spaces available in childcare centers and provision of housing benefits—remains unclear. Regardless, fertility rates in Russian and other Slavic regions followed a downward trajectory similar to that in Western Europe, while remaining relatively high in the Central Asian Republics.

Explicit efforts to increase women's participation in paid employment, beginning in the 1920s, were accompanied by emancipatory rhetoric. Yet policymakers seemed to assume that day care for children and ample maternity leave would eliminate parental care burdens. They did not. Children, like other dependents, require care after factories and childcare centers close. That care was provided primarily by mothers and grandmothers. The scarcity of food required shoppers—predominantly women—to spend long hours waiting in line, and the high cost of consumer durables such as refrigerators, dishwashers, and vacuum cleaners left them far out of reach for many.[96] The central planning process, based on a narrow and dogmatic definition of economic output, impeded investments from which all Soviet families, but especially women, would have benefited.

The resulting constraints on women's time nullified some of the empowering effects of public childcare provision and increased employment. Discrimination against women also remained widespread. Even in the 1920s, a period of intense postrevolutionary idealism, male resistance to female competition for skilled jobs was palpable. In an eerie foreshadowing of later US policies, job shortages led to rules that discouraged the employment of married women, on the grounds that families needed only one wage earner.[97] Despite much higher levels of educational attainment and entrance into scientific and technical occupations, Soviet women failed to reach higher levels of management in either industry or government. As Gail Lapidus wrote in 1976 with considerable prescience, an end to occupational segregation would have required "not merely the partial assimilation of women to male roles, but the reciprocal redefinition of both."[98]

The concentration of political power in a few big hands meant that processes of privatization inaugurated in the 1990s led to an unparalleled concentration of private wealth. While these changes have often been described as a (re)transition to capitalism, they also entailed the open embrace of patriarchal institutions. In recent years, Russian political leadership has invited the support of the Russian Orthodox Church and its titular head, the Patriarch of Moscow and All Russia.[99] In 2012, five members of the feminist group Pussy Riot staged a protest performance against Orthodox Church support for Vladimir Putin. They were sentenced to two years' imprisonment for "hooliganism motivated by religious hatred."[100]

In Russia, as elsewhere in Eastern Europe, rapid large-scale privatization and cuts in public services increased economic insecurity and stress, causing abrupt spikes in mortality rates.[101] Women proved less susceptible to "deaths of despair" from alcoholism and suicide than men, but their economic lives deteriorated more as a result of cutbacks in public services. Their history of high participation in wage employment did little to improve their relative earnings: the gender gap in Russian wages remains quite high by comparison with other developed countries.[102] While data on Russian poverty and inequality are sparse, analysis of postsocialist countries of the European Union shows particularly high gender poverty gaps in countries that reduced spending pensions and family support.[103]

Socialist revolution in China, partly driven by the mobilization of the rural peasantry against Japanese invasion, did not lead to changes in family law as expansive as those in the Soviet Union or to reversals as extreme. As Judith Stacey puts it, patriarchy "kowtowed" to the new regime but remained influential: women were scarcely visible in political leadership.[104] Arranged marriage and foot-binding were outlawed, but Confucian traditions and son preference shaped Chinese economic policies from the outset.[105] The initial collectivization of agriculture reduced the economic power of male household heads over their own children and mobilized women's labor. In the 1980s, however, Chinese policy moved toward a "household responsibility system" that maintained nominal state ownership but guaranteed use-rights and stable tenure to individual households. Their limited specification and application fell far short of gender parity, even if women gained some legal rights.[106]

The initial success of Chinese Communist policies in improving living standards and reducing mortality led to rapid population growth, which in turn stoked fears of demographic pressure. In the post-Mao era, the party moved toward more market-oriented development policies that could mimic the performance of neighboring capitalist success stories such as Japan and South Korea. Socialist ambitions devolved into authoritarian schemes using the promise of higher living standards to justify intrusive controls over daily life.[107]

The desire to promote growth in GDP per capita prompted Chinese leadership to implement strict one child per family rules in 1979. This coercive policy stoked political resentments and boosted short-run economic production at the expense of long-run economic reproduction: it amplified incentives for sex-selective abortion, contributing to severely tilted sex ratios that threaten future family formation. It also contributed to shortfalls in the family safety net, leaving many elderly people with no one to care for them.[108]

Growing awareness of the stresses created by especially rapid fertility decline contributed to the easing of one-child restrictions in 2013, and, recently, endorsement of a two-children-per-family goal. Chinese rulers, facing the looming costs of public support for the elderly, have minimized responsibility for public or enterprise-level pensions by passing a new law stipulating adult children's responsibilities toward parents.[109]

Women are vulnerable to intergenerational crossfire: on the one hand, adult daughters without brothers are important sources of potential financial support for parents; on the other hand, daughters are often expected to provide hands-on personal care, which limits their potential for paid employment.[110] Reliance on children and grandchildren for support in old age also encourages the stigmatization of nonconformists who prefer not to become parents.[111]

The Chinese have implemented strict controls over rural–urban migration that seem designed to keep the costs of family care (as well as agricultural production) relatively low. In a spatial configuration not unlike that in South Africa, women, children, and the elderly are disproportionately concentrated in rural areas, where they provide low-cost services that subsidize both capital accumulation and higher urban living standards.[112] At the same time, wage-earning mothers in urban areas have relatively little access to either family-based or publicly provided childcare, making it difficult for them to compete in a labor market that does little to discourage gender discrimination.[113]

Chinese policymakers do not seem to realize that legal policies aimed to enforce family responsibilities are at odds with economic policies that render such responsibilities especially costly. It remains to be seen whether Chinese birth rates will revive or whether filial piety can be restored from the top down. Yet the experience of China, like that of the former Soviet Union, demonstrates that unequal distribution of reproductive costs is not unique to purely capitalist systems. The introduction of market reforms thirty years ago led to a significant decline in women's earnings relative to men, and President Xi recently called on women to "shoulder the responsibilities of taking care of the old and young, as well as educating children."[114] The Chinese "developmental state" is trying far harder to improve the development of men than that of women.

## The Plot Thickens

Economic dictators who control most private wealth and political dictators who control most state authority have much in common: the power to claim an unfair share of gains from cooperation. They pursue strategies of individual and collective aggrandizement that occasionally create openings for political reconfiguration. Workers and peasants, men and women, groups defined by national or racial/ethnic identity and other common interests all bargain for a larger share of the economic pie while also hoping to increase its overall size.

Technological and environmental changes often jolt institutional arrangements formed under different circumstances. Some economists argue that technical progress automatically triggers feedback loops that encourage human capital accumulation and empower women, further promoting economic growth.[115] If this were true, the historical record would reveal steady advances toward gender equality and higher living standards. Instead, we see uneven patterns of progress, serious threats of environmental disruption, intensified racial/ethnic and national conflict, and significant pushback against feminist goals. The so-called process of "creative destruction" seems increasingly destructive.

In the early twentieth century, Rosa Luxemburg famously argued that capitalism was dependent on precapitalist modes of production for its expansion.[116] Her argument resonates today, as unpriced resources and reproductive work continue to subsidize capital accumulation. Yet Luxemburg's argument did not go far enough. Capitalist development also depends on precapitalist—and noncapitalist—institutional hierarchies that inhibit the development of class solidarity.

The historical record shows that early forms of collective conflict based on class moved through corridors carved by preexisting inequalities.[117] The same processes of collective realignment that weakened some hierarchical legacies also intensified the class differences imprinted upon them. Inequalities based on many dimensions of collective identity other than class and gender remain conspicuous, and their long-run trajectory depends primarily on the vitality of alliances that can effectively champion more egalitarian and sustainable structures of institutional governance.

# 8
## Welfare State Tensions

One of the great ironies of capitalist development in now-affluent countries is that success in the accumulation of private wealth led to the expansion of public spending. Both the desirability of dampening social conflict and the need to address market failures help explain this trend, but changes in the relationship between families and the economy also came into play. Debates over the welfare state have always had a reproductive subtext. Invocations of the national interest have appealed to family loyalty writ large, invoking the fatherland and the mother tongue. Conservatives in the United States and the United Kingdom have derogated the "nanny state," and feminists have denounced the "daddy state," or, in more academic terms, "public patriarchy."[1] Bargaining over political priorities and social spending has paralleled bargaining in private households; in both cases, shifting fallback positions altered the space for many forms of collective negotiation.

Capitalist expansion created a disjuncture between production and reproduction that helps explain a strategy of social reproduction implemented by modern welfare states: tax corporate profits and the working-age population to finance education for the young, pensions for the elderly, and public subsidies for health care. The political system often described as social democracy can be better understood as socialization of the intergenerational transfers built into the patriarchal family economy.

For much of the twentieth century, public spending on health, education, retirement, and social safety nets in affluent countries grew rapidly, only to slow in recent decades—until hit by the global Covid-19 pandemic.[2] Welfare-state policies took different shapes in different countries, but their general momentum was retarded, and, in some cases, reversed, by forces similar to those that earlier weakened traditional patriarchal families. Increased capital mobility energized a neoliberal narrative that touted the virtues of competition over any and all forms of social obligation. Taxes and wages too high, regulations too onerous in this country? Invest elsewhere. A patriarchal undertone exaggerated the threats of free riding by "welfare moms" while celebrating the top riding achievements of overpaid executives.

The increased concentration of wealth and income, its global effects amplified by increasingly precarious employment and international migration, began to destabilize the political coalitions that once effectively promoted welfare state policies in affluent countries. Some groups, frustrated by their reduced share of the global economic pie, dug in to defend advantages based on citizenship, race/ethnicity, and gender—a more familiar and more easily achievable goal than a challenge to global corporate power.[3]

The payoff to this so-called populist strategy once seemed high in the United States, as a realigned Republican coalition jettisoned earlier slogans of fiscal conservatism and used tax cuts to increase the federal deficit, boost aggregate demand, and drive the unemployment rate down. The unequal distribution of the payoff was evident from the very outset, as the tax cuts—targeted to owners of capital—could only exacerbate the already highly polarized distribution of wealth and income.

In early 2020, however, any gains that had been made slipped into the maw of the Covid-19 pandemic, a health shock that sent unemployment through the roof, and threatened to send the stock market through the floor, creating unstoppable political demand for public assistance. Contagion—whether in families, communities, or markets—has a way of highlighting interdependence and the need for mutual aid.

## Why the Welfare State?

The future of the welfare state is changing before our very eyes, making it all the more important to understand its past. Neoliberal rhetoric often blames social spending for economic slowdown, treating the production and maintenance of human capabilities as a private project rather than a joint enterprise. Cuts in public social spending shift costs from taxpayers onto women and families.[4] Such cuts have been easy to sell partly because a divided electorate has been persuaded to think of social spending as a luxury for "others" rather than a form of investment with benefits for everyone.

National income accounts designate public spending as consumption expenditures and assign value to the services of care industries such as health and education based merely on what was spent on them. Both private and public spending on human capabilities creates huge benefits that go uncounted because they are unmonetized. The subtle devaluation of the welfare state recapitulates the devaluation of women's unpaid care in the home.

### The Social Wage vs. Market Failure

The neoclassical tradition has long treated public social spending either as a response to market failure or as a byproduct of rent-seeking by special interest groups.[5] Both explanations fall short. Like families, states provide services that markets cannot provide in the first place (including military defense and old age insurance), and gain-seeking is by no means limited to the public sector. The Marxian tradition treats collective conflict over social spending as a form of class struggle—workers trying to increase the social wage, or the total bundle of payment they receive for their labor.[6] This too is only partially correct: public social spending is shaped by many different forms of collective tussle.

Conventional prescriptions for the future of the welfare state also disappoint. Most countries describing themselves as socialist developed more egalitarian systems of social reproduction than their more capitalist counterparts, and re-establishment of capitalist institutions sometimes led to immediate public health shocks, as in the case of the former Soviet Union.[7] Yet as indicated earlier, socialist policies often exploited women as care providers. Blueprints for socialist planning—generally short on details—have seldom included specific attention to care provision either by families or the state, except as a means of increasing women's paid employment.[8] This shortcoming remains salient today. Proposals for market socialism typically focus on the coordination of for-profit enterprises without explaining how workers employed in health and education (much less those doing family work) would fare.[9]

Many conservatives, averse to state planning, pine for a society in which families ruled by benevolent dictators and cared for by altruistic women counterbalance competitive markets, making public services (and public oversight) superfluous. Their vision relies heavily on the belief that government expenditures reduce private expenditures dollar for dollar, a process of crowding out that neutralizes any benefits. By this assumption, public pensions for the elderly induce their adult children to reduce support for them, and public school lunch programs induce parents to skip feeding breakfast to their school-age children.[10]

The same reasoning is embedded in the anti-Keynesian claim that deficit spending will never stimulate economic growth because parents will anticipate the higher tax rate that their grown children will need to pay in order to finance the debt and reduce their own consumption in order to save more on their children's behalf.[11] Even if families sought such a perfect balance of consumption between their current and future members, the notion that they have sufficient information to optimize dynastic calculations is, to say the least, far-fetched. None of us know exactly how long we will live or what disasters may befall us, which is exactly why risk pooling through social insurance offers huge benefits.[12]

The crowding-out assumption is seldom extended to intrafamily transfers, although it should in principle apply. In his essay "The Samaritan's Dilemma," libertarian economist James Buchanan points out that private charity, like public transfers, can undermine self-sufficiency, but he stops short of considering the ways in which parents may spoil children.[13] Becker's Rotten Kid Theorem (discussed in Chapter 5) ignores the sometimes perverse consequences of bribing children for good behavior. Carried to its logical conclusion, crowding out implies that adult children would decline to assist parents who have accumulated sufficient financial wealth to purchase care, and grandma's cookies would displace mom's cupcakes. If public transfers can sometimes discourage work effort, so too can inherited wealth and privilege.

Both positive and negative transfers can have unintended consequences. However, as John Stuart Mill observed over a century ago in his *Principles of Political Economy*, "Energy and self-dependence are liable to be impaired by the absence of help, as well as by its excess."[14] Considerable research shows that the social context in which rewards are offered (or punishments administered) determines their effects.[15] Altruistic transfers often generate reciprocity, and both social and legal obligations can reinforce personal attachments. Even profit-maximizing employers recognize that gifts to their employees can enhance productivity.[16]

Neither families nor welfare states should be idealized. For most of recorded history, families have been governed by patriarchal power structures enforced by state authority. Commitments to the care of others cannot be entirely voluntary or self-enforcing, especially in economic systems that encourage individual competition.[17] Even gender-neutral rules defining the responsibilities of spouses for mutual support and the financial obligations of noncustodial parents have coercive power. Yet families and states are also capable of forms of coordination that are democratically constituted and fairly applied.

**The Social Investment State**

Like economists, sociologists tend to picture welfare state dynamics as purely redistributive processes. The widely used concept of "decommodification," for instance, implies that social spending reduces workers' dependence on paid employment.[18] But most social spending either substitutes for or complements family commitments that were never commodified on a pay-per-unit basis in the first place.[19] Nor can welfare state dynamics be accurately termed "defamilialization."[20] While some programs that provide childcare or eldercare services provide partial substitutes for unpaid care provision in the home, they have the overall effect of subsidizing family care.

Family and state care provision often go hand-in-hand: purchased childcare services typically cover only a portion of the day, teachers need parents to help children learn, and hospitals rely on family members to help heal the sick. Welfare state policies socialize a relatively modest share of the total costs of reproduction, and a significant portion of the support they provide goes directly to families in the form of tax subsidies, health care, education, and social insurance.

Basic economics texts often describe government spending as a drag on economic growth and characterize taxes as a greater threat to efficiency than looming gaps between private and social costs. Neoliberal rhetoric justifies emphasis on market outcomes, promoting policies that shift reproductive costs onto families and the women who care for them.[21] Yet social investment in health, education, and family support promotes sustainable economic development. Cross-national comparisons of the historical record show a strong positive relationship between social spending and gross domestic product (GDP) growth.[22] Effects on measures like the Genuine Progress Indicator (GPI) discussed earlier would show even stronger positive effects.

Market-based measures of output diverge sharply from measures of human capabilities such as the Human Development Index, with huge implications for international comparisons of economic efficacy.[23] Infant mortality in the United States is far higher—and life expectancy somewhat lower—than in many poor countries.[24] If a reasonable market value based on willingness to pay were assigned to literacy and life expectancy as outputs of social investment, the Cuban economy would appear far larger and more successful than conventional measures indicate.

While market metrics can sometimes approximate the rate of return on social investment, they offer, at best, a lower bound estimate. Improved access to education from an early age contributes to higher lifetime earnings and reduces defensive social expenditures such as crime and public assistance.[25] Improvements in life expectancy and reductions in morbidity improve labor productivity.[26] Other spillover effects are difficult to measure. Good educational outcomes improve the productivity of future parents and citizens, not just wage earners. Early childhood education reduces inequalities of opportunity that undermine the effort of disadvantaged groups.[27]

The investment metaphor is often applied too narrowly, prioritizing children above all others and ignoring the value of maintaining and enhancing existing human capabilities.[28] The value of improved health cannot be reduced to consequences for market income. Ask anyone what they would pay for an additional year of pain-free life.[29] Their answer depends almost entirely on how much money is at their disposal. The Covid-19 pandemic prompted much discussion of health versus jobs, lives versus livelihood, but these abstract trade-offs conceal underlying questions: whose health versus whose wealth? Whose lives versus whose livelihoods?

Many researchers have documented the negative effects of extreme economic inequality on physical and mental well-being.[30] The pandemic highlights an even darker downside: the anger and frustration engendered by inequality undermines solutions to problems that require cooperation rather than competition. Commitment to the intrinsic rather than merely instrumental value of human capabilities could reinforce norms of mutual aid. Yet the fear that others will be unwilling to cooperate prompts individuals to ask, "What's in it for me?"

The economic value of social spending helps explain why the welfare state itself has become a site of distributional conflict that reaches far beyond tensions between capital and labor. Many groups vie for a greater share of the net benefits of access to health, education, and social insurance that, along with access to well-paying jobs, make citizenship in an affluent country a valuable asset. Because these investments are subject to at least some democratic control, they are easier to contest than ownership of financial capital, which is firmly concentrated in a small number of private hands. This contestation, however, has splintering effects, making it difficult to form the alliances necessary to redistribute wealth and redirect investment.

Patriarchal power structures have always relied on public rules to reinforce private power; in this sense, public patriarchy is nothing new. What has and continues to change is the role of the state in promoting and capturing the benefits of reproductive investments. Partial capture of the benefits of reproductive work through taxation of the working age population gives the polity some incentive to invest in human capabilities, but also creates opportunities to free ride on parental and, especially, maternal commitments. In a health crisis like the Covid-19 pandemic, our dependence on the moral courage of care workers becomes salient. In April 2020, most of the workers on the health care frontlines in the United States were women.[31]

A more equitable distribution of the costs and risks of care work requires greater social provision. Still, families—defined as units of personal connection and mutual commitment rather than legal marriage or biological kinship—will continue to play a crucial role. The development of more diverse egalitarian family forms should supersede "defamilialization." Care responsibilities should be distributed more equally in families and in the polity, a goal sometimes be described as "degenderization."[32] The differing implications of these two fancy words is nicely illustrated by the recent history of interaction between families and states in the now-affluent capitalist economies.

## Capitalist Development and Family Change

Capitalist development does not push families in a single direction, but wage employment tends to have defamilizing effects, rewarding individual efforts that can be easily monetized, reducing adult children's economic dependence on their parents, and encouraging geographic mobility. In its later stages, capitalist development rewards the accumulation of human capital but offers little direct reward to those who invest in the human capital of others. As a result, it has contradictory effects on women, imposing new risks on those who specialize in family care even as it increases their options for reducing such specialization.

### Disruption

Many early critics of capitalist development noted that workers with many dependents to support were forced to compete in the labor market with individuals who were unencumbered, reducing wages below the level necessary to support a family. While reluctant to pay a family wage to address this problem, employers faced political pressure to do so, and some, at least, recognized the potential long-term benefits of public investment in a healthy and capable supply of labor. In early nineteenth-century Britain, Robert Owen expressed this view in particularly eloquent terms, encouraging passage of legislation restricting the factory employment of young children.[33]

The spread of wage employment and migration in nineteenth-century Europe, Canada, Australia, and the United States reduced the economic cohesion of most families even as it nudged them toward more egalitarian forms. The growth of opportunities outside the family economy increased the bargaining power of young people in particular. Even abysmally low wages could offer a better future than poor rural—and often dispossessed—parents could provide. Access to whole new continents seized by colonial powers offered migrants new freedoms along with new risks. The reduced labor supply in the areas that they left behind may well have strengthened the bargaining power of those who would otherwise have been forced into low-wage employment.

Patriarchal institutions made it harder for women than men to take advantage of the increased scope for individual mobility. Indeed, they were often literally left behind, and the demographic structure of migrant-sending regions tilted toward women and the elderly. It became easier for men in general, and fathers in particular, to default on family commitments. Patriarchal families that successfully function as somewhat self-sufficient units of production can be exploitative, but they can also meet the subsistence needs of dependents and offer parents some reward for child-rearing. The uneven concentration of economic resources that often results from capitalist development—even in the absence of colonialism or other forms of tribute extraction—creates new forms of exploitation. The process of enclosure in late eighteenth and early nineteenth-century England, for instance, lowered women's potential to contribute food and fuel to their families and made it more difficult for families to meet their own subsistence needs.[34]

The earliest critics of wage employment in Great Britain bewailed its disruptive effects on both patriarchal authority and the family economy.[35] Labor mobility contributed to increased national income, but reduced family coresidence, income-pooling, household economies of scale, and mutual aid. In traditional patriarchal systems, elder male ownership of property provided economic leverage over both women and the younger generation that improved chances of economic security in old age.[36] In the late eighteenth century, fertility rates in the global North began a slow, uneven, but significant decline that has persisted to the present day. Changes in the direction and magnitude of intergenerational income flows were both cause and consequence of significant changes in family size.[37]

The economic pressures driving fertility decline in Western Europe and its former colonies also increased the economic insecurity of the elderly. While men and women working in household-based enterprises such as farms and artisanal businesses could modify the duration and intensity of work according to their capabilities, capitalist employers were less flexible. The risks of unemployment, forced retirement, poor health, and low wages often precluded accumulation of sufficient savings for retirement. Intergenerational leverage based on control over resources was increasingly limited to wealth-owning families that could promise dowries or bequests as rewards for filial loyalty.

Such families were also better positioned to invest in their own children's capabilities. This class differential did not completely disable families that lacked property or were properties of others. When forces of altruism, solidarity, and mutual aid prevailed, they fostered more resilient and probably more emotionally rewarding relations among kin than those based on economic self-interest. On the other hand, families at the lower end of the wealth distribution—whether as a result of slavery, debt peonage, discrimination, or sheer bad luck—were susceptible to enormous centripetal forces.

As the preceding chapter showed, the slavery and colonialism that facilitated early capitalist development encouraged practices that directly undermined the families of subaltern groups. The durable legacy of such practices was reinforced by patterns of segregation encouraging disregard for the well-being of other people's children. Economic inequalities based on class, race/ethnicity, and citizenship fueled the market for sexual services, which seldom thrives when buyers and sellers are on an equal footing; prostitution, in turn, undermined family-based commitments and the shared support of dependents.

In the early twentieth century, fertility decline itself caused a certain moral panic. In an era in which the size of a country's army heavily influenced its chances of military success, national population size was perceived as a public good. In the United States, Theodore Roosevelt warned against the prospect of race suicide, singling out upper-class women for their signal failure to breed.[38] Adult children were called out for their failure to adequately care for—or even stay in touch with— their elderly parents. Husbands were called out for deserting their wives and children.

Such problems were generally attributed to declining morals or cultural depravity. Yet the unfortunate side effects of economic transformation were also acknowledged. Conservatives argued that women could and should buffer the effects of capitalist individualism as angels in the house. Resistance to feminist efforts to secure access to political suffrage and better paying jobs was often based on the claim that these could destroy family life. Indeed, women provided a kind of bridge between the two colliding worlds of social obligation and individual freedom, making it easy for men to walk right over them.

### Family Wages

The difficulty of transitioning from family-based to individual employment was powerfully encapsulated in debates over a "family wage" that influenced public policies in many now-affluent countries. The concern that a large supply of single workers would drive wages down below the level required for married fathers with children was not misplaced.[39] On the other hand, the notion that men, but not women, required a family wage reflected collective interests based on gender.[40] The principle that employers should help pay for the creation of a future labor force defied capitalist principles of work organization, as did the concept that child rearing was an economically productive activity.

Nonetheless, in the early twentieth century, many employers in some countries—notably France—bowed to pronatalist pressure from both the national government and religious authorities and agreed to pay workers with dependents a premium.[41] Once most firms agreed to the premium, any competitive disadvantage they experienced was probably small. As was apparent from the outset, however, such policies gave employers an incentive to hire workers who were unencumbered.

Noting this perverse incentive, the British Fabian socialists argued that national family allowances offered a better way of addressing the problem.[42] During World War I, the British military paid its soldiers on the basis of family size as well as rank, a practice that dramatically improved working-class living standards and lowered child mortality.[43] Indeed, the need to successfully reproduce soldiers by providing them with food, housing, medical care, and family benefits was, until recently, a military priority.[44] In 1924 the English feminist Eleanor Rathbone made a persuasive case for national family allowances in some detail, observing that men earning a wage premium were not necessarily husbands or fathers and that many women were important contributors to household income.[45]

Great Britain and many other European countries eventually adopted family allowances out of concern for children's welfare and enthusiasm for population growth. High levels of war-related mortality, anxieties about declining fertility, and increases in women's participation in wage employment drove family policy innovations that varied substantially according to historical circumstance. Nordic countries took the lead, with Southern European countries lagging behind. The gender-specific effects varied, often determined by the strength of feminist mobilization.[46]

The United States remained an outlier, partly because racial/ethnic divisions militated against provision of universal benefits. Explicit family allowances never materialized. Nonetheless, implicit family-based subsidies were built into a number of specific public policies.[47] For instance, the retirement provisions of the US Social Security Act passed in 1935 were built upon family wage principles, providing greater transfers to married than to single workers with the same employment history. Men with spouses received benefits 50 percent higher than those of unmarried men with the same earning history. This spousal benefit, an indirect recognition of nonmarket work, at least partially recognized the costs of family care. Many of the gender asymmetries in the Social Security program have been corrected, but workers—primarily men—with a stay-at-home spouse continue to enjoy disproportionate benefits. Other features of the US tax system have long subsidized marriage in ways that work to the disadvantage of single employed mothers in particular.[48]

Early debates over minimum wage legislation in the United States also drew on family wage logic, particularly the notion that a full-time wage earner should receive sufficient earnings to keep his family above the poverty line. As more women entered wage employment, some claimed that it represented a contribution to family support that, while less than her husband's, could be construed as an excuse for a lower minimum wage for him. This claim ignored the decline in unpaid work once performed by full-time housewives and its contribution to household living standards. Even today, the US poverty line is set at the same family income level for families with two income-earning parents (for instance, two adults earning $25,000) and those with a full-time housewife/care provider (for instance, with one adult earning $50,000) if they have the same number of children. Yet the first family has far larger out-of-pocket costs for childcare, meals away from home, and other paid work-related expenses.[49]

Over time women's entrance into paid employment contributed to a gradual degendering of the family wage for men, renamed a "living wage" for families. In the United States, political campaigns to require local employers to pay more than the national legislative minimum gained momentum in many states and municipalities in the closing decades of the twentieth century. Up until the 1990s, the legal threshold was often defined by the needs of a single wage earner supporting spouse and children, but it was gradually revised to include consideration of different family types and household structures.[50] Today it is typically defined as a wage that would allow two fully employed parents with two children to meet basic expenses that include payment for high-quality childcare.[51] By this definition, the federal minimum wage in the United States remains strikingly inadequate: a typical family with two wage earners would need to work four full-time minimum wage jobs (75 hours each) to reach this standard.[52]

Political campaigns for living wages have gone global, highlighting variations in the gap between individual wages and family needs.[53] The methodologies developed for calculating appropriate living wage levels take household size and composition into account.[54] Such calculations place moral and political pressure on global employers, but seem far more difficult to implement than state policies targeted to families with children, such as the conditional cash transfers that many Latin American countries have adopted.[55] On the other hand, in the absence of effective taxes on accumulated wealth, such transfers represent an implicit subsidy for employers, allowing them to pay lower wages.

### Income Security and Social Investment

Public support for child-rearing was only one of the motivating forces behind the development of the welfare state, and it was quantitatively swamped by three other priorities. Patriarchal norms favored pensions for the elderly that would give primacy to male wage earners, while employer demand for a skilled and disciplined labor force favored the expansion of public education. Improvements in health care that could lower the costs of producing labor power (also known as human capital) required the development of efficient insurance systems. These were reproductive investments that women and families could not make on their own.

In 1881, Chancellor Otto Bismarck of Germany announced the first state-financed old-age pension system, explicitly describing it as a way of enforcing collective commitments to the elderly.[56] Germany provided public pensions for manual workers in 1889, and other European countries gradually followed suit.[57] In the United States, the first steps toward a public pension system emerged in the aftermath of the Civil War, when Congress guaranteed old-age assistance to veterans of the Union Army, a substantial share of the male population in northern states. In the early decades of the twentieth century, some private employees began to offer pensions, and some states experimented with policies that presaged the national Social Security legislation enacted in 1935.[58]

The costs were only partially borne by employers, who could offset their tax contributions by paying lower wages. Most pension systems depended heavily on an age-based redistribution of tax revenues from wage earners to retirees, in a pay-as-you-go system. This arrangement could be interpreted as a form of payback for investments made by the working-age population in public education, increasing their productivity and helping increase the earnings on which they would later be taxed to assist those who helped finance their education.[59] It essentially socialized the traditional patriarchal system of support for parents, in which elderly married women and widows derived only indirect benefits from income under male control.

The similarities between private and public transfers are illustrated by laws in some countries (and some states within the United States) that hold adult children responsible for the support of their indigent parents.[60] Some proposals have gone further. One US economist suggests that working-age adults pay approximately 15 percent of their earnings directly to their own parents rather than contributing to the Social Security system.[61] Similar, though less clearly specified obligations are currently in effect in the largest country in the world. Chinese policies designed to minimize public expenditure rely on mandatory family support rules.[62]

At the opposite extreme, individuals can be held responsible for their own income security in old age through personal savings and investment, making any intergenerational transfers to the older generation entirely voluntary. Men and women who devote no time or resources to raising the next generation are generally in a better financial position to build a cash nest egg. As one advertisement for an Individual Retirement Account (IRA) puts it, "Your IRA is like your child." Indeed, it offers property rights over a far more reliable rate of pecuniary return.

The pension systems adopted in many countries idiosyncratically combined individual, family-based, and socialized intergenerational transfers, with little understanding of their long-run implications. In Europe, as in the United States, most transfers to retirees rely heavily on pay-as-you-go financing, in which taxes paid by the working-age generation directly finance retirement beneits.[63] In most developing countries, the level of pension coverage is uneven, limited to formal sector workers, including government employees. East Asian and Latin American economies provide significantly greater coverage than the still largely family-based economies of Sub-Saharan Africa.[64] China has adopted some policies that go beyond family support laws, but these are largely restricted to the urban population.[65]

National investment in education is the other half of the socialized intergenerational contract. When Robert Owen argued that public education should replace child labor, he anticipated the diagnosis of market failure later developed by neoclassical economist Gary Becker: many parents lacked sufficient wealth to invest in their children's education, even though they knew it would be worthwhile.[66] Employers largely dependent on a national or local labor force often endorsed this reasoning, even if they sought to minimize their own share of the costs. In the United States, public schools were primarily financed by taxes on the most widely owned form of family wealth: home ownership.

Much of the payoff was tangible. Public education promoted a high rate of economic growth in the United States and Europe in the late nineteenth and early twentieth centuries.[67] In addition to increasing overall levels of literacy and numeracy, schools helped socialize children to the new forms of routinized discipline likely to be imposed upon them at work.[68] The expansion of higher education fostered a new class of professional and managerial employees who provided a buffer of sorts between owners and workers. Not incidentally, most of the benefits were captured by affluent white families, but public education provided at least some potential for upward mobility.

The development of health insurance systems was driven in part by demands from citizenries cognizant of the need to buffer their unexpected financial costs of valuable new medical technologies. Working-class organizations and voters deserve considerable credit for a global trend toward increased public spending on health, whether in the form of direct provision or insurance subsidies. They were generally more successful in this effort when less divided by race/ethnicity and class. As Jacob Hacker puts it in his overview of the experience of British, Canadian, and US policies, "no country has acquired national health insurance without a fierce and bitter political fight."[69]

In the early stages of welfare state expansion, capitalist employers hoped to blunt the political threats posed by the socialist and left-wing parties that demanded more social spending. Because health care did not initially provide lucrative opportunities for profit, opposition from the private sector was not always deeply entrenched. In addition, many employers who were largely reliant on their fellow citizens as potential workers and consumers anticipated significant benefits from public provision, especially where it would reduce their financial liability for the health of their own employees.

Countries that developed strong public investments in health care at a relatively early stage were those that subsequently developed the most robust and successful programs. Germany established a public health insurance system in 1883, Great Britain in 1911, Japan in 1927, and France began developing such a system in 1930.[70] The Soviet Union put universal health care into place in the 1920s, and after World War II most Soviet-bloc countries developed similar systems. South Korea began expanding coverage in the 1970s, China in 2000. Once established, these programs gained a constituency that made them difficult to revoke.

In many countries where public provision initially lagged, however, resistance to it appeared to grow over time. The United States took a

large step toward public insurance provision in 1965–66, with the establishment of Medicare for the elderly and Medicaid for the indigent, but
efforts to expand these programs met concerted opposition as a result of
slower rates of growth in GDP and concern about burgeoning costs. In
many areas of the developing world, social spending on health also
languished. Some countries, including Chile, Costa Rica, Thailand, and
Rwanda, cover large percentages of their population.[71] For the most
part, however, public health insurance that pools risks and contributions remains an aspiration rather than a reality.[72] According to a recent
report from the World Bank and the World Health Organization, at least
half the world's population lacks access to essential health services.[73]

By the end of 2019, the global momentum that welfare state policies
enjoyed in the second half of the twentieth century had largely dissi-
pated. The optimistic expectation that democratic governments would
be able to generously distribute the fruits of economic growth proved
misplaced. Many voters would have preferred "capitalism with a human
face" but found it increasingly difficult to imagine, much less achieve.
Shifts in the relative bargaining position of powerful intersecting groups
led to a structural realignment that both intensified class inequality and
aggravated persistent nonclass divisions. Whether the global Covid-19
pandemic will reverse this trend remains unclear.

## Welfare Hits the Wall

When nominated by the president for a major cabinet post in 1953,
General Motors Chief Executive Officer Charlie Wilson famously
explained his belief that "what was good for the country was good for
General Motors, and vice versa."[74] The vice versa part of his statement
was widely quoted, but there was far more truth in the first part. From
the late nineteenth century to the early twenty-first century, the interests
of capitalist employers in affluent countries were sufficiently aligned
with racial and national interests to promote the development of public
policies that socialized some of the costs of creating and developing
human capabilities. This alignment, however, proved temporary.

In some countries, the very enlargement of the welfare state undermined its forward progress. As public social expenditures grew, their
distribution became more consequential, often intensifying racist,
nationalist, and gendered allegiances. Democratic support for social

programs made them resistant to cutbacks but did not enable expansion in the face of fiscal pressures created by the growing difficulty of taxing corporate profits or the super-rich. The threat of increased capital mobility and the growing ease of international tax evasion shifted the perceived burden of taxation toward workers with stagnant earnings. Another pressure on the welfare state derived from its persistent patriarchal bias: by socializing the benefits of raising the next generation of taxpayers more generously than the costs, it encouraged a decline in birth rates to below replacement levels, threatening the sustainability of its intergenerational transfers.

**Whose Welfare?**

The habit of taking the production of human capabilities largely for granted has obscured important dimensions of collective conflict. Welfare state policies shape access to the means of social reproduction. As their relative size grows, they become more susceptible to conflicts over the allocation of their spending, especially when starved of resources by the multinational employers who are their most economically powerful beneficiaries.

This distributional struggle sometimes led to favorable outcomes in the reproductive economy. In the United States in the early twentieth century, for instance, women's groups mobilized successfully on behalf of state-level assistance for mothers who had been widowed or deserted by their husbands even before women gained the federal franchise.[75] Once allowed the ballot box, women threw much of their weight behind increases in spending on public health that significantly reduced child mortality rates.[76]

Yet US public policies in the early twentieth century also limited women's job market opportunities. Most states and localities enforced rules that required teachers to resign from their jobs if they married or became pregnant.[77] As unemployment intensified during the Great Depression, the Roosevelt administration directed the federal civil service to lay off workers whose spouses also worked for the government, with disproportionate consequences for women employees. This was only one manifestation of the ways in which it reinforced patriarchal norms.[78]

In the same era, racist priorities channeled public spending. Federal complicity enabled the implementation of segregationist policies in the South, including severe restrictions on civil rights. Facing political pressure from the segregationist South, the architects of the New Deal implemented relief policies that have been described as "affirmative action for whites."[79] Landmark legislation, including the Social Security Act of 1935 and the National Labor Relations Act of 1937, excluded Black-dominated occupations such as domestic workers and farm laborers from both coverage and protection.[80] Residential segregation, reliance on local tax bases, and overt racism combined in ways that condemned Black students to underfunded schools.[81]

The civil rights movement that began to take shape in the 1950s contributed to the political and economic empowerment of women and people of color, with noticeable effects on the evolution of welfare state policies. The most visible pieces of legislation, such as the Civil Rights Act of 1964, were both preceded and succeeded by many other changes, including expansion of Social Security coverage to previously unrepresented workers. The Medicare and Medicaid programs extended public health care to the elderly and to the extremely poor.

The history of social policy in the United States clearly shows that racial/ethnic coalitions made it difficult for anti-poverty efforts to gain greater political traction.[82] Racial stereotyping has long been endemic; media depictions of families receiving public assistance have often over-represented African Americans, particularly women.[83] Even as public social spending expanded, it provided more significant benefits to white men than other groups, especially when the hidden welfare state—tax policies subsidizing middle- and higher income families—is brought into view.[84]

Still, the expansion of social spending in the United States, along with affirmative action and anti-discrimination laws put in place in the 1960s and 1970s, threatened some advantages based on gender and race/ ethnicity, contributing to a political backlash against the welfare state itself. This perceived threat was intensified by steady increases in both legal and illegal migration. Despite evidence that immigrants to the United States do not represent a significant burden, the fear that noncitizens free ride on public assistance permeates anti-immigrant campaigns.[85] Restrictions on public assistance to noncitizens were a significant aspect of changes to means-tested public assistance implemented in 1996, and the Trump administration doubled down on this strategy.

Flames were fanned by the structure of US social spending. Tax breaks for affluent families' expenditures on health and education remain invisible to most voters, while means-tested programs such as Food Stamps and Medicaid are publicized. The universal benefits that build a stronger constituency for public spending have been concentrated on the predominantly white elderly population.[86] When public benefits are means-tested, families with incomes that are just above the eligibility level often feel aggrieved. If benefits are phased out as income goes up, the benefit-reduction rate represents a high implicit tax rate.[87]

Class differences in political power clearly intensified in the United States. The deregulation of political campaign spending, congressional redistricting, and population shifts amplified the already disproportionate influence of the affluent on political outcomes. Strategic investments funded by many of the richest families in the country were cleverly designed to weaken democratic processes.[88] The views of most Americans on social spending issues are not accurately represented by their elected representatives.[89]

Similar trends unfolded in many other countries. The increased flow of refugees and other migrants following upon the opening of European Union borders led to significant political realignments, particularly in France, Germany, Hungary, and the United Kingdom. Though much depends on political context, racial and ethnic heterogeneity appears to undermine support for government provision of public goods in both developed and developing countries.[90] Generous social benefits can certainly buffer the effects of free trade and job loss, but they can also fuel nativist fears of their dilution by unrestricted migration.

Within this intersectional matrix, gender conflict left its mark. A large gap between men's and women's voting preferences became apparent in the United States and many European countries in the twentieth century, with women (particularly those not pooling income with men) more supportive of public spending.[91] In the United States, Democrats were often described as the "mommy party" and Republicans as the "daddy party." Differences based on biological sex were less telling than differences in attitudes toward traditional norms of femininity and masculinity.[92] The battleground encompassed even the smallest details of public policy. In their efforts to dismantle Planned Parenthood, the largest nonprofit organization providing reproductive health care services in the United States, some Republicans expressed outrage that men were being taxed to help pay for prenatal care and mammograms.[93]

In the international arena, women's political representation altered patterns of public spending. A cross-national comparison of political reforms between 1995 and 2012 found that gender quotas that resulted in a large increase in women's parliamentary representation resulted in greater expenditures on public health and relative declines in military spending.[94] A randomized policy experiment in India examining the impact of gender quotas for village councils found greater spending on public goods that would benefit women and higher aspirations and educational attainment for young girls.[95] Pushback, however, quickly became apparent. Orchestrated campaigns emerged to bolster traditional gender norms, restrict reproductive rights, and deny protections to lesbian, gay, bisexual, or transsexual people. Their advocates often described themselves as "friends of the family" aiming to prevent its destabilization by the state.[96]

A better descriptor would be "friends of the patriarchal family" desperate to prove that no other viable family forms exist. Structures of collective power based on gender, age, and sexual orientation derive much of their resilience from their complementarities with structures of collective power based on race/ethnicity, citizenship, and class, and vice versa. These evolving social divisions explain the difficulty of adapting welfare state institutions to new sources of economic risk. They also explain the shocking level of international vulnerability to a previously unknown, highly contagious, and terrifying coronavirus.

**Whose Labor?**

As global inequalities in the distribution of wealth have metastasized in recent years, the specific impact of class conflict on the welfare state has become increasingly apparent. Like a landowner who can charge higher rents if his tenant farmers increase their output, or a stationary bandit who can command greater tribute from prosperous victims than from poor ones, capitalist employers can benefit from increases in the productivity of their workers. This partial alignment of interests can be weakened, however, by increased mobility of employers and workers and by technological changes that reduce the demand for skills embodied in living human beings.

Steady improvements in transportation and communication technologies have increased the economic permeability of political boundaries, giving employers greater access to a global labor pool and reducing the ability of democratic governments to tax profits or control capital flows. The mere threat of relocating or automating jobs has put downward pressure both on wages and on levels of redistributive social spending. Employers' economic incentives to support or help finance social investment have declined, with denationalizing as well as defamilizing effects.

The threat that increased capital mobility poses to the sustainability of the welfare state, and, indeed, to the living standards of wage earners everywhere, has been widely recognized.[97] Some economists argue that such mobility could have a salutary disciplinary effect, pressuring national governments to operate more efficiently and reduce unproductive social spending.[98] The terminology used in this argument reveals its specious foundations: social spending is a form of public investment and public investment is not unproductive. It is a necessary aspect of sustainable development—a cost of doing business—that those in advantageous positions would prefer not to pay.

Political coalitions, rather than economic constraints, define the policy space of the welfare state. In some European countries, free public higher education and extensive job training have gone hand-in-hand with increased international competitiveness. Some countries have successfully adapted to the reduced economic significance of national borders by reducing the threat of job loss.[99] Even where significant austerity measures have been implemented, such as the United Kingdom and the United States, overall social spending continues to comprise a significant share of public budgets.

Yet increased globalization drove a wedge between national interests and the interests of large employers (and those invested in them). Even in European social democracies, the forward progress of the welfare state stalled until the Covid-19 pandemic hit.[100] Efforts to improve, expand, or innovate were blocked by budgetary stringency. Even where citizens were willing to tax themselves to strengthen their national human capabilities, their reduced ability to tax corporate profits—or the individuals who derive the bulk of income from them—undercut the social investment agenda.

Poor countries have long been familiar with the problem of capital flight exacerbated by political corruption, a process that has severely undermined economic development in Sub-Saharan Africa in particular.[101] Tax shelters themselves are nothing new. But the sheer size of international transfers, documented by new forensic accounting methods and leaked records, revealed startling transfers of wealth across national borders.[102] The very threat of increased tax evasion was used to justify recent corporate tax rate reductions in the United States.

Both the actual and the threatened relocation of capital abroad through off-shoring of production facilities increased the bargaining power of firms relative to employees, regulators, and tax collectors.[103] In the United States, state and local communities often engaged in bidding wars to attract investment, guaranteeing tax exemptions and rebates in return for often unenforceable promises of job creation.[104] Even multi-national corporations with secure profit margins based on technological innovation and brand loyalty, such as Apple, actively used international strategies to minimize their taxes and labor costs.

By the late twentieth century, the United States, once in the international vanguard of public higher education for its citizens, had begun to lag behind.[105] Many developing countries, seeing the flip side of international capital mobility, increased their educational spending in the hope of attracting foreign capital. In 1970, the United States represented 6 percent of the world's population and accounted for 29 percent of the world's college students; by 2005–2006, its share of total college students had declined to 12 percent. By the early twenty-first century, almost 75 percent of global tertiary education enrollments were in developing countries, including China, India, and Mexico.[106]

This is a remarkable accomplishment that bodes well for global productivity, but it also reduces the bargaining power of college-educated workers in affluent countries. Why should large businesses pay taxes to support public higher education in their own countries when they can capture the payoffs to investments made by other states or countries?[107] Migrants from low-income to high-income countries provide a source of labor that is doubly cheap: no taxpayer money was expended on their care or education to adulthood, and many are unmarried and/or separated from dependent family members. Uneven economic development has created such enormous pressures to seek improved living standards that many migrants are willing to risk their lives—and those of their children—to relocate.

State policies often explicitly reduce the bargaining power of migrants, making them an inexpensive source of labor not just for capitalist employers but also for a wide swath of consumers. In the Arab emirates such as Qatar, migrants have virtually no enforceable rights and can simply be deported if they become unemployed or unable to work.[108] In the United States, the undocumented status of many Latin American workers puts them in virtually the same situation.[109] Migrant domestic servants and care providers are among the most economically vulnerable workers in the world.[110]

Like patriarchs weathering the decline of family-based enterprise, nation-states are weathering the decline of nation-based enterprise with varying degrees of indignation and backlash. Nationalism is resurgent in part because it invokes collective commitments that capitalist institutions devalue. There are positive precedents: many patriarchal families remain committed to the well-being of their sons and daughters even as they recognize the increased difficulty of capturing economic benefits from them. By contrast, capitalist firms intent on cutting costs regardless of the consequences for fellow-citizens are like absentee fathers intent on avoiding child support payments.

### Whose Children?

The larger distribution of the costs of raising children offers the most tangible example of tensions between current and future generations. Early welfare states socialized the benefits of raising the younger generation more than they compensated parents for the private costs.[111] These policies speeded a process of fertility decline that was initially viewed as a potential boost to economic growth but went farther and faster than expected, reaching below-replacement rates that could well lead to the steady decline of some national populations.

Parents raise children for reasons of their own that obviously cannot be reduced to calculations of pecuniary gain to themselves or others. Nonetheless, children in many countries today grow up to become workers who pay taxes to help finance care for many older persons who devoted very little time or effort to the younger generation.[112] Many elderly parents enjoy significant help from their own children in managing illness and disability, but the general direction of intergenerational transfers within families is from older to younger, and within the public sector, from younger to older.[113] In explicit acknowledgement of this pattern, the German Constitutional Court recommended in 2001 that parents pay lower taxes than nonparents for public eldercare insurance.[114] Less attention has been devoted to the gendered aspects of net transfers: mothers in general and lone mothers in particular pay a disproportionate share of the costs of producing future citizens and the tax revenues they will generate.

The size of transfers between cohorts that overlap in time is significantly influenced by demographic trends. In a rapidly growing population with high fertility rates, the youngest generation tends to be large, the working-age population smaller, and the elderly population smaller still, making pay-as-you go pension financing expeditious. As life expectancy expands, however, the tax burden on the working age population also increases. This increase is not inevitable. Support for the elderly could, in principle, be financed by a tax on wealth or profits, but this option is often foreclosed by entrenched interests and institutional inertia. As a result, state-financed pensions continue to channel inter-generational transfers that resemble earlier patriarchal bargains.[115]

Most public pension systems were put into place during a period of declining but still relatively high fertility rates, making them relatively easy to finance. On top of demographic change, slow growth in real wages and employment in affluent countries have lowered the living standards of younger generations relative to their elders. Not surpris-ingly, real and potential increases in the per capita tax liabilities of the working age population have exacerbated distributional tensions caused by reluctance to openly confront or negotiate issues of intergenerational justice.

The elderly population is not to blame for declines in fertility, increases in longevity, or costly new medical technologies that have increased the fiscal burden of the transfers promised to them. Yet their political clout—including the simple fact that in most democracies they have votes while those under 18 do not—augments their collective power. In the United States the share of the federal budget devoted to the elderly has increased rapidly over time, even as the share devoted to children has declined.[116] The comparative budget analyses of the National Transfer Accounts project arrive at similar conclusions for many other countries.[117]

In the United States, the combined impact of immigration and differ-ences in birth rates between migrants and native-born Americans gives public generational transfers racial/ethnic dimensions. White non-Hispanic children now represent less than 50 percent of all newborns in the United States. By 2020, more than half of all children under 18 will be designated members of a minority race or ethnic group. The elderly population, by contrast, will remain predominantly white and non-Hispanic.[118] Not surprisingly, elderly voters are less likely than others to support spending on the younger generation.[119]

Privatization of pension systems does not offer an easy solution to this problem. A working-age cohort forced to save more money to finance its own retirement and health care would have far less money to spend on its own children. Indeed, "refamilialization" would make the problem worse. Parents would face even greater fears regarding their children's future success in the labor market than they do today. Adults worried about their income security and care in later years would weigh the net benefits of raising children against the net benefits of private savings that would enable them to purchase the care they need. This, too, would discourage child-rearing.

Many countries that have done little to promote gender equality or to provide public support for family commitments are now headed for especially rapid population decline. Russia, Italy, Spain, Greece, Japan, and Korea are all near the top of this list.[120] Among developing countries China stands out, with especially low fertility rates in urban areas.[121] Other countries may soon enter the category of those whose population is projected to decline. In 2016, US fertility rates reached a record low, slightly below the replacement level of 2.1 births per woman.[122] If net immigration begins to decline, so too will the total US population.

By contrast, Nordic and other northwestern European countries that provide relatively generous supports for employed mothers such as paid family leaves and universal childcare have stabilized their birth rates closer to replacement levels, offering a smoother transition to a likely future of population decline. Their social investment and environmental policies promise increases in the productivity of future generations that could help compensate for the decline in their relative cohort size. These welfare states have not yet achieved gender equality, but they have, at least, recognized and rewarded reproductive commitments laying a new social foundation for postindustrial economies.[123]

The process of fertility decline now underway in virtually every part of the world intensifies pressures to renegotiate the social institutions that govern the distribution of the costs of caring for dependents, including the welfare state. The term "birth strike" may not be entirely accurate, but it testifies to increases in women's collective bargaining power.[124] It also helps explain why political resistance and backlash remain ferocious. Women in many countries still lack basic reproductive rights.[125] In the United States, legislative efforts to ban abortion and restrict contraception have reached epic levels.

Declining birth rates, if accompanied by institutional changes that buffer the resulting economic stresses, offer huge benefits. A continuing shift from quantity to quality of investments in human capabilities would improve the productivity and the bargaining power of both women and workers. Stabilization, or even contraction of the global population in the near future could help reduce environmental degradation and climate change. Some redistribution of the global population through politically sustainable levels of migration could dramatically reduce poverty and inequality.

Still, the short-run costs of rapid transition to below-replacement fertility rates, which threaten the sustainability of current transfers to the elderly, should be acknowledged. Both pension and health-care delivery systems require more creative long-range planning and institutional reform. The complex forms of distributional conflict that impede adaptation to new economic circumstances—and new viral threats— must be transmuted into forms of solidarity based on the need to recognize, reward, and redistribute the work of caring for others.[126]

## Changing the Narrative

Families and welfare states have coevolved in ways heavily inflected by demographic trends. Conflicts and complementarities between patriarchal and capitalist institutions reach far beyond gender differences to encompass many other dimensions of collective identity. The costs of creating, developing, and maintaining human capabilities are distributed unequally not only between men and women, but also among many other socially assigned groups, including those based on age, sexual orientation, race/ethnicity, citizenship, and class. Stark inequalities in health outcomes, including mortality from Covid-19, testify to the complex dynamics of social reproduction.

The productivity of social investment has been obscured by accounting methods that understate the value of public goods, influenced by the androcentric assumption that women's unpaid work is not really work. A spurious narrative that takes most reproductive work for granted has pictured commitments to families, friends, and communities as discretionary expenditures akin to luxury goods. The false claim that social spending necessarily crowds out intrafamily transfers and weakens family ties has been used to justify cuts in public assistance and social insurance.

Women's unpaid contributions to the creation of both private and social wealth are vital. The difficulty of privately capturing and capitalizing these contributions—like the difficulty of privately capturing and capitalizing natural assets and ecological services—dramatizes the limitations of any economic system that relies too heavily on capitalist institutions. The democratic negotiation of contributions to public goods is intrinsically difficult but absolutely necessary. Its achievement depends, in large part, on a convincing explanation of the need to bridge the gap between the private costs and the social benefits of reproductive work.

# 9
## Gender and Care Costs

Men are not the only beneficiaries of collective power structures that offload an unfair share of reproductive costs onto women. Nonetheless, unequal distribution of the costs of caring for others has obviously gendered implications. When labor economists acknowledge the cost of specialization in care provision, they typically assume that it represents a price freely paid for the intrinsic satisfaction it affords. This assumption ignores the economic, political, and ideological institutions that both shape preferences and reduce women's ability to capture the value of the care services they provide. Even when capitalist expansion offers women more space to pursue traditionally masculine prerogatives, it increases the relative cost of commitments that do not yield a private return.

Some feminist theorists have described the cost of care as a kind of reproductive tax, applying a tax metaphor that some labor economists use to describe the child support obligations of noncustodial parents.[1] Since textbook economic theory holds that taxes create inefficiencies known as deadweight losses, the latter usage implies that absent fathers should be allowed to choose whether to pay up or not. This, in turn, helps explain why women pay a metaphorical reproductive tax: their specialization in care provision is not entirely voluntary, and its benefits redound not only to care recipients but also to society as a whole. The economic penalties that caregivers pay are not legislatively stipulated, officially measured, or even widely acknowledged, but they are nonetheless significant. Their incidence helps explain the persistence of gender inequality.

Investments in other people are enforced by normative pressures and emotional commitments that help ensure high-quality care but weaken the bargaining power of care providers. The strategic dilemma resembles the stylized game of Chicken, in which two players may threaten to do something—whether to drive head-on into another car or to ignore a baby's dirty diaper—in the hope that the other player will capitulate. Where diaper changing is concerned, the person most worried about the baby is the one whose bluff is least convincing. She is likely to do most of the dirty work.[2]

The consequences of such gender asymmetry are often amplified by health shocks such as Covid-19. That women do a disproportionate share of work entailing a high risk of viral infection does not imply that all women are equally burdened or that many men do not also pay a price for providing care. It does, however, reveal linkages between gender, care, and economic disadvantage.

## The Costs of Family Care

Increases in the cost of raising children help motivate the transition to lower fertility rates but can also intensify conflict between mothers and fathers over the distribution of these costs. Who should sacrifice leisure time or career opportunities to look after the kids? Net transfers between parents and children over the life cycle can also change in ways that cause economic strain. Should parents pay the full cost of higher education, graduate school, or buying a home? Adult children may or may not provide a partial payback to their aging parents or a pay-forward to children of their own. It is not uncommon for them to default on normative obligations held dear by earlier generations. Recent changes in family and household structure have left many women with more responsibility than men for both the care and support of dependents.

### Within Marriage

Family members living under the same roof typically have similar living standards, because they share household public goods such as living space and utilities. Men typically earn more than women, and women typically perform more unpaid family care; husbands and wives may nonetheless pool their market income, make joint decisions about how to spend it, and share responsibilities for dependent care. Even in stable married-couple families, however, wives often have less economic bargaining power, less control over major consumption decisions, and less unencumbered leisure time than their husbands.[3]

Family care providers do not receive an individual paycheck, and the emotional rewards they hope for can be variable and unpredictable. Once committed, it is difficult for them to threaten exit.[4] Specialization in care provision intensifies personal attachments and cultivates person-specific skills that are not always transferable. Productive contributions to family living standards and capabilities are not fungible outside the family, unlike employment history, which often pays off both in marketable skills and pension credits.[5] Reductions in paid labor force experience lower women's future earnings and reduce their fallback position in household bargaining.

The effects of family care on individual earnings are most apparent in countries where the postponement of child-rearing and fertility decline have generated significant variation in maternal commitments. Responsibilities for young children typically constrain choices regarding hours and location of employment, type of occupation, and industry. Even statistical analyses that take these factors into account show that children tend to lower the earnings of mothers but increase those of fathers, especially over the life cycle.[6] Mothers are especially likely to reduce their employment hours when children have health-related disabilities.[7] The motherhood penalty is particularly significant among educated women in career tracks where employers prize long hours and continuity of employment.[8]

In affluent countries, responsibilities for the care of sick, disabled, or frail family members also bear more heavily on the employment of women than on men.[9] Women in the United States report that they provide substantially more care to their elderly parents than men do in large part because they feel a greater obligation to do so.[10] Daughters provide more care than sons, and sons with sisters manage to provide less care than those without.[11]

In married-couple families in which income is pooled over an entire lifetime, the economic costs of care are often redistributed in equalizing ways. Wives without independent access to wealth or income, however, remain economically vulnerable to any diminution of spousal altruism or affection, especially that which might lead to physical abuse. Analysis of data from the US state of California shows that reported levels of domestic violence are lower in areas where women's wages are higher relative to men's.[12] British data shows that employment has protective effects for women: an increase in male unemployment leads to a decrease in intimate partner violence, while an increase in female unemployment has the opposite effect.[13] On the other hand, increases in female economic power often prompt male backlash. A study of families in Mexico where some mothers received public transfers through the Oportunidades program reported a significantly reduced incidence of domestic violence but a higher incidence of threats.[14]

Efforts to examine how married couples allocate family income and consumption reveal less dramatic but nonetheless significant disparities, with implications for other family members.[15] Income under the control of mothers is more likely to be spent on children (especially daughters) than income under the control of fathers.[16] Nationally representative time-use surveys reveal another dimension of intrafamily inequality: differences in the amount of time individuals devote to self-care (including sleep) and leisure. Most surveys focus on specific care activities, with scant attention to supervisory or on-call constraints that often require a caregiver to stay close to home. As a result, they underestimate the impact of care responsibilities.[17] Nonetheless, gender inequality in total work hours, calculated as the sum of hours of market plus nonmarket work, is strongly associated with parenthood. Across countries, the greater women's specialization in unpaid family care, the longer the length of their total workday relative to men.[18]

Participation in paid employment strengthens women's fallback position in household bargaining, but its effects often seem modest. Gender norms exert a powerful independent influence on the division of labor, and women often sacrifice leisure time rather than reduce family care, especially if no alternatives are available. Analysis of time use surveys from countries as diverse as the United States, India, and Ecuador show that an additional hour of paid work reduces women's unpaid work by considerably less than one hour, effectively increasing the length of their work day.[19] In rural Indian households, one of the few factors that has been shown to reduce the length of an adult woman's workday is the presence of a daughter-in-law who assumes part of the care burden.[20] These quantitative results are supported by qualitative evidence: women in many countries testify to the stress of the "double day."[21]

Nonetheless, women's economic bargaining power is increasing, with tangible consequences. Empirical research in two affluent countries, the

United States and Australia, show that higher earnings for women are associated with a reduction in the share of total household work that they perform. Wives either persuade their husbands to do more, or they purchase goods and services that reduce their own workload.[22] This bargaining effect is particularly strong in households where wives contribute a substantial portion of family market income. The effect disappears, however, in households where wives contribute more than their husbands do. Beyond this point, women increase their relative contribution to household work as if to compensate for violating traditional gender norms.[23]

No statistical analysis of household-level data can fully capture the complex negotiations of family life. Market earnings are not the only factors that influence bargaining power, and divorce is not the only threat to reduced cooperation. Many different social institutions—ranging from family law to community-level factors such as childcare centers or police practices—have differential effects. Norms themselves constitute fallbacks: rather than making explicit decisions, couples may simply conform to cultural expectations that they specialize in "separate spheres."[24] Yet norms are altered by the cumulative effects of nonconformity, and cultural negotiation can alter the meanings of femininity and masculinity.

**Outside Marriage**

Patriarchal rules once common to many countries gave husbands direct authority over wives. Contestation of such rules has clearly benefited women, but the decline of marriage itself has had ambiguous effects. On the one hand, gender roles in nonmarital partnerships tend to be less specialized, offering more autonomy and flexibility. On the other hand, women in such partnerships are less likely to enjoy long-term financial assistance from the fathers of their children. Lack of respect or remuneration for the work of raising children is a form of social and paternal free riding that can leave women just as vulnerable to exploitation as patriarchal top riding.

In the mid-1980s, economist Victor Fuchs argued that declines in income pooling between men and women had countervailed increases in women's individual earnings relative to men in the United States between 1959 and 1983.[25] This claim rests on strong assumptions about sharing in married-couple households, but it is not implausible for mothers with poor prospects in the labor market. Divorce rates increased in the United States during this period as a result of the adoption of no-fault divorce provisions, and women often paid a high price in the form of reduced family income.[26] This negative impact began to diminish in the 1980s, largely as a result of increases in women's employment. Even today, however, divorce lowers wives' total income far more than that of their husbands.[27] Similar effects have been well-documented for British, Canadian, and German married couples.[28]

In recent years, cohabitation outside of marriage has increased significantly in many affluent countries; in the United States, equitable coparenting outside marriage seems especially difficult to achieve.[29] The extent to which cohabiting couples pool their income and share family care responsibilities remains unclear, but like marital divorce, the dissolution of such relationships is often most costly for women.[30] Men are increasingly insulated from both the direct experience and financial demands of fatherhood.[31] In 2017, about 27 percent of children in the United States were living in households without a biological, adoptive, or stepfather compared to 11 percent in 1960.[32] Perfectly comparable statistics for other countries are hard to come by, but in the United Kingdom, the percentage of men ages twenty-six to thirty living with a dependent biological child dropped steadily from 58 percent among those born between 1940 and 1949 to 28 percent among those born between 1980 and 1989.[33]

Fathers need not live in the same household to coparent a child, but physical absence often goes along with minimal contributions of both money and time. Poor specification and enforcement of child support increases financial demands on custodial parents—primarily mothers—and leaves many children vulnerable to poverty. One most recent estimate for the United States indicates that only 54 percent of noncustodial fathers paid any child support at all.[34] Only about four out of every ten nonresident fathers had legal child support orders, and only 20 percent paid all the child support they are owed.[35] Divorced mothers are far more likely than unmarried mothers to receive such payments.

The economic value of the time that parents devote to children, even when based on a lower bound estimate of the cost of hiring a replacement caregiver, far exceeds direct expenditures on shelter, food, and clothing.[36] Household structure has marked effects on the total amount of time devoted to direct interaction with children. One recent study analyzing family care time in the United States reported negligible attention from both nonresident fathers and cohabiting men with no biological tie or legal responsibility (for example, stepfathers or adoptive fathers) to the children they were living with.[37] Coresident grandparents by contrast tend to provide significant amounts of care.

In the United States, children living in two-parent or multigenerational households typically benefit from higher family income and greater quantities of adult time than those in other households, contributing to better educational attainment and higher future earnings.[38] In Japan, Australia, and the European Union, as well as the United States, mothers with college degrees have more bargaining power in both the labor market and the marriage market: they are more likely than other women to pool resources with relatively high-earning men.[39]

Although intrafamily transfers of income and time are often viewed as purely private and personal matters, they have enormous impact. The percentage of families maintained by women alone has increased significantly in recent years in many areas of the world, including the United States, Europe, and Latin America.[40] In these regions, changes in family and household structure are just as relevant to gender inequality in disposable income as trends in relative labor market earnings.[41] Measures of women's empowerment would look very different if they went beyond comparisons of market earnings to assess changes in men's relative contributions to the care and support of children and other dependents.[42]

## The Pauperization of Motherhood

Poverty is generally defined in terms of family income, and families maintained by women alone represent a large share of all families with children in poverty in the United States and many other countries.[43] There is less evidence of feminization of poverty than pauperization of motherhood; overrepresentation of women among the poor is far less significant than the overrepresentation of mothers of children under age eighteen.[44] This distinction is often overlooked by researchers examining poverty among female-headed households, traditionally defined as households that do not include an adult male.[45] These households include two groups that bring up average income for the larger category: single women who are employed full-time and widows who have inherited property and pensions from their husbands; young children are not necessarily present.[46]

Mothers supporting children on their own face the difficult task of combining childcare with income-generating employment. This task is particularly stressful in countries where most income-earning opportunities lie outside the home, where other family members are not available as supplementary caregivers, and where public provision of childcare is inadequate. All these factors, as well as the income available to spend on feeding, clothing, and educating children, influence family living standards.

Poverty thresholds are typically based on market income adjusted for differences in household size and composition. Equivalence scales based on assumptions regarding economies of scale and the consumption requirements of children relative to adults provide a basis for such adjustment, but most such scales significantly underestimate the cost of young children. Household surveys conducted in the 1950s showed that expenditures on food for a child averaged half as much as food for an adult. As a result, many scales discount children by 50 percent relative to other household members. In many countries today, however, food represents a very small share of total expenditures on children, dwarfed by the costs of childcare and education.[47] Accurate estimates of increases in relative expenditures on children over time would almost certainly raise poverty thresholds for families maintained by mothers alone, increasing estimates of the percentage living in poverty.[48]

Attention to changes in intrafamily income flows does not imply that global capitalist dynamics are unimportant. As emphasized in Chapter 7, formal sector employment in many developing countries has grown at painfully slow rates for both men and women. The resulting economic stress and forced migration has contributed to greater variance and unpredictability in family support. Many successful migrants send large remittances home to children and/or aging parents, but others are unable to find employment, and some simply lose touch with their families. Women from poor countries who cross international borders to find jobs pay a high price in separation from their families and communities.[49] Global care chains, like deforestation, overfishing, and carbon emissions, offer short-run gains at the expense of long-run sustainability.

These intersectional dynamics illustrate the contradictory impacts of modern economic development. Capitalist celebration of individual self-interest and economic mobility has contributed to a process of deregulation that has weakened the patriarchal bargain but has left caregivers vulnerable. Many women view the vaunted benefits of modernization with some skepticism, because they confront the worst of both worlds—weakened support for family commitments yet limited opportunities for secure employment.

## Care Penalties in Paid Employment

Inequalities in the amount of time that women and men devote to family care have huge consequences for their relative earnings over the life cycle.[50] Even among full-time employees, women typically devote fewer hours to market work than men, a factor that helps explain why the gender gap in wages has remained so persistent even in advanced capitalist countries such as the United States.[51] Though the size of the motherhood penalty appears to be declining in the United States today, the gender differential in earnings continues to reflect differences in family commitments.[52]

Whether or not they become mothers, women often enter traditionally feminine occupations and industries in which workers have little bargaining power. Many of the jobs in the expanding service sector in affluent countries, including those requiring high levels of education, involve care provision in health, education, and social services. These jobs are vulnerable to the same undervaluation as family care: they often involve person-specific interactions that create benefits that are difficult to commodify. Even within the medical profession, doctors who specialize in family practice or pediatrics earn considerably less money than those specializing in elective procedures—a factor that helps explain why the Covid-19 pandemic, which crowded out such procedures, put enormous financial pressure on US hospitals.[53]

### The Motherhood Penalty

Men are able to devote more time than women to paid employment because they can more easily rely on someone else to provide direct care for family members and friends. Many firms prefer to hire workers for high-end jobs who can work long hours, be available evenings and weekends, and travel on short notice. Since employers cannot always reliably identify job applicants who will fit this description, they tend to discriminate against those they consider statistically unlikely to be "ideal workers," namely women.[54]

Covert, perhaps even unconscious, bias clearly affects employment outcomes. In a now-famous experiment, sociologists sent fictional job applications to US employers that were closely matched in every respect but one—some included a signal that the applicant was the mother of a young child, such as participation in a Parent-Teacher Organization.[55] Such signals reduced the likelihood that the applicant would receive further consideration. This experiment, like others focusing on signals of racial difference, confirms the economic impact of subtle forms of discrimination.[56]

Employers often treat mothers and fathers differently.[57] As the US Equal Opportunities Employment Commission noted in 2007,

> women with caregiving responsibilities may be perceived as more committed to caregiving than to their jobs and as less competent than other workers, regardless of how their caregiving responsibilities actually impact their work. Male caregivers may face the mirror image stereotype: that men are poorly suited to caregiving. As a result, men may be denied parental leave or other benefits routinely afforded their female counterparts.[58]

Family responsibility discrimination is a version of gender discrimination that "polices men into traditional breadwinner roles and women out of them."[59]

Some jobs seem intrinsically more flexible than others. In pharmacy, for instance, both men and women work highly variable hours and earn virtually the same.[60] Yet the premia most employers pay for conformity to the stereotype of the ideal worker cannot be wholly explained by differences in productivity or value added to the firm.[61] Other factors come into play: lingering male discomfort with women in authority, sheer institutional inertia, and the ability to cut costs by forcing workers to accept long hours at the expense of their personal and family lives.[62]

Declines in worker bargaining power result not only in slower wage growth, but also in less control over schedules. Even as total work hours in managerial and professional jobs have increased in the United States, many employers have increased their reliance on part-time workers, often resorting to just-in-time scheduling to cut labor costs. Unpredictable and inadequate work hours are just as problematic for some employed caregivers as mandatory overtime for others.[63]

Unless they face labor shortages, employers have little economic incentive to organize employment in more family-friendly ways. In the United States, many women in high-level professional and managerial jobs have sufficient bargaining power to win access to employer-provided benefits such as scheduling flexibility and paid family leaves.[64] As more women have become obstetricians and veterinarians, they have developed group-based practices where on-call and after-hours responsibilities can be rotated. By contrast, women in low-wage jobs are often forced to quit jobs when childcare falls through or a child or parent falls ill, further increasing their economic vulnerability.

In many countries, the expense of paid childcare, the length of the school day, and school vacations make it difficult to combine parenting with long hours of paid employment. In the United States, many working parents sign up for split shifts, sacrificing time they might otherwise spend together in order to make sure their children are looked after.[65] Scheduling problems are ubiquitous in developing countries as well as affluent countries. Yet they could be effectively addressed. One study of the cut-flower industry in Colombia found that the practice of starting and ending the work day early—while flowers are fresher—created new employment opportunities for mothers who were able to clock out before their children came home from school.[66]

Unfortunately, in the absence of labor shortages and strong trade union pressure, employers have little incentive to implement family-friendly practices, and relatively few countries implement these on the national level. Even some public sector institutions rely heavily on unpaid family care: for many years German school systems sent children home in the middle of the day to eat hot lunches prepared by their mothers. Similarly, many hospitals in developing countries expect families to supply meals for patients. The pressure to maximize profits or minimize costs often distracts attention from achievement of social outcomes that don't improve employers'—or managers'—bottom lines.

### Segregation and Sorting

When employers know that women often work for lower wages than men, they make lower wage offers, reproducing preexisting inequalities based on gender. This downward pressure helps explain why men feel threatened when women enter a previously male-dominated occupation and tend to flee once the percentage of women exceeds a certain threshold.[67] The significant effect of previous earnings on current and future earnings has prompted some cities and states in the United States to prohibit employers from asking for job applicants' earnings histories.[68]

Yet important supply-side factors, including decisions made by women themselves, help explain occupational segregation. Just as competing demands on women's time affect the number of hours they supply to the labor market, competing cultural pressures affect the types of jobs they enter. On a global level, patterns of gender segregation in traditionally female occupations and industries cannot be entirely explained by direct employer discrimination.[69] The threat of sexual harassment by male coworkers often deters women from holding traditionally masculine jobs.[70] Women's own preferences to work in certain occupations and industries—despite their lower levels of average compensation—also exert influence.

Neoclassical economists sometimes argue that women derive sufficient subjective satisfaction from their job choices—a kind of psychic income—to fully compensate them for lower wages, and some scholars believe that women are simply drawn to feminine work.[71] One can acknowledge women's agency, however, without ignoring the institutional constraints on their choices. Gender norms put women in a contradictory position in which gains in the labor market can be neutralized by losses in the dating and marriage market. Men in high-paying occupations are prized as partners, while women in high-paying occupations—especially traditionally male occupations—are not.[72]

Many men feel threatened by women who compete with them on their own turf. A recent study of the behavior of women in the Harvard Masters of Business Administration program, for instance, found women more likely to express commitment to their own professional success when classmates who were potential marriage partners were not present.[73] In the US, lesbians fare better in the labor market than heterosexual women with similar characteristics, in part because they are more likely to enter nontraditional occupations.[74] Men who are openly gay, on the other hand, pay a wage penalty compared to similar heterosexual men.

The forces constraining women's occupational choices cannot be reduced to a desire for social approval. Moral commitments to children and other dependents also influence their decisions. In affluent countries such as the United States, women are disproportionately concentrated in industries such as health, education, and social services, often in jobs that involve face-to-face, hands-on, or first-name interactions with people whose welfare they genuinely care about.[75] By their own account, they enter such jobs partly out of a desire to help others.[76]

Whether women are naturally predisposed or socially conditioned to greater concern for others than men matters less than the economic penalties that result. In the long run, the greater care penalties become, the less care will be voluntarily supplied. Punish good deeds and they will eventually dwindle. The evolutionary theories of multilevel selection outlined in previous chapters explain why altruism requires institutional reinforcement—if not the coercion of women, then new forms of collective commitment to value and reward care for others.

### The Wages of Care

Such rewards cannot be based on simple market forces. Whether waged or unwaged, commitments to other people do not yield standardized commodities that are easily substitutable.[77] As noted in Chapter 4, it is difficult, if not impossible, to measure and capture the value of individual contributions to the maintenance and development of human capabilities, which helps explain why care work is underpaid even when performed for pay. Studies of the United States and the United Kingdom show that employment in care occupations and industries lowers the earnings of both women and men relative to other jobs, even controlling for a variety of personal and workplace variables.[78]

This care wage penalty reflects the specific characteristics of jobs, rather than the people who fill those jobs, a theme explored in earlier studies of comparable worth and pay equity. It has long been observed, for instance, that parking lot attendants in the United States have higher median wages than childcare workers.[79] Earlier arguments regarding the comparable worth of male- and female-dominated jobs focused on so-called compensable factors such as educational requirements, levels of responsibility or stress, and working conditions.[80] Attention to these factors has now been supplemented by attention to other aspects of the labor process (such as emotional attachment and collaboration with others, or team production) and also to characteristics of the product or service (such as its lack of standardization and its spillover effects).

Many care workers find great satisfaction in their jobs. This does not justify the low levels of pay they receive relative to the social value of the services they provide. Care wage penalties differ considerably across countries because they are strongly influenced by specific labor market institutions that also shape overall levels of earnings inequality.[81] Reliance on market forces leads to undervaluation.

In the United States and the United Kingdom, turnover rates in many poorly paid care jobs, especially childcare and eldercare, are relatively high, often with emotionally wrenching and quality-lowering effects.[82] Taken to an extreme, market logic holds that "an underpaid nurse is a good nurse" because low wages discourage workers who lack the intrinsic motivation necessary to do their jobs well.[83] The notion that nurses (but not employers or doctors) should be selected for their altruistic preferences reflects profound gender bias. It ignores the reality that care workers need wages sufficient to support themselves and their families. It also assumes that altruistic preferences (like other unpriced resources) will never be depleted.

Care penalties in wage employment are sharply crosscut by differences in bargaining power based on class, race, and citizenship. Relatively cheap domestic servants have always been available to the very wealthy; cheap service-sector employees replicate their effects, often in similarly racialized ways. In the United States, a large supply of low-wage immigrant women keeps the cost of childcare and eldercare services—as well as restaurant meals—relatively low. Native-born, college-educated, high-earning women reap many of the benefits.

Global care chains ensure an ample supply of nannies for children and in-home care providers for the elderly for families who can pay out-of-pocket and/or under the table in informal employment. These care workers often leave their own children or parents behind—usually in the care of other women—because of a pressing need to provide financial support for them. They typically remit a larger share of their earnings home than male migrants, despite their lower wages.[84] It is hard to imagine a group that experiences more intersectional disadvantage.

Empirical research shows that increases in number of low-wage immigrants in major US cities have boosted both the labor supply and the fertility of highly educated women.[85] Similar effects have been measured in Spain, Italy, and Hong Kong.[86] In the short run, low-wage women benefit from expanded employment opportunities, while high-wage women find it easier to combine paid work and family work. In the long run, however, large class inequalities have the effect of redistributing care penalties, reducing incentives for high-wage women to support public care initiatives.[87] What will happen if and when international migration is curtailed?

Some economists hold women lucky to inhabit caring occupations, because these are more difficult to automate or outsource than the manufacturing jobs held predominantly by men.[88] By this logic, the miraculous forces of supply and demand will reduce gender inequality by encouraging men to enter traditionally female fields. This cheerful narrative assumes that earnings are determined primarily by the quantity and quality of work performed, largely unaffected by collective bargaining power or the difficulty of capturing value created. It overlooks the distinctive characteristics of care work that make it vulnerable to undervaluation, whether it is provided by women or by men. It also overlooks the extraordinary risks and stresses that health care workers, in particular, endure when global pandemics strike.

## Public Policies and Care Penalties

Despite their potentially equalizing effects, many state policies are gendered: they assign women disproportionate responsibility for meeting care needs. Restrictions on reproductive rights, along with reluctance to enforce men's family responsibilities, exploit women's willingness to be care providers of last resort, as the "reserve army of feminine self-sacrifice."[89] Levels of public support for unpaid care work—like levels of poverty among families with dependents—vary enormously across countries, but even the most generous European social democracies reinforce a gender division of labor that is costly for women.

Different groups of women are obviously affected in different ways. The economic bargaining power of primary caregivers profoundly affects the well-being of those they care for: rates of child poverty are highest among families that are maintained by single parents. In the United States, family subsidies were long linked to marital status, imposing significant costs on those who violated heterosexual norms.[90] Employment discrimination on the basis of sexual orientation or gender identity remains a problem.

While declining birth rates have motivated increased public support for child-rearing in many countries, public subsidies compensate only a small percentage of the costs and risks of raising children and typically reinforce the traditional division of labor. Many affluent countries now provide at least some public support or services for individuals with disabilities and the frail elderly, but family caregivers, primarily women, continue to bear most of this burden. Likewise, many public pension systems provide benefits based primarily on earnings in paid employment, putting women at an economic disadvantage in old age.

## Reproductive Rights and Responsibilities

Lack of access to contraception and medically safe abortions, as well as effective protection against domestic violence, represents a serious health risk for women in many countries.[91] Restricted access to contraception and early abortion violates women's right to control their own bodies and exploits the fierce attachment that most mothers feel for newborn infants. Mothers need to plan parenthood precisely because it is likely to lead to irrevocable commitment.

Vulnerability is intersectional. In the United States, as in many other countries, unintended pregnancies are concentrated among less-educated, low-income women, disproportionately women of color. Economic stress is often the most cited reason for seeking an abortion, and abortions typically increase during periods of economic stress such as recessions.[92] A recent study in the United States found that carrying an unwanted pregnancy to term quadrupled the odds that a new mother and her child would live below the federal poverty line.[93]

Many regimes that deny women reproductive rights also fail to strictly define the child-support responsibilities of noncustodial fathers. Under many versions of Islamic law, fathers remain legally responsible for the support of children after separation or divorce, but few enforcement mechanisms exist. In much of sub-Saharan Africa, customary rather than formal laws govern custody and maintenance, sometimes bypassing maternal rights altogether. In eastern Nigeria, for instance, custody rights over children revert to the mother's father if her husband failed to pay the bride price.[94] Few developing countries collect even basic statistics on the percentage of families maintained by mothers alone. In Peru, one of the few exceptions to this rule, only about 35 percent of single mothers received child support payments in 2012.[95]

While most affluent countries have developed child support enforcement policies, lack of comparable statistics hampers cross-country comparisons. The most recent data from the Organisation for Economic Co-operation and Development (updated in 2010) lump private transfers from nonresident parents together with transfers from the state, showing that the percentage of sole parents receiving any child maintenance payments was "not available" in fourteen out of twenty-one countries in 2004 and was below 40 percent in the United States, the United Kingdom, and Australia. In Denmark and Sweden, by contrast, the percentage receiving assistance was more than 98 percent.[96]

Low levels of transfer from noncustodial fathers have been well documented in the United States and the United Kingdom, with attention to the difficulty of enforcing payment from men who lack adequate income to support themselves. The economic vulnerability of Black and Latino men is reflected in punitive policies implemented in the United States, resulting in high levels of incarceration. Efforts to bludgeon "deadbeat dads" into compliance have proved remarkably unsuccessful.[97] Yet mothers who are typically even more economically disadvantaged than the fathers of their children manage to provide financial as well as direct care. They are often willing to sacrifice regular financial support from fathers in return for continued paternal engagement with children or freedom from abusive treatment.[98]

Enforcement problems are not unique to the Anglo-American context. In Russia, legal provisions for child support are almost completely ineffectual, and social expectations for paternal contributions are extremely low.[99] In Japan, legal protections for single mothers are weak and public support minimal, despite rising divorce rates.[100] The growth of international migration also complicates the picture, with millions of parents now living in countries distant from those of their children. Legal rules for cross-border enforcement of family maintenance responsibilities remain underdeveloped.[101]

Many countries of northwestern Europe, including Scandinavia, provide public insurance for parental child support that guarantees a minimum level of family income, significantly reducing poverty among both mothers and children.[102] Scandinavian policies also challenge the traditional caregiver/breadwinner model by promoting joint custody and shared parenting. Their example suggests that a combination of effective public governance and efforts to strengthen norms of paternal engagement can improve parental collaboration.[103]

### Public Support for Child-rearing

Many other public policies subsidize child-rearing, among them publicly subsidized health care, childcare, and education. Two specific types of programs, more narrowly targeted to parents, have become standard in most affluent countries: paid family leaves from work and family allowances. Expenditures on these programs represent a substantial transfer of income from taxpayers to parents and children, and because mothers are more likely than fathers to take parenting responsibility, from taxpayers to mothers. These programs have somewhat contradictory implications for women: on the one hand, they provide compensation for family care; on the other hand, they encourage women's specialization in care provision, increasing their personal vulnerability.

A global trend toward greater support for child-rearing has been driven by a variety of factors, including women's political empowerment, growing recognition of the payoffs to social investment, and concerns about the intergenerational viability of social spending. Probably the most important factor, however, has been growing fear of national population decline resulting from below-replacement fertility. Scandinavian family support policies that embrace the goal of gender equality have stabilized birth rates at close to replacement levels, in sharp contrast with the extremely low rates now evident in Spain, Italy, Greece, Japan, and Korea.[104]

As a result, some demographers and policymakers now argue that achievement of greater gender equality is central to the goal of maintaining stable national population levels.[105] One need not agree with this goal to appreciate the force of this argument, which suggests that women—who are seldom willing to withhold care from those they are emotionally attached to—can exercise considerable bargaining power by preemptively minimizing such attachments. Paradoxically, when many women postpone, minimize, or avoid motherhood altogether, their actions give mothers greater leverage.

Public support for child-rearing is clearly shaped by intersectional collective bargaining. The European Union has strongly encouraged benefits to parents in the form of paid family leaves, rights to reduced working hours, and family allowances. The form these benefits take is even more important than their overall level. When they are universal, rather than means-tested, they tend to enjoy widespread public support. If paid leaves are taken predominantly by women, rather than men, or if paid maternal leaves are too long, they tend to reduce mothers' attachment to paid employment, reducing their lifetime earnings. Empirical research suggests that leaves in excess of six months probably have this negative effect, making high-quality publicly subsidized childcare a necessary supplement.[106]

Nordic countries have modeled ways of encouraging greater participation from fathers by offering relatively high wage replacement rates
for family leaves combined with "use-it-or-lose it" provisions. Take-up
rates by fathers have increased significantly over time, though their
overall leave time remains far lower than that of mothers.[107] Greater
paternal participation in childcare at an early stage often leads to greater
engagement with children as they grow older. Recent evidence from
Denmark suggests that paternal leaves help mothers return to work and
increase overall family earnings.[108]

Even in the Nordic countries, however, parental leave equality has
not been achieved. There, as elsewhere, many public policies continue to
encourage maternal specialization.[109] Mothers continue to put fewer
hours into paid employment and are disproportionately concentrated in
relatively low-paying public sector jobs.[110] A recent analysis of twenty-
one European countries and their influence on men's behavior found
that Iceland's parental leave policies are the most egalitarian, but "no
country has equal, nontransferable, and well-paid leave for each
parent."[111]

Family policies in other affluent capitalist countries reveal a similar
tendency to reinforce gender specialization.[112] In developing countries,
patterns are more complex. The traditionally "maternalist" Latin
American approach to public policy is now being contested.[113] In Asia,
the legacy of Confucian norms has made gender roles particularly resistant to change. China's political rulers, focused on gross domestic product
growth, have reduced care services, reducing women's ability to participate in paid employment.[114] In Japan and South Korea, by contrast, a
growing commitment to social investment has driven significant changes
in both employment and welfare policy, influenced by women's groups.[115]

Unlike paid leaves from work, family allowances (and related tax
subsidies for children) are not conditional on paid employment. They
give parents, including mothers, more individual choice, but also nudge
them toward decisions that are far riskier in terms of long-run economic
security for themselves and their children. Further, most family allowances cover only a relatively small share of the overall expenditures on
children, especially when the costs of parental time devoted to care are
taken into account.[116] Similar concerns apply to many proposals for a
universal basic income.

Whether allowance-based approaches can help prop up birth rates
remains to be seen. Particularly when they are inconsistent and variable,

they have a greater effect on the timing of births than on their number. Recent Russian policies provide a clear example of disregard for long-term effects. In the Soviet Union, family allowances were universal (along with extensive childcare and education services). Russia initially continued such policies but cut them back in 2001, restricting them to families with income at or below the subsistence level. Then, in 2006, President Putin decided that birth rates should be increased, and provision of family subsidies expanded, including large lump-sum payments termed "maternity capital," to mothers of two or more children.[117] Effects to date on birth rates have been modest, perhaps as a result of distrust regarding future levels of support.[118]

Among affluent capitalist countries, the United States remains a significant outlier. Only a few states and cities have implanted universal pre-kindergarten programs or paid family leave.[119] Many US families with dependents who pay lower taxes than their European counterparts probably have less disposable income once their out-of-pocket payments for childcare, health insurance, education, and eldercare are accounted for.

Because tax subsidies for children and childcare expenses in the United States are complex, uneven, and difficult to understand, they have a divided constituency.[120] Eligibility for means-tested cash benefits and childcare assistance is largely conditional on participation in paid employment. Many low-income parents who are currently unemployed could gain support through the Earned Income Tax Credit if they simply swapped children from 9 to 5 every weekday and paid one another exactly the same wages for care, thus qualifying as employed.[121] Paltry forms of public support in the United States have contributed to high rates of poverty among children, stunting the development of human capabilities and intensifying class and racial/ethnic inequalities.[122] Not surprisingly, birth rates in the United States have recently fallen below replacement levels.[123]

Policies that make it easier for mothers and fathers to take time out of paid employment reduce at least some of the tensions between family work and market work. In countries like Sweden with generous public support, most women have at least one child; in the United States, a much larger percentage of women remain childless.[124] Partly as a result, the gender gap in earnings is particularly high in Sweden at the upper end, in professional and managerial jobs.[125] However deplorable this failure, women's success should not be measured simply in terms of their relative labor market earnings: the economic opportunity to become a parent is also precious.

**Public Support and Transfers to the Elderly and Adults with Disabilities**

Many public policies providing pensions and health care to adults carry implicit care penalties. Those who take time out of paid employment to provide family care often reduce their pension eligibility and/or credits as a result, leaving them susceptible to poverty in old age. The United Kingdom, France, Germany, and Sweden, among other countries, offer earnings credits to family caregivers, but these are capped at a relatively low level.[126] US policies are even worse: as noted in the previous chapter, the provisions of the US Social Security system provide special support for married spouses who do not work for pay, with a spousal benefit set at a percentage of the employed spouse's earnings. Single parents, however, are doubly penalized by Social Security: their nonmarket work goes unrewarded and they often end up in intermittent, poorly paid employment that reduces their eligibility for Social Security benefits. As a result, they typically receive far less retirement income from the state than men who have devoted little time or effort to raising the future taxpayers who help finance Social Security payments to the older generation.

Like paid family leaves, public policies that support family provision of eldercare can reinforce traditional gender roles. On the other hand, when combined with public policies that offer adequate pay and benefits to paid providers, they give family members more flexibility, making it easier for them to contribute to family income.[127] Indeed, publicly supported but consumer-directed home care can make it economically feasible for family members to provide full-time paid care for a disabled or elderly relative.[128] Paid family leaves can also increase flexibility by protecting job security for those who require only temporary time off from employment.[129]

Here again, the United States is an outlier. While some individual states have adopted such woman- and family-friendly policies, federal health insurance for the elderly does not reimburse costs for the nursing home services or home care required by those suffering chronic but untreatable conditions such as dementia.[130] Because many men marry women younger than themselves who also have a longer life expectancy, they can often rely on spousal care. Elderly women often cannot. They are far more likely than elderly men to end up in nursing homes where they do not enjoy any means-tested public assistance until they qualify as indigent.

Public assistance for home and community-based care of needy adults through the means-tested Medicaid program imposes a kinship penalty: in many states, participants can use public funds to pay for the services of a daughter or a son, but not a spouse, the family member most likely to provide care. (Ex-spouses typically are eligible, creating a financial incentive to divorce.)[131] Surveys of home caregivers suggest that when family members are hired, they are often paid significantly less than caregivers hired through an agency and provide many more hours of care than they are paid for.[132]

Some mothers and fathers receive some payback from their adult children in the form of assistance in old age, sometimes reinforced by the promise of a bequest. Evidence from both affluent and poor countries shows that parents often use their accumulated wealth strategically to reward services from their adult children but also respond to financial need.[133] As noted in Chapter 8, this familial safety net has economic as well as social value: childless older adults in the United States are significantly more likely than parents to receive public assistance.[134] Levels of parental engagement also matter: unmarried and divorced fathers are less likely than others to receive assistance from their children.[135] Still, within families, intergenerational transfers from old to young far exceed those in the other direction.[136]

In many low-fertility countries with aging populations, international migrants play an even greater role in eldercare than childcare.[137] In the United States, administrative rules have long denied the predominantly Black, Latino, and immigrant workforce in home-based eldercare basic labor rights—such as payment of a minimum wage—under the Fair Labor Standards Act. Racial animus helps explain why many states in the US South allocate their Medicaid funds primarily to nursing homes rather than home and community-based care. Such institutions are far more expensive on a per capita basis, but conditions are so poor that many eligible persons choose not to apply, keeping total costs low. Policymakers express concern that expansion of home and community-based care would be too expensive because so many potential beneficiaries might "come out of the woodwork" to apply for assistance.[138]

By any indicator, in virtually every country for which data is available, elderly women are more susceptible to poverty than elderly men.[139] This outcome is no accident, and it cannot be portrayed as the result of entirely voluntary choices. It reflects collective power structures that lead to the exploitation of many caregivers—predominantly women— over their entire life cycle. Some women enjoy sufficient bargaining power to substantially buffer this effect, but most do not, and the overall quality of care provision is compromised in ways that intensify other dimensions of inequality. The disproportionate impact of the Covid-19 pandemic on people of color and the working poor in the United States provides poignant evidence of intersectional vulnerability.[140]

## Care Futures

Just as care represents a kind of reproductive tax, those who minimize their payments of it enjoy a kind of patriarchal dividend.[141] The book-keeping above reveals entries on both sides of the ledger that are signifi-cantly influenced but not entirely determined by gender. It also indicates the growing threat of care deficits in which the need for care far outstrips its supply. The word "need" is more appropriate here than the word "demand," which economists use, restrictively, to describe mere purchas-ing power. Reliable, high-quality care cannot simply be bought, because it requires empathy, connection, and commitment.

Obviously, the future is unclear. Whether for reasons of biology or culture, women may have stronger preferences for the care of others than men do. The cost of these preferences, however, is largely determined by structures of collective power that are vulnerable to contestation. Moreover, caring preferences are shifting, as indicated by the emerging significance of new family forms that depart from gendered stereotypes, and typically lead to less specialization than traditional heterosexual families.[142] The very concept of social assign-ment based on a gender binary is unravelling. Gendered or not, extreme specialization in care provision will continue to lead to economic vulnerability unless and until reproductive costs are distrib-uted in more equitable ways.

Much depends on how institutions governing the costs of caring commitments are perceived, interpreted, and contested. Their complex-ity defies simplistic proposals for reducing gender inequality, especially those that do not recognize interlocking inequalities based on age, sexual orientation, race/ethnicity, citizenship, and class. Neoliberal poli-cies have taken care work for granted, reassured by its longstanding historical provision through patriarchal channels. As these channels narrow and other inequalities widen, market forces are likely to intensify care deficits.

Any sustainable vision of social justice must specify both equitable rights to care and mutual obligations for its provision. As women devote more energy and effort to activities that offer them economic security and political voice, they are also pressing men to take more responsibility for traditionally female priorities. The global organization Promundo puts it this way: "working with men and boys to transform harmful gender norms and unequal power dynamics is a critical part of the solution to achieving gender equality."[143] The dual earner/dual carer model that feminist scholars outlined years ago is gaining traction.[144] Unfortunately, progress toward this model is discouraged by employers' incentives to minimize labor costs and taxes.[145]

Stronger alliances between women and men aimed to strengthen the care economy are crucial, but the abolition of gender itself as a category would not solve the larger problem. Discrimination against women would clearly diminish if it became "commonplace that fathers are as responsible for the care of children and home as mothers."[146] Care penalties, however, would remain in force. Any competitive market economy that fails to adequately support care work penalizes caregivers regardless of gender: a "daddy track" in employment is just as potentially harmful to career advancement and job security as a "mommy track"; men as well as women earn less in jobs that generate more social benefits than private revenues.

Nor can imported care solve the problem. The "cheap migrants" solution to care provision in affluent countries resembles the cheap-natural-gas-as-a-substitute-for-coal solution to global climate change: a short-run gambit that postpones a more serious reckoning. Reliance on a global care chain simply offloads care deficits onto others, with especially negative consequences for disempowered groups and low-income countries.[147] The servants of globalization deserve better rights, better working conditions, and better pay.[148]

The threat of long-run deterioration in care services could, like the threat of climate change, unify otherwise disparate constituencies. In the absence of stronger collective efforts to support care provision, including more international cooperation to protect public health and limit climate change, the global economy will suffer. The poet Tony Hoagland imagines a modern Karl Marx explaining, "I was listening to the cries of the past, / When I should have been listening to the cries of the future."[149] Patriarchal constraints can no longer restrict women to reproductive tasks, and most capitalist investors demand returns that they can easily capture and control. The competitive pressure to offload the costs of creating and maintaining human capabilities creates a dilemma that—like climate change and ecological disruption—can be solved only by fostering commitments to the welfare of other people.

# 10

# Division and Alliance

Once upon a time, Ariadne decided to explore the dark maze to which the dangerous Minotaur had been confined; to ensure that she could find her way back, she tied a red thread to its entrance and unspooled it behind her. When she finally found the beast, she spoke softly to it, promising to release it from captivity if it followed her in peace. Yet she also carried a sword, knowing that the beast, crazed by its years of captivity, might turn upon her. We don't yet know what happened to the two, only that the story widely told about them—involving a brash young hero, a brutal slaying, elopement, and betrayal—was fake news.

We inhabit a pyramidal maze of our own making, packed with institutional structures that significantly influence our probabilities of economic success. The theoretical claims and historical narratives outlined in this book expose social divisions that are both cause and effect of these articulated structures. We don't yet know how best to alter them but can follow a process that logicians call Ariadne's thread—a careful examination of all possible routes. To do this, we must keep a clear record of where we have been and what dead ends we have encountered. We should also consider the possible need to tear down walls.

Economists often invoke models of economic organization that either should not be tampered with or cannot possibly be changed. Some warn against interference with individual choice, ignoring the value of collective commitments. Some warn that capitalism is a hegemonic system based entirely on class conflict that, once eliminated, would allow collective commitments to easily thrive. Both paradigms are simplistic: no economic system has ever been organized entirely around voluntary exchange or the extraction of surplus by a single ruling class. The feminist critique of institutional structures that have disempowered women strengthens an intersectional political economy attentive to many forms of cooperation and conflict, choice and constraint. This conceptualization of the multiple incarnations of institutional power could help build stronger coalitions of the disempowered, including women.

## Game Changing

Games are not just for fun and sport. Some are deadly, some are exploitative, and some are even self-destructive. Most of the games that people play involve a combination of effort, luck, and teamwork and are governed by enforceable rules. In the absence of such governance, lack of trust can encourage individuals to act in ways that leave everyone worse off. Formal games such as the prisoner's dilemma, Chicken, and Stag Hunt metaphorically illustrate such coordination problems. Institutional structures of collective power help solve these problems, enforcing cooperation. In the process, however, they generate costly forms of conflict and exploitation. Game design is itself a game. We live subject to rules that previous winners designed to perpetuate their advantage, until we devise ways to change them. Simply leveling the playing field is not enough.

### Agency and Structure Revisited

The mutually constitutive dynamics between agency and structure parallel the dynamics between players and games of survival. Players hope to improve their position in a pyramidal maze and, in the process, to reconfigure the structure to their advantage. Players are often socially assigned to a variety of teams and sub-teams but exercise some choice regarding their commitments to these. One player's gains are not inevitably based on another's losses. The gains from cooperation may be unequally distributed but may also increase the total rewards the players can potentially enjoy.

This set of games cannot be reduced to survival of the fittest; it is not always winners-take-all, because the winners often depend on the losers to help create the available rewards. Players are preoccupied with how to rise, or at least survive, and group membership significantly influences their chances of success. They are molded by the rewards and punishments they experience, becoming, in a sense, products of the very game they play. Debates over its design may seem like a distraction, especially to those who are comfortably ahead. Yet the game is always changing, and the stakes are high: life or death, freedom or submission, prosperity or poverty.

The complexity of intersectional inequalities helps stabilize large hierarchical systems through both cooptation and countervailing forms of collective conflict. On the other hand, it creates a social environment that is somewhat unpredictable and difficult to control. Shifting alliances can have tipping effects, leading to abrupt political realignments. Excessive conflict can weaken the entire pyramid from within. Some games are zero-sum games, all gains coming at the expense of others' losses. In some games, everybody loses—mutually assured destruction.

External shocks and pressures can destabilize articulated structures, as can internal dynamics. The pyramidal maze represents a human project in a natural environment that emerged and evolved long before we made our appearance as a species. We have become increasingly adept at extracting energy and resources from this environment and dumping increasing quantities of waste into it, dirtying our diapers and soiling our own nest. Those at the top may remain above the stench, but those at the bottom already find it difficult to breathe. The pyramid itself may sink into the sludge.

### The Patriarchal Rules

Women have long been assigned the greatest responsibility for future generations; if men were prone to neglect such responsibility, it was because, for a while, they could. Many now-obsolete patriarchal institutions tied men and women together in ways that intensified their differences, confining them to binary roles and separate spheres. These institutions reduced women's bargaining power relative to men but also provided some economic incentives for male support of dependents and their caregivers—at least within groups that escaped extinction, expropriation, slavery, or other forms of direct coercion. Often, institutional power over subaltern groups seemed explicitly designed to undermine familial solidarities and kinship networks. At the same time, the exploitation of subaltern groups could and did provide women in powerful groups with compensation in the form of higher living standards.

Capitalist dynamics had mixed consequences for women, depending on configurations of collective power. In some areas of the world, including Western Europe and the United States, technical innovation and the expansion of wage employment both destabilized feudal inequalities and loosened the grip of patriarchal institutions. Capitalist expansion did, occasionally, create temporary engines of liberation. Yet it also generated new forms of exploitation that were particularly intense when and where preexisting inequalities based on race/ethnicity, citizenship, and class were extreme.

Demographic consequences could be transformative: increases in the cost of rearing children, driven partly by reductions in their contribution to family subsistence as youngsters and their increased economic independence as adults, encouraged fertility decline and reduced women's specialization in family care. Yet when women gained new opportunities for employment outside the family, these were constrained by the difficulty of combining remunerative with reproductive work. Increased reliance on market exchange increased the relative costs of activities that were not amenable to market logic. Where men have been unable to retain their traditional economic advantage, they have been tempted to opt out of family support.

Women could never entirely overcome the differences among themselves, but they could occasionally reconcile them, demanding changes in the gender game that reached well beyond inequalities in earnings to encompass the distribution of the cost of caring for dependents and the emergence of welfare states. Their collective success varied according to coalitional possibilities and the strategic insights necessary to seize them. The consequences have been momentous.

**Liberal and Neoliberal Feminisms**

In nineteenth- and early twentieth-century Great Britain and the United States, relatively rapid capitalist development and rising living standards within the white population encouraged a particularly liberal form of feminism with an emphasis on individual rights. The principles that men invoked in challenging the authority of fathers could be turned against the authority of men in general and husbands in particular. Many women's interests were aligned with those of an ascendant class well served by expanded freedom to pursue individual self-interest. In this respect liberal feminism could be seen as a moral failing, an opportunistic adaptation to the capitalist status quo.[1]

On the other hand, the rights-based strategy proved remarkably successful, not only because it reduced the resistance of influential men, but also because it expanded the scope of democratic governance. Like political democracy writ large, it initially took incomplete, inconsistent, even hypocritical forms, but nonetheless created an opening wedge that could later be driven home. Over time, the discourse of political rights has expanded in subversive ways to include economic rights.[2] Among these rights, many feminists argue, are the "right to care and be cared for."[3]

This transcendence of the liberal feminist agenda contrasts vividly with neoliberal feminism, which takes all structures of collective power as a given and urges women to try harder to climb to the top. Facebook executive Sheryl Sandberg's 2013 book, *Lean In*, exemplifies this strategy. As one critic put it, the book provided a self-help guide to our "turbo-capitalist, what's-in-it-for-me world."[4] A blog post advising women to "become the men they want to marry" explains, "Acting selfishly will get you much further in life than if you're constantly worried about everyone around you."[5] This recycled version of Ayn Rand's libertarian philosophy succeeds only if life is reduced to the competitive upscale labor market.

In this narrow universe, women's success is measured by their access to traditionally male prerogatives: participation in formal employment, access to professional or managerial jobs, and political leadership. Money can buy everything, and family care becomes just another management challenge that can be accomplished through no-nonsense delegation, exhaustive checklists, and nerves of steel. Most women live in a very different place, where family responsibilities pose a substantial risk of poverty for themselves and their children, making even a modicum of assistance from men more than welcome.

Neoliberal feminism is even more divisive than its liberal antecedents, tying its agenda to the coattails of an increasingly small, if prodigiously rich, economic minority. As an intersectional strategy, it is unlikely to succeed, because capitalist development is no longer delivering on its promise of opportunities for widespread upward mobility and appears increasingly vulnerable to external shocks—the "externalities" that economists have long acknowledged but also relegated to the margins. Dangerous new pathogens, the threat of global climate change, and intensified social conflict are only the most visible of a spate of looming problems that can only be solved by cooperation rather than competition. Not surprisingly, another strand of feminist theory is now returning to the fore.

### Socialist Feminisms

In 1825 the Irish socialist feminists William Thompson and Anna Wheeler argued that any economic system based on individual competition would disadvantage those who took responsibility for the care of others.[6] Their argument, scarcely acknowledged at the time, prefigured the research on care penalties described in previous chapters and helps explain the emergence of welfare state policies designed to socialize at least some of the costs of developing and maintaining human capabilities. Such policies, vulnerable to shifting political coalitions, remain subject to reversal. They cannot be sustained, much less expanded, in the absence of social institutions that (to apply the terminology developed in Chapter 4) discourage both free riding and top riding.

Socialist feminists have generally had a stronger vision of their goals than of the means to achieve them. An emphasis on the need to recognize, reward, and distribute family work highlights the particular risks of for-profit provision in the care sector of the economy: health, education, and social services. The policy agenda often labeled social democracy could also be termed "care socialism."[7] Achievement of the right to care and be cared for requires, at the very least, negotiation of a new reproductive bargain that could reduce socially constructed inequalities. Some feminist economists call it Plan F.[8]

At least some pieces of such a larger plan are already apparent. Nordic countries offer a number of specific, publicly funded policies that reduce care penalties, but many other countries have recently moved in this direction. UN Women's recent report "Families in a Changing World" estimates that a package of family-friendly social transfers and services aimed at supporting diverse families and protecting women's rights is affordable, costing less than 5 percent of GDP for most countries.[9] Its contribution to genuine economic progress would far exceed the costs.

The International Labour Office urges efforts to simultaneously address emerging crises in both unpaid and paid care. "High-road" strategies in paid care employment offer the potential for coalitions between workers and consumers to boost compensation and reduce turnover.[10] Recent examples include the successful unionization of paid home care workers in California, widespread public support for increases in teacher pay in the United States in response to walkouts in 2018, and a historic pay equity adjustment for New Zealand residential and home care workers in 2017.[11]

Public services will not displace the need for personal engagement with family, friends, and community. Paid care leaves and reduced penalties for part-time employment can strengthen the moral and emotional commitments crucial to a healthy care economy. Challenges to compulsory heterosexuality can create safe space for sexual self-expression and also encourage the emergence of new family forms. Many married couples today embrace egalitarian principles, including shared responsibility for family care.[12] In the United States, a majority of young women and men say they would prefer to share work and family responsibilities equally.[13] Gay and lesbian couples have fought long and hard for the right to define marriage on their own terms.[14]

Bargaining over reproduction inevitably entails bargaining over production. Progressive taxes on income and wealth, long criticized as a deterrent to labor supply (defined as labor supply to the market), encourage people to reallocate their time and devote more energy and effort to the unpaid care of family, friends, and neighbors. Standards of living must be redefined in broader terms than per capita gross domestic product (GDP). The global economy doesn't need to stop growing; it needs to grow in better directions. The phase out of forms of production with environmentally harmful effects could make room for the expansion of care services and enhancement of human capabilities.

Changes in the current distribution of gains from cooperation are not likely to be achieved merely through moral exhortation and appeals to long-run efficiency. The current concentration of wealth impedes democratic negotiation largely through the threat of withdrawal: "Tax our wealth and we will take it elsewhere." Complex overlays of group advantage make many people reluctant to risk changes to the status quo. Hence the need to develop a clear picture of interlocking structures of collective power.

## Capitalism?

The conventional concept of capitalism as a unitary system overstates both the significance and the success of capitalist institutions, which have not existed and probably cannot exist in the absence of other hier-archical structures. Karl Polanyi made a similar point years ago when he noted that markets tend to disrupt the embedded social relations they must rely on.[15] Polanyi's view of these social relations, however, was romantically gender blind, overlooking structures of patriarchal power that preceded the development of capitalist institutions and shaped their evolution.

While Marxian theory offers keen insights into this historical drama, its vision of a hegemonic mode of production as the source of all exploi-tation is both incomplete and obsolete. Neither private property, nor capitalism, nor patriarchy is the root of all evil, because evil is not a tree that grows naturally from the ground, but a more complex construction whose blueprint we are just beginning to understand. The "economy" cannot be equated with the extraction of surplus value, any more than it can be equated with a marketplace denominated in dollar values.

However important financial wealth may be, its value is dwarfed by other forms of capital: embodied human capabilities, the natural assets of a planetary ecosystem, the social wealth of inherited knowledge and technology, and our ability to work together. The future success of human cooperation depends on the successful management of this larger set of assets, a task for which capitalist institutions are ill-suited. The concentrated private ownership of financial assets now impedes the development of institutions required for democratic governance, the protection of public health, and environmental sustainability.

**Extending Exploitation**

Employers can often pay workers less than the value of what they produce simply because their control of financial capital—regardless of how it is acquired—puts them in a stronger fallback position. Many other socially constituted groups enjoy similar forms of collective power, played out in appropriation, production, reproduction, and the social reproduction of groups themselves. The threat of physical violence morphs into economic power and commitments to the care of depend-ents morph into economic vulnerability. The production of a good or service whose benefits can be quickly and easily captured is more lucra-tive than the production of a good or service necessary for future generations.

This broad approach to social division dethrones wage earners from the unique category of "the exploited" yet also helps explains how their exploitation has been reproduced and intensified over time. In the modern global economy, the intergenerational transmission of financial, human, and social capital within socially assigned groups strongly affects opportunities for economic success. In the past, progressive taxes, including inheritance taxes, have had leveling effects; over the last several decades, the increased political bargaining power of the wealthy has largely reversed them.[16]

When Thomas Piketty, famous for his research on the global concentration of financial wealth, visited my university several years ago, a graduate student asked him why he was putting so much emphasis on taxation rather than on class struggle. He quietly replied that taxation is a form of class struggle. So it is. But taxation is also a form of struggle over the distribution of the cost of public investments that could potentially improve the relative well-being of women, people of color, poor people, inhabitants of poor countries, and future generations. The dimensions of this struggle are largely obscured by economic theories that gloss over the dramas of intersectional collective conflict.

The intergenerational transmission of nonfinancial resources and access to modern technology privileges a far broader swath of the global population than the financial wealth now so concentrated among the top 1 percent.[17] Differences in parental spending and education, and more broadly, differences in neighborhoods and social networks, have significant effects in countries like the United States, characterized by high levels of residential segregation based on race/ethnicity and class.[18] The impact of large lump-sum transfers such as gifts or bequests to adult children appears to have increased in recent years, even in relatively egalitarian countries such as Norway.[19] Inherited inequalities are far greater on the global level, making access to residence in affluent countries an extremely valuable resource.[20] Opportunities for migration from desperately poor to comfortably prosperous countries will prove increasingly consequential, especially as many areas of the global South suffer the impact of climate-related economic stress.[21]

An intuitive understanding of apocalyptic possibilities surely helps explain the resurgence of nationalist political movements that are inconsistent with the capitalist neoliberal agenda, yet prone to co-optation by it. In an age of capital mobility and digital outsourcing, protectionist policies affect only a subset of firms, leaving large corporations inconvenienced, but unharmed. As a result, such policies prolong coalitions that leave a small global elite of wealthy men with far more political influence than they could purchase on their own. Like feudal lords promising their minions protection from invading hordes, they can use this narrative to justify their intensified exploitation of all the disempowered.

The specific solution to this political dilemma remains unclear, partly because it reflects the type of interaction between class and nonclass dynamics that traditional paradigms of left political economy have downplayed. Debates over the impact of immigration in affluent countries focus largely on whether it has, in the past, hurt or helped workers, without much consideration of how an extrapolation of current trends could change the economic calculus. They remain focused on short-term policies rather the long-term dilemma: how to reinterpret and reconfigure public policies to distribute the significant benefits of immigration in equitable but politically sustainable ways.

**Crises of Reproduction**

The disjuncture between short-term and long-term benefits also characterizes demographic trends. In heavily patriarchal systems, families and communities often benefited from high fertility rates, even when these led to accumulated population pressures. A combination of institutional and technological changes mitigated the adverse consequences but created the opposite problem. The transition to below-replacement birth rates in many areas of the world will likely have dislocating economic and political effects even though, in the longer run, it will benefit the global ecosystem. In the very longest run, fertility must regain replacement levels in order to prevent extinction.

The future quantity of children matters less for the economic future than the quality of the capabilities they develop, along with the opportunities they have to put those capabilities to productive use. Human and social capital represent the real future wealth of nations, yet the institutional incentives to invest in them are weak.[22] High rates of child poverty on the global level as well as low levels of education in many countries testify to an enormous waste of unpriced human resources that is not factored into the level or growth of GDP.[23]

Children are not the only victims of underinvestment in human capabilities. Unemployment, underemployment, poverty, and income inequality all have toxic consequences for the social environment. Rates of suicide, drug addiction, and mortality in both rich and poor countries have all been linked to levels of absolute and relative economic stress.[24] Investments in better social insurance and economic opportunities could improve physical and mental health. Such investments offer a high rate of social return, but not one that individual investors can easily capture in the form of profits.

While concentration of wealth is heightened by capitalist dynamics, it leads to virtually feudal consequences. Members of the global elite can insulate themselves from the degradation of the natural and social environment, retreating to mountaintop resorts to minimize the inconvenience of global warming and relying on gated communities, country clubs, and private schools to minimize exposure to uncomfortable dysfunctions. Inequalities of wealth and income lead powerful groups to undervalue public goods and discourage the policies needed to protect them.[25] How paradoxical that the term "capitalism" is applied to a system so destructive of natural, human, and social capital writ large.

### Intersectional Hierarchies

Collective conflicts over the distribution of the costs of social reproduction help explain the persistence of alliances based on race/ethnicity and citizenship as well as gender. Interactions among these and other dimensions of socially assigned group membership cannot simply be described as varieties of capitalism. Multiple layers of collective conflict make the "dark side of the force" loom large, yet also contradict any view of global capitalism as an unstoppable juggernaut, against which any resistance must seem futile.[26] Capital may be manly, but it is not self-sufficient.

A care economy that can never be fully commodified remains central to its social reproduction. Even in the United States, a country widely considered the epitome of modern capitalism, more than half of all the work performed on a daily basis is unpaid, involving the provision of goods and services for oneself or others. While employers reap many of the benefits, so too do many others, including women. Families, friends, and neighbors will continue to negotiate mutual aid and informal safety nets. The very persistence of unpaid work reveals the contributions and capacities of people getting important jobs done without the so-called discipline of the market or the supervision of highly paid managers.

The historical narratives outlined in preceding chapters suggest that tensions between the pursuit of individual self-interest and the fulfillment of responsibilities of care for others were once partially reconciled by a culturally prescribed and legally enforced division of labor between men and women. Men would enter the competitive marketplace to seek their fortunes; women would dedicate themselves to homes and families no matter what the costs. As this division of labor continues to weaken, the valuation of care for others hangs in the balance, with implications that reach far beyond family life.

The Covid-19 pandemic in the United States, in particular, brought care issues to the fore. Long-standing and recurrent sequestration (whether mandated or voluntary) resulted in many families staying at home for months, caring for young children or trying to home-school students affected by changes in school schedules. They were unable to visit with—or supervise the care of—family members living away from home, whether in nursing homes or distant cities. Most grandparents were unable to see, much less care for, their grandchildren. A little less than 30 percent of all workers, mostly with college degrees, were initially able to work for pay from home—if they could manage this on top of the increased responsibilities for provisioning themselves and others.[27]

No systematic time-use data are yet available, but previous patterns and the force of habit suggest that many women took on a disproportionate share of new tasks. Sequestration forced many men to stay home, increasing their perception of—and dependence on—family care, possibly enhancing their appreciation of it. The high percentage of women among "essential workers" in public and private enterprises that were allowed to continue operating could also have altered the division of labor.[28] On the other hand, it also increased family tensions and left potential victims of domestic violence with no escape.

It quickly became apparent that health care workers—more than 75 percent female—would become particularly vulnerable to infection with Covid-19.[29] Often forced to work without adequate protective equipment, both medical personnel and care workers tending to the elderly and disabled put their health on the line. Relatively young women accounted for most early Covid-19 cases among health care workers, and while mortality rates for the disease proved significantly lower for women than for men, the illness was frightening and debilitating.[30] Many essential workers in relatively low-paid occupations not usually associated with care, including grocery store clerks, bus drivers, and delivery people, also suffered from poor protections against infection and lack of hazard pay.

Pandemic-related mortality was driven not just by level of exposure to contagion, but also by preexisting medical conditions such as hypertension, diabetes, and heart disease, especially widespread among low-income families of color in the United States who lack adequate access to health care. In New York City, the epicenter of the epidemic, mortality rates for Black and Latino people were twice as high as those for whites.[31] Widespread dependence on employer-provided health insurance meant that the millions of people who lost their jobs in the pandemic-caused recession also lost their health care coverage.

Reliance on the private sector and state-level governments for provision of basic protective equipment and testing kits prolonged the costly and traumatic period of sequestration. Many people asked, "Why was no vaccine under development for pathogens of this type?" In general, the United States, like many other countries, has underinvested in public health. Vaccine development is not a profitable investment for large pharmaceutical companies, at least not until a global crisis offers fame and fortune to the winner of a late-starting race to the rescue.[32]

The logic of cooperative conflict (outlined in Chapter 5) suggests that groups will often tolerate an unequal share of the gains from cooperation as long as this leaves them better off than what they perceive to be their next best alternative. The health crisis caused by Covid-19, along with its attendant economic shocks, exposes the major fault lines of global inequality. Like the structure of patriarchal power at an earlier point in human history, the current structure of capitalist power may appear natural and inevitable, but it is not invulnerable. If the distribution of its benefits continues to narrow and its health and environmental costs to accumulate, it will begin to bend and shake. It could and should be democratized.

## Coalitional Strategies

Explicitly intersectional approaches to understanding patriarchal systems emerged from the subjective experience of women's simultaneous membership in groups with conflicting interests and often dwelt on the experience of being defined as "other." From the outset intersectionality had strategic consequences that were discouraging to groups struggling to unify and consolidate their own campaigns for institutional change. Acknowledgement of difference itself can seem divisive. Widespread derogation of "identity politics" on the left grew out of the assumption that inequalities based on gender, race/ethnicity, citizenship, and sexual orientation were more subjective and less substantial than inequalities based on class. Yet all forms of collective inequality are constructed from cultural as well as economic institutions: identities and interests hang together.

Class, however defined, has long served as an example for other dimensions of inequality. After a long conversation with fellow musician Pete Seeger in 1989, Billy Bragg welcomed small but telling changes to the traditional version of the socialist anthem, the Internationale, adding, "So come, brothers and sisters," "let racist ignorance be ended," and "Stand up, all victims of oppression."[33] Recognition of divisions has always been the first stage in the development of political alliances, including the left-wing strategy of a popular front. The next stage requires concerted efforts to overcome those divisions.

### Anxieties and Solidarities

Strategic intersectional analysis does not lead to easy political prescriptions, but it does help explain political realities. The policy packages developed by conservative political parties often reflect alliances based on gender, race, and citizenship as well as class. They typically promise rich rewards or, at the very least, protection of the status quo, in return for acquiescence to the dictatorship of the wealthy. In the past, the wealthy have often been able to deliver on this promise. It is unlikely, for the reasons outlined above, that they will be able to continue doing so.

The recent success of conservative parties reflects many contingent factors, including backlash against the growing political and cultural influence of women, racial/ethnic minorities, and immigrants. In the United States, in particular, conservatives gained electoral ascendance partly because the mainstream of the Democratic Party proved reluctant to acknowledge, much less remedy, the declining living standards of non-college-educated workers and their families. In this respect, criticism of identity politics has a ring of truth: moral outrage was more easily directed at overt forms of discrimination and abuse than at the vulnerabilities created by globalization and automation.

In 2016, Donald Trump convinced a significant portion of the US electorate that single women, immigrants, workers of color, and citizens of other countries posed a greater economic threat to them than plutocratic aggrandizement. He also capitalized on widespread resentment of highly educated managers and professionals clustered in metropolitan areas, whose air of personal achievement grates heavily on those they have left behind. His was not the only victory of this sort: conservative coalitions in many countries have deployed similar rhetoric. Still, Trump's language was particularly telling in its generalization of capitalist logic. As he put it in one campaign speech that brought cheers from the crowd: "I've been greedy. I'm a businessman . . . Take, take, take. Now I'm going to be greedy for the United States."[34]

Sexism, racism, and xenophobia are not mere attitudes; they are typically built into policy packages with significant distributive consequences.[35] Because these consequences simply reinforce existing inequalities, they often seem more credible than promises of future class-based redistribution. Conservatives often argue that egalitarian principles, extended to the global economy, would harm Americans. As conservative economist Gregory Mankiw puts it, "Imagine a candidate for president who campaigned on a platform of imposing a one-third tax on the average American's income and transferring the entire proceeds of the tax to poor nations around the world. Would you be inclined to support this candidate?"[36] He cleverly describes an arbitrary level of mandatory charity, rather than a change in the larger structure of economic opportunities and rewards that could leave everyone better off.

Still, his remark illustrates the distributional anxieties that are likely to sap most coalitions of the left until they are able to devise a plausible plan for achieving structural change based on redistribution of wealth and power from the very rich rather than from the average taxpayer, average man, or average white person. In the short run, the national interests of affluent countries seem to clash with ideals of international solidarity, but in the long run, they converge. Sustainable economic development requires global cooperation, and vice versa.

Once-denigrated theories of evolutionary dynamics based on multilevel selection authenticate this paradox. Nature may be red in tooth and claw, but over time cooperative species have outmatched others. Some desire to overcome divisions is embedded in our history, whether in religious language (we are all God's children), a pledge of allegiance ("one nation, indivisible, with liberty and justice for all"), or allegories of science fiction such as the film *Independence Day*, in which the furious desire to defend Earth from alien invaders brings nations together, overcomes racial animus, empowers women, and delivers victory.

Internal threats are more difficult to discern than attacks from outer space, making it more difficult to mobilize against them. Yet the notion that people should pursue their own self-interest has never helped caregivers in general, or women in particular, and it offers no hope of successfully confronting the cumulative hazards of pandemics, ecological devastation, economic exploitation, and social dysfunction. Economic institutions based entirely on the pursuit of private profit offer little incentive to invest in public goods. Women generally dedicate more effort to such investments than men do, so they have a particularly large stake in advancing them.

**Lessons**

Sometimes structures of collective power interlock in ways that can block incremental change, but sometimes they tip each other over like a line of dominos. Modular systems are more transformable, at least, than blocks of solid granite. Sociologist Erik Olin Wright offers many examples of what he calls nonreformist reforms, steps toward real utopias.[37] Proposals to move beyond the traditional gender division of labor and provide more public support for family care fit squarely into this agenda.[38] As economist Julie Matthaei explains, women also have much to gain from developing the cooperative enterprises of the "solidarity economy."[39]

Democracy cannot be expanded without successful efforts to defend and improve existing democratic institutions and mobilize effectively within them. Nothing is more important than the development of resilient progressive coalitions, and feminists must lean in to this task. The theoretical compass developed in this book points toward "feminism for the 99%."[40] A powerful example is offered by the United Nations Sustainable Development Goals, which emphasize long-run investments in human capabilities, setting bold targets for universal health and education and a social safety net for the global economy.[41]

Socialist institutions are often derogated as a slippery slope to authoritarian rule. Historically, however, regimes labeled capitalist have proved just as susceptible to the overthrow of democracy as those labeled socialist. It is hard to imagine a greater threat to democracy than the current concentration of global wealth capable of evading national regulation. There is no greater threat to sustainable economic development than institutional arrangements that reward private profit at the expense of natural, social, and human assets.

Intersectional political economy utilizes some concepts that emerged from the neoclassical tradition, such as coordination problems, game theory, externalities, and bargaining. At the same time, it affirms Marxian emphasis on the complex, often self-destructive dynamics of hierarchical systems, explaining the need for new political alliances. We need a democratic counterweight to what Thomas Hobbes dubbed "the war of all against all" and Langston Hughes described as "the same old stupid plan / Of dog eat dog, of mighty crush the weak."[42]

### Divided but Not Conquered

An early despot first uttered the phrase "divide et impera" (divide and conquer), and it has long been the watchword of territorial conquest. It sometimes represents an explicit strategy but may also take a more subtle form. A third party can simply stand back and allow preexisting divisions and disagreements among its opponents to fester. The Latin term for such exploitation of divisions is "Tertius gaudens" ("the third party rejoices"). In hierarchical systems, this rejoicing group is likely to hold a powerful position because its members are relatively homogeneous, easily allied, and adept at enforcing allegiance through the strategic distribution of rewards.

Yet social division does not always block collective commitment. Feminist movements, always prone to division, have also been dividers, sometimes embracing racist or imperialist rhetoric or succumbing to corporate cooptation. Nonetheless, demands for gender equality have often proved subversive of the larger status quo. In their political protests, many feminists have promoted individual rights, democratic governance, and commitments to the future. In their economic protests, they have asserted that workers do not always get what they deserve, challenging the metric of the market.

While the centuries-long campaign against patriarchal institutions is far from over, its successes testify to potential for international cross-class, cross-race, and cross-gender coalitions that learned how to improvise and adapt to unexpected circumstances.[43] These coalitions often wavered, but sometimes persisted. Occasional waves of political success crashed into longer lasting troughs of regress and retrenchment. Periods of relative unity were riven by factional splits. Feminism was initially derided as immoral, then as unnatural; later, it was labeled impractical and utopian. Today its critics complain that it has been too successful.

Diversity can be a source of strength as well as weakness. James Madison, one of the authors of the US Constitution, argued that only a well-orchestrated balance of powers could avert tyranny.[44] However difficult it may be to build alliances of the disempowered, a better under-standing of social division can strengthen the process. The feminist embrace of intersectional analysis offers encouragement, and recent trends set the stage for new political alignments. The financial wealth of the world is now concentrated in a very few hands, increasing the poten-tial gains from greater democratic claims upon it. Similarly positioned groups facing the same hegemon are more likely to form a coalition than those fighting a variety of unrelated battles.

Sometimes, necessity is the mother of coalition. Sometimes, the metaphorical payoff matrix reveals a single best payoff for all players: cooperate or die. But such situations are rare. For the most part, coali-tions grow out of explicit efforts to create a shared commitment that overlays but does not displace other forms of collective identity. People's propensity to engage in collective struggle is affected both by the history of their grievances and their prospects for success.[45] Broad solidarities do not simply fall from the sky or grow from the ground—they are created, nurtured, and developed through personal efforts, small-scale experiments, collective organizing efforts, and coherent public policies.

## Partial Victories

What conservatives share is the "felt experience of having power, seeing it threatened, and trying to win it back."[46] Patriarchal institutions may not continue their decline. A backlash against neoliberal globalization, fueled by nationalism and white supremacy, could reinforce and rein-state them. New kinds of hybrid systems could emerge, including neofeudal domination by corporate moguls with loyalties to no one but themselves. Giant insects from outer space could conquer us or we could destroy the planet on our own. Or we might sow the seeds of more cooperative social institutions hardy enough to survive predatory attacks. At least we know more than we once did about our capabilities for change. Let us learn something from both our failures and our successes.

Many people, not just a small minority, benefit from exploitative social institutions. Powerful competitive pressures have generated outcomes that might have been similar even if winners and losers had traded places. We can dismiss the complacent claim that we live in the best of all possible worlds but reject the accusation that only a small group of villains deserve the blame. We can seek to modify structures of collective power and unfair advantage without denouncing all those who have unwittingly benefited from them.

Our successes stand. Many women and men have benefited from the process of economic development, the expansion of democracy, the efflorescence of human knowledge, and the weakening of patriarchal institutions. The rise, decline, and indefinite future of patriarchal systems show that political rights must be accompanied not only by economic rights but also by obligations to care for one another and for generations to come. As the poet Carolyn Forché observes, "the history of our time does not allow for any of the bromides of progress, nor for the promise of successful closure."[47] Still, it invites the recognition of partial victories and the determined grasp of new possibilities.

# Notes

## Chapter 1. Intersectional Political Economy

1 Heidi Hartmann, "The Unhappy Marriage of Marxism and Feminism: Toward a More Progressive Union," *Capital and Class* 3: 2, 1979, 1–33.

2 Nancy Folbre, "Gender Bargaining in the Labor Market," Working Paper. Washington, DC: Economic Policy Institute, forthcoming.

3 Anne Marie Goetz, "The Politics of Preserving Gender Inequality: De-institutionalisation and Re-privatisation," *Oxford Development Studies* 48: 1, 2019, 2–17.

4 Sarah Ashwin and Jennifer Utrata, "Revenge of the Lost Men: From Putin's Russia to Trump's America," *Contexts*, 2019, in press.

5 Oxfam Briefing Paper, "An Economy for the 99%," January 2017, oxfam.org; Gerry Mullany, "World's 8 Richest Have as Much Wealth as Bottom Half, Oxfam Says," *New York Times*, January 16, 2017, nytimes.com.

6 Liam Stackmarch, "'Fearless Girl' Statue to Stay in Financial District (for Now)," *New York Times*, March 27, 2017, nytimes.com.

7 See the Online Etymological Dictionary at etymonline.com.

8 Roxane Gay, *Bad Feminist*, New York: Harper Perennial, 2014, 17.

9 Audre Lorde, "The Master's Tools Will Never Dismantle the Master's House," in *Sister Outsider: Essays and Speeches*, 110–14, Berkeley, CA: Crossing Press, 1984, collectiveliberation.org.

10 Kate Pickett and Richard G. Wilkinson, *The Spirit Level: Why Greater Equality Makes Societies Stronger,* London: Bloomsbury, 2009.

11 Nancy Folbre, "Children as Public Goods," *American Economic Review* 84: 2, 1994, 86–90.

12 Ellen Gabler, Zach Montague, and Grace Ashford, "During a Pandemic, an Unanticipated Problem: Out-of-Work Health Workers," *New York Times*, April 3, 2020, nytimes.com.

## Chapter 2. Defining the Patriarchal

1 Bina Agarwal, "'Bargaining' and Gender Relations: Within and Beyond the Household," *Feminist Economics* 3: 1, 1997, 1.
2 Deniz Kandiyoti, "Bargaining with Patriarchy," *Gender and Society* 2: 3, 1988, 274.
3 Nancy Folbre, *Greed, Lust and Gender: A History of Economic Ideas*, New York: Oxford University Press, 2009.
4 For instance, Gerda Lerner (whose research on the origins of patriarchal systems is described in Chapter 6) defines "patriarchy" as the "manifestation and institutionalization of male dominance over women and children in the family and the extension of male dominance over women in society in general." Gerda Lerner, *The Creation of Patriarchy*, New York: Oxford University Press, 1986, 239.
5 Douglass North, "Institutions," *Journal of Economic Perspectives* 5: 1, 1991, 92.
6 Nancy Folbre, *Who Pays for the Kids? Gender and the Structures of Constraint*, New York: Routledge, 1994.
7 Larry Neal and Jeffrey G. Williamson, eds., *The Cambridge History of Capitalism*, New York: Cambridge University Press, 2014.
8 Sylvia Walby, *Theorizing Patriarchy*, New York: Blackwell, 1990, 20; Göran Therborn, *Between Sex and Power*, New York: Routledge, 2007.
9 Nancy Folbre, "The Political Economy of Human Capital," *Review of Radical Political Economics* 44: 3, 2012, 281–92.
10 Therborn, *Between Sex and Power*.
11 Mala Htun and S. Laurel Weldon, "The Civic Origins of Progressive Policy Change: Combating Violence Against Women in Global Perspective, 1975–2005," *American Political Science Review* 106: 3, 2012, 548–69.
12 Timothy Besley and Maitreesh Ghatak, "Property Rights and Economic Development," in *The Handbook of Development Economics*, Vol. 5, Dani Rodrik and Mark Rosenzweig, eds., Amsterdam: Elsevier, 2009, 4525–96.
13 Steven N.S. Cheung, "The Enforcement of Property Rights in Children and the Marriage Contract," *Economic Journal* 82: 326, 1972, 641–57.
14 David Brion Davis, *The Problem of Slavery in Western Culture*, Ithaca, NY: Cornell University Press, 1966, 35.
15 Orlando Patterson, *Slavery and Social Death*, Cambridge, MA: Harvard University Press, 1982.
16 August Bebel, *Woman Under Socialism*, translated from the original German of the 33rd edition by Daniel De Leon, New York: Schocken Books, 1971, 216.

17  See, for instance, Thomas A. McGinn, *The Economy of Prostitution in the Roman World*, Ann Arbor: University of Michigan Press, 2004.

18  Therborn, *Between Sex and Power*, 25.

19  A. Sachs and J. H. Wilson, *Sexism and the Law*, Oxford: Martin Robinson, 1978, 149.

20  Siwan Anderson, "The Economics of Dowry and Brideprice," *Journal of Economic Perspectives* 21: 4, 2007, 151–74.

21  Sheetal Sekhri and Adam Storeygard, "Dowry Deaths: Response to Weather Variability in India," *Journal of Development Economics* 111, 2014, 212–23.

22  Francesca Bettio and Tushar K. Nandi, "Evidence on Women Trafficked for Sexual Exploitation: A Rights Based Analysis," *European Journal of Law and Economics* 29: 1, 2010, 15–42.

23  World Health Organization, "Global and Regional Estimates of Domestic Violence Against Women: Prevalence and Health Effects of Intimate Partner Violence and Non-partner Sexual Violence," Geneva: Author, Department of Reproductive Health and Research, 2013, who.int.

24  Elaine McCrate, "Trade, Merger and Employment: Economic Theory on Marriage," *Review of Radical Political Economics* 19: 1, 1987, 73–89.

25  Elissa Braunstein, and Nancy Folbre, "To Honor or Obey: The Patriarch as Residual Claimant," *Feminist Economics* 7: 1, 2001, 25–54.

26  Katherine Silbaugh, "Turning Labor into Love: Housework and the Law," *Northwestern University Law Review* 91: 1, 1996–97, 3–86.

27  Elizabeth Cady Stanton, Susan B. Anthony, and Matilda Jocelyn Gage, *History of Woman Suffrage*, Vols. 1–3, New York: Fowler & Wells, 1882; Reva B. Siegel, "Home as Work: The First Woman's Rights Claims Concerning Wives' Household Labor, 1850–1880," *Yale Law Journal* 103: 5, 1994, 1073–217.

28  Therborn, *Between Sex and Power*, 66.

29  Betsey Stevenson and Justin Wolfers, "Bargaining in the Shadow of the Law: Divorce Laws and Family Distress," *Quarterly Journal of Economics* 121: 1, 2006, 267–88.

30  Jeffrey Gettleman, Kai Schultz, and Suhasini Raj, "India Gay Sex Ban Is Struck Down. 'Indefensible,' Court Says," *New York Times*, September 6, 2018, nytimes.com.

31  "Women Caned in Malaysia for Attempting to Have Lesbian Sex," *The Guardian*, September 3, 2018, theguardian.com.

32  It is worth noting the historical significance of an ancient patriarchal civilization that was highly tolerant of homosexual behavior but had little concept of homosexual identity: Ancient Greece. On the distinction between identity and behavior, see John D'Emilio, "Capitalism and Gay Identity," in *The Gender/Sexuality Reader*, Roger N. Lancaster and Micaela Di Leonardo, eds., New York: Psychology Press, 1999, 169–78; Julie Matthaei, "The Sexual Division of Labor, Sexuality, and Lesbian/Gay Liberation," *Review of Radical Political Economy* 27: 2, 1995, 1–37.

33  Alexandra Rosenberg, Amanda Gates, Kate Richmond, and Stefanie Sinno, "It's Not a Joke: Masculinity Ideology and Homophobic Language," *Psychology of Men and Masculinity* 18: 4, 2017, 293–300; J. D. Wellman and S. K. McCoy, "Walking the Straight and Narrow: Examining the Role of Traditional Gender Norms in Sexual Prejudice," *Psychology of Men and Masculinity* 15: 2, 2014, 181–90.

34  Andrew Byrnes and Marsha Freeman, "The Impact of the CEDAW Convention: Paths to Equality," Gender Equality and Development Background Paper for the World Development Report, Washington, DC: World Bank, 2012, siteresources.worldbank.org.

35  Christian Morrisson and Johannes P. Jütting, "Women's Discrimination in Developing Countries: A New Data Set for Better Policies," *World Development* 33: 7, 2005, 1065–81; Johannes P. Jütting, Christian Morrisson, Jeff Dayton-Johnson, and Denis Drechsler, "Measuring Gender (In)Equality: The OECD Gender, Institutions and Development Data Base," *Journal of Human Development* 9: 1, 2008, 65–86.

36  Boris Branisa, Stephan Klasen, Maria Ziegler, Denis Drechsler, and Johannes Jütting, "The Institutional Basis of Gender Inequality: The Social Institutions and Gender Index (SIGI)," *Feminist Economics* 20: 2, 2014, 29–64.

37  Stefan Klasen, "Gender, Institutions, and Economic Development: Findings and Open Research and Policy Issues," Courant Research Centre: Poverty, Equity and Growth, Discussion Paper No. 211, 2016.

38  Stephan Klasen and Dana Schüler, "Reforming the Gender-Related Development Index and the Gender Empowerment Measure: Implementing Some Specific Proposals," *Feminist Economics* 17: 1, 2011, 1–30.

39  George A. Akerlof, J. L. Yellen, and M. L. Katz, "An Analysis of Out-of-Wedlock Childbearing in the United States," *Quarterly Journal of Economics* 108: 447, 1996, 278–317.

40  Nancy Folbre, *Who Pays for the Kids?* New York: Routledge, 1994, Chapter 6.

41  Julia Twigg and Alain Grand, "Contrasting Legal Conceptions of Family Obligation and Financial Reciprocity in the Support of Older People: France and England," *Ageing and Society* 18: 2, 1998, 131–46.

42  Katherine C. Pearson, "Filial Support Laws in the Modern Era: Domestic and International Comparison of Enforcement Practices for Laws Requiring Adult Children to Support Indigent Parents," *Elder Law Journal* 20, 2012, 269–92.

43  Mead Cain, "The Consequences of Reproductive Failure: Dependence, Mobility, and Mortality Among the Elderly of Rural South Asia," *Population Studies* 40: 3, 1986, 375–88; Monica Das Gupta, Jiang Zhenghua, Li Bohua, Xie Zhenming, Woojin Chung, and Bae Hwa-Ok, "Why Is Son Preference so Persistent in East and South Asia? A Cross-country Study of China, India and the Republic of Korea," *Journal of Development Studies* 40: 2, 2003, 153–87.

44  Ray Serrano, Richard Saltman, and Min-Jui Yeh, "Laws on Filial Support in Four Asian Countries," *Bulletin of the World Health Organization* 95: 11, 2017, 788–90.

45  Peter Whiteford and Willem Adema, *What Works Best in Reducing Child Poverty: A Benefit or Work Strategy?* Paris: OECD, 2007.

46  Sylvia Chant, "Exploring the 'Feminisation of Poverty' in Relation to Women's Work and Home-Based Enterprise in Slums of the Global South," *International Journal of Gender and Entrepreneurship* 6: 3, 2014, 296–316.

47  Nancy Folbre, *Valuing Children*, Cambridge, MA: Harvard University Press, 2008.

48  Nancy Folbre, "The Political Economy of Human Capital," *Review of Radical Political Economics* 44: 3, 2012, 281–92.

49  Tom W. Smith, Jaesok Son, and Jibum Kim, "Public Attitudes Toward Homosexuality and Gay Rights Across Time and Countries," Working Paper, Williams Institute, School of Law, University of California at Los Angeles, 2014, https://escholarship.org/uc/item/4p93w90c

50  Paula England, "The Gender Revolution: Uneven and Stalled," *Gender and Society* 24: 2, 2010, 149–66.

51  For a classic description, see Pierre Bourdieu, *Outline of a Theory of Practice*, New York: Cambridge University Press, 1977.

52  Edward Ross, *Social Control: A Survey of the Foundations of Order*, New York: Macmillan, 1901.

53  Edna Ullmann-Margalit, *The Emergence of Norms*, Oxford: Clarendon Press, 1977, 189.

54  For a historical account, see John Boswell, *Christianity, Social Tolerance, and Homosexuality*, Chicago: University of Chicago Press, 2015.

55  The classic formulation of the "just world hypothesis" is Melvin Lerner's *Belief in a Just World: A Fundamental Illusion*, New York: Plenum, 1980. For instance, in one experiment, participants incorrectly reported that a student who won a cash lottery worked harder than the loser. In another, individuals who were randomly punished (with a fake electric shock) were derogated, especially if they appeared to have no way of avoiding punishment

56  William Ryan, *Blaming the Victim*, New York: Pantheon, 1971; Timur Kuran, "Social Mechanisms of Dissonance Reduction," in *Social Mechanisms: An Analytical Approach to Social Theory*, Peter Hedström and Richard Swedberg, eds., New York: Cambridge University Press, 1998; Daniel Kahneman, *Thinking, Fast and Slow*, New York: MacMillan, 2011.

57  Herbert A. Simon, "A Mechanism for Social Selection and Successful Altruism," *Science* 250: 4988, Dec. 21, 1990, 1665–68.

58  For a classic description of self-blame among economic losers, see Richard Sennett and Jonathan Cobb, *The Hidden Injuries of Class*, New York: Norton, 1993.

59  Arthur T. Denzau and Douglass C. North, "Shared Mental Models: Ideologies and Institutions," *Kyklos* 47: 1, 1994), 3–31.

60 Susan Pinker, *The Sexual Paradox: Men, Women and the Real Gender Gap*, New York: Scribner, 2009.

61 Irene Browne and Paula England, "Oppression from Within and Without in Sociological Theories: An Application to Gender," *Current Perspectives in Social Theory* 17, 1997, 77–104.

62 Candace West and Don H. Zimmerman, "Doing Gender," *Gender and Society* 1: 2, 1987, 125–51.

63 Hilary Land and Hilary Rose, "Compulsory Altruism for Some or an Altruistic Society for All?" in *In Defence of Welfare*, P. Bean, J. Ferris. and D. Whynes, eds., London: Tavistock, 1985; Nancy Folbre, "Should Women Care Less? Intrinsic Motivation and Gender Inequality," *British Journal of Industrial Relations* 50: 4, 2012, 597–619.

64 Folbre, *Greed, Lust and Gender*.

65 *International Herald Tribune*, June 11, 1998, 1.

66 Nancy Chodorow, *The Reproduction of Mothering*, Berkeley: University of California Press, 1978.

67 UNICEF, *Harnessing the Power of Global Data for Girls*, New York: Author, 2018.

68 Claire Cain Miller, "A 'Generationally Perpetuated' Pattern: Daughters Do More Chores," *New York Times*, August 8, 2018, nytimes.com.

69 West and Zimmerman, "Doing Gender."

70 Kingsley Browne, *Divided Labours*, New Haven, CT: Yale University Press, 1998; W. Farrell, *The Myth of Male Power*, New York: Simon & Schuster, 1993; George Gilder, *Sexual Suicide*, New York: Quadrangle, 1973.

71 Mandy Boehnke, "Gender Role Attitudes Around the Globe: Egalitarian vs. Traditional Views," *Asian Journal of Social Science* 39, 2011, 57–74.

72 Kristin Donnelly, Jean M. Twenge, Malissa A. Clark, Samia K. Shaikh, Angela Beiler-May, and Nathan T. Carter, "Attitudes Toward Women's Work and Family Roles in the United States, 1976–2013," *Psychology of Women Quarterly* 40: 1, 2015, 1–14; David Cotter, Joan M. Hermsen, and Reeve Vanneman, "The End of the Gender Revolution? Gender Role Attitudes from 1977 to 2008," *American Journal of Sociology* 116: 4, 2011, 259–89; David A. Cotter, Joan M. Hermsen, and Reeve Vanneman, "Back on Track? The Stall and Rebound in Support for Women's New Roles in Work and Politics, 1977–2012," research brief for the Council on Contemporary Families, 2016, https://contemporaryfamilies.org/gender-revolution-rebound-brief-back-on-track/.

73 Carol Corrado, Charles Hulten, and Daniel Sichel, "Measuring Capital and Technology: An Expanded Framework," in *Measuring Capital in the New Economy*, C. Corrado, J. Haltiwanger, and D. Sichel, eds., Studies in Income and Wealth, Vol. 65, Chicago: University of Chicago Press, 2005.

74 Mary Murray, *The Law of the Father: Patriarchy in the Transition from Feudalism to Capitalism*, New York: Routledge, 2005.

75 See, for instance, Colin D. Harbury and David Hitchens, "Women, Wealth and Inheritance," *The Economic Journal* 87: 345, 1977, 124–31.

76  Carole Shammas, "Re-assessing the Married Women's Property Acts," *Journal of Women's History* 6: 1, 1994, 9–30; Lee Holcomb, *Wives & Property: Reform of the Married Women's Property Law in Nineteenth-Century England*, Toronto: University of Toronto Press, 1983.

77  Carole Shammas, "A New Look at Long-Term Trends in Wealth Inequality in the United States," *The American Historical Review* 98: 2, 1993, 427.

78  Carmen Diana Deere and Magdalena Leon De Leal, *Empowering Women: Land and Property Rights in Latin America*, Pittsburgh: University of Pittsburgh Press, 2014.

79  Ruth S. Meinzen-Dick, Lynn R. Brown, Hilary Sims Feldstein, and Agnes R. Quisumbing, "Gender, Property Rights, and Natural Resources," *World Development* 25: 8, 1997, 1303–15; Susan Lastarria-Cornhiel, "Impact of Privatization on Gender and Property Rights in Africa," *World Development* 25: 8, 1997, 1317–33.

80  Bina Agarwal, *A Field of One's Own: Gender and Land Rights in South Asia*, New York: Cambridge University Press, 1994.

81  Mariko Lin Chang, *Shortchanged: Why Women Have Less Wealth and What Can Be Done About It*, New York: Oxford University Press, 2010.

82  Carmen Diana Deere and Cheryl R. Doss, "The Gender Asset Gap: What Do We Know and Why Does it Matter?" *Feminist Economics* 12: 1–2, 2006, 1–50.

83  Shing-Yi Wang, "Property Rights and Intra-Household Bargaining," *Journal of Development Economics* 107, 2014, 192–201.

84  Nancy Folbre, "The Political Economy of Human Capital," *Review of Radical Political Economics* 44: 3, 2012, 281–92.

85  Jérôme Pelenc and Jérôme Ballet, "Strong Sustainability, Critical Natural Capital and the Capability Approach," *Ecological Economics* 112, 2015, 36–44.

86  Robert Trivers, "Parental Investment and Sexual Selection" in *Sexual Selection and the Descent of Man*, B. Campbell, ed., New York: Aldine, 1972, 136–79.

87  Bobbi Low, *Why Sex Matters*, Princeton: Princeton University Press, 2000.

88  Mukesh Eswaran and Ashok Kotwal, "A Theory of Gender Differences in Parental Altruism," *Canadian Journal of Economics/Revue Canadienne D'économique* 37: 4, 2004, 918–50.

89  Carol Tavris, *The Mismeasure of Woman*, New York: Simon and Schuster, 1992.

90  See, for instance, Frans de Waal, "Evolutionary Psychology: The Wheat and the Chaff," *Current Directions in Psychological Science* 11: 6, 2002, 187–90.

91  Jane B. Lancaster, "A Feminist and Evolutionary Biologist Looks at Women," *Yearbook of Physical Anthropology* 34, 1991, 1–11; Barbara Smuts, "Male Aggression Against Women: An Evolutionary Perspective," *Human Nature* 3, 1992, 1–44; "The Evolutionary Origins of Patriarchy,"

*Human Nature* 6: 1, 1995, 1–32; Patricia Gowaty, ed., *Feminism and Evolutionary Biology*, New York: Springer, 1997.

92 Robert Putnam, *Bowling Alone: The Collapse and Revival of American Community*, New York: Simon and Schuster, 2000.

93 Stephen Knack and Philip Keefer, "Does Social Capital Have an Economic Payoff? A Cross-Country Investigation, *"Quarterly Journal of Economics* 112: 4, 1997, 1251–88.

94 Charles Tilly, *Durable Inequalities*, Berkeley: University of California Press 1999.

95 James S. Coleman, "Social Capital in the Creation of Human Capital," *American Journal of Sociology* 94, 1988, S95–S120.

96 George Borjas, "Ethnicity, Neighborhoods, and Human–Capital Externalities," *American Economic Review* 85, 1995, 365–90; Shelly J. Lundberg and Richard Startz, "Inequality and Race: Models and Policy," in *Meritocracy and Economic Inequality*, Kenneth Arrow, Samuel Bowles, and Steven Durlauf, eds., Princeton: Princeton University Press, 2000.

97 James M. Buchanan, "An Economic Theory of Clubs," *Economica* 32: 125, 1965, 1–14.

98 Steve McDonald, "What's in the "Old Boys" Network? Accessing Social Capital in Gendered and Racialized Networks," *Social Networks* 33: 4, 2011, 317–30.

# Chapter 3. Gender, Structure, and Collective Agency

1 For a complete quote in context, see margaretthatcher.org.

2 Ashe Schow, "A Yearly Reminder that the Gender Wage Gap Is Due to Choice, Not Discrimination," *Washington Examiner*, April 14, 2015, washingtonexaminer.com. For other discussions of the view that women choose to earn less than men, see Lindsay Olson, "Do Some Women Choose to Make Less Than Men?" *US News and World Report*, February 12, 2015, money.usnews.com, and Mike Burns, "Fox Attempts to Revive Myth About Personal Choice and Gender Pay Gap," Media Matters, August 6, 2013, mediamatters.org.

3 Marx and Engels used the term "patriarchal" in the *Communist Manifesto* but never probed its specific meaning. For more discussion of their relationship to feminist thinking, see Nancy Folbre, *Greed, Lust, and Gender: A History of Economic Ideas*, New York: Oxford University Press, 2010.

4 John T. Jost, "Negative Illusions: Conceptual Clarification and Psychological Evidence Concerning False Consciousness," *Political Psychology* 16, 1995, 400.

5 August Bebel, *Woman Under Socialism*, trans. from the original German of the 33rd edition by Daniel De Leon, New York: Schocken Books, 1971.

For a longer discussion of the relationship between Engels and Bebel, see Folbre, *Greed, Lust and Gender.*

6 Mariarosa Dallacosta and Selma James, *The Power of Women and the Subversion of the Community*, London: Falling Wall Press, 1972.

7 See, for instance, Lise Vogel, *Marxism and the Oppression of Women*, Rutgers, NJ: Rutgers University Press, 1987.

8 Christopher Middleton, "The Sexual Division of Labour in Feudal England," *New Left Review* 113, 1979, 147–68; Wally Seccombe, *A Millennium of Family Change*, London: Verso, 1995.

9 Perry Anderson, *In the Tracks of Historical Materialism*, New York: Verso, 1988; Ira Katznelson, "Working Class Formation: Constructing Cases and Comparisons," in *Working–Class Formation*, Ira Katznelson and Aristide R. Zolberg, eds., Princeton, NJ: Princeton University Press, 1986, 4–42.

10 See, for instance, Alice Clark, *Working Life of Women in the Seventeenth Century*, New York: Augustus Kelley, 1967. (Original work published 1919).

11 Immanuel Wallerstein, *The Modern World-System I: Capitalist Agriculture and the Origins of the European World-Economy in the Sixteenth Century*, New York: Academic Press, 1974, and *Historical Capitalism*, London: Verso, 1983.

12 Theda Skocpol, "Wallerstein's World Capitalist System: A Theoretical and Historical Critique," *American Journal of Sociology* 82: 5, 1977, 1075–90.

13 Silvia Federici, *Caliban and the Witch: Women, The Body, and Primitive Accumulation*, New York: Autonomedia, 2004.

14 See, for instance, Jason W. Moore, *Capitalism in the Web of Life*, London: Verso, 2015.

15 Herbert Simon, "Rational Choice and the Structure of the Environment," in *Models of Man*, New York: John Wiley and Sons, 1957, Chapter 15. In his autobiography, Simon writes, "The metaphor of the maze is irresistible to someone who has dedicated his scientific career to understanding human choice": *Models of My Life*, New York: Basic Book, 1991, xvii.

16 Gary Becker, *The Economics of Discrimination*, Chicago: University of Chicago Press, 1957.

17 Victor Fuchs, *Women's Quest for Economic Equality*, Cambridge, MA: Harvard University Press, 1988; Catherine Hakim, *Work–Lifestyle Choices in the 21st Century: Preference Theory*, New York: Oxford, 2000.

18 Gary Becker, *A Treatise on the Family*, Cambridge, MA: Harvard University Press, 1981. See also Robert Evenson, "On the New Household Economics," *Journal of Agricultural Economics and Development* 6, 1976, 87–103.

19 Nancy Folbre, "Hearts and Spades: Paradigms of Household Economics," *World Development* 14: 2, 1986, 245–55.

20 Gary Becker, *Accounting for Tastes*, Cambridge, MA: Harvard University Press, 1996, 128, 50.

21 Claudia Goldin, *Understanding the Gender Gap: An Economic History of American Women*, New York: Oxford University Press, 1990.

22  Rick Geddes and Dean Lueck, "The Gains from Self-Ownership and the Expansion of Women's Rights," *American Economic Review* 92: 4, 2002, 1079–92.

23  Jeremy Greenwood, Ananth Seshadri, and Mehmet Yorukoglu, "Engines of Liberation," *Review of Economic Studies* 72: 1, 2005, 109–33.

24  Martha J. Bailey, Brad Hershbein, and Amalia R. Miller, "The Opt-In Revolution? Contraception and the Gender Gap in Wages," *American Economic Journal: Applied Economics* 4: 3, 2012, 225–54.

25  Anthony Giddens, *The Constitution of Society*, New York: John Wiley and Sons, 2013. Geoffrey Hodgson, "Reconstitutive Downward Causation: Social Structure and the Development of Individual Agency," in *Intersubjectivity in Economics: Agents and Structures*, Edward Fullbrook, ed., New York: Routledge, 2003, 159–80; Geoffrey M. Hodgson, "Hayek, Evolution, and Spontaneous Order," in *Natural Images in Economic Thought*, Philip Mirowski, ed., New York: Cambridge University Press, 1994, 408–47.

26  Alec Nove, *The Economics of Feasible Socialism*, New York: Taylor and Francis, 1983.

27  Adam Przeworski, *Capitalism and Social Democracy*, New York: Cambridge University Press, 1985; Vivek Chibber and Rosie Warren, eds., *The Debate on Postcolonial Theory and the Specter of Capital*, New York: Verso, 2016.

28  Peter A. Hall and David Soskice, *Varieties of Capitalism: The Institutional Foundations of Comparative Advantage*, New York: Oxford University Press, 2001.

29  Hadas Mandel and Michael Shalev, "Gender, Class, and Varieties of Capitalism," *Social Politics* 16: 2, 2009, 161–81; Nancy Folbre, "Varieties of Patriarchal Capitalism," *Social Politics* 16: 2, 2009, 204–9.

30  David M. Kotz, Terrence McDonough, and Michael Reich, eds., *Social Structures of Accumulation*, New York: Cambridge University Press, 1994.

31  Robert Pollin, *Contours of Descent*, New York: Verso, 2005; David M. Kotz, *The Rise and Fall of Neoliberal Capitalism*, Cambridge, MA: Harvard University Press, 2015.

32  David Kotz, "Household Labor, Wage Labor, and the Transformation of the Family," *Review of Radical Political Economics* 26: 2, 1994, 24–56.

33  Erik Olin Wright, *Classes*, New York: Verso, 1997.

34  Erik Olin Wright, *Envisioning Real Utopias*, New York: Verso, 2010.

35  Harold Wolpe, ed., *The Articulation of Modes of Production*, Boston; Routledge & Kegan Paul, 1980.

36  Bruce J. Berman, "The Concept of 'Articulation' and the Political Economy of Colonialism," *Canadian Journal of African Studies* 18: 2, 1984, 407–14; see also John Haldon, *The State and the Tributary Mode of Production*, New York: Verso, 2017.

37  Antonella Picchio, *Social Reproduction*, New York: Cambridge University Press, 1992, 7, 116.

38 Meg Luxton, "Feminist Political Economy in Canada and the Politics of Social Reproduction," in *Social Reproduction*, Kate Bezanson and Meg Luxton, eds., Montreal: McGill-Queen's University Press, 2006, 11–44.

39 Heidi Hartmann, "The Unhappy Marriage of Marxism and Feminism: Toward a More Progressive Union," *Capital and Class* 3: 2, 1979, 1–33; Ann Ferguson and Nancy Folbre, "The Unhappy Marriage of Capitalism and Patriarchy," in *Women and Revolution*, Lydia Sargent, ed., Boston: South End Press, 1981, 313–38.

40 Wally Seccombe, *A Millennium of Family Change*, New York: Verso, 1992; *Weathering the Storm*, New York: Verso, 1993.

41 Cedric Robinson, *Black Marxism*, Chapel Hill: University of North Carolina Press, 2000.

42 David McNally, "Intersection and Dialectics: Critical Reconstructions in Social Reproduction Theory," in *Social Reproduction Theory*, Tithi Bhattacharya, ed., London: Pluto, 2017, 94–111.

43 Gary S. Becker, "Altruism in the Family and Selfishness in the Market Place," *Economica* 48: 189, 1981, 1–15.

44 David Sloane Wilson, *Does Altruism Exist? Culture, Genes, and the Welfare of Others*, New Haven, CT: Yale University Press, 2015.

45 For a broad overview of the ways that economists have engaged with the issue of group selection, see Jeroen C. J. M. van den Bergh and John M. Gowdy, "A Group Selection Perspective on Economic Behavior, Institutions, and Organizations," *Journal of Economic Behavior and Organization* 72, 2009, 1–20.

46 Herbert Gintis, Samuel Bowles, and Ernst Fehr, "Explaining Altruistic Behavior in Humans," *Evolution in Human Behavior* 24: 3, 2003, 153–72.

47 Robert Trivers, "Parental Investment and Sexual Selection," in *Sexual Selection and the Descent of Man*, B. Campbell, ed., New York: Aldine, 1972, 136–79; Robert Trivers, "Parent–Offspring Conflict," *Integrative and Comparative Biology* 14: 1, 1974, 249–64.

48 Marjorie B. McElroy and Mary Jean Horney, "Nash-Bargained Household Decisions: Toward a Generalization of the Theory of Demand," *International Economic Review*, 1981, 333–49; Shelly Lundberg and Robert A. Pollak, "Bargaining and Distribution in Marriage," *Journal of Economic Perspectives* 10: 4, 1996, 139–58.

49 Nancy Folbre, "Gender Coalitions: Extrafamily Influences on Intrafamily Inequality," in *Intrahousehold Resource Allocation in Developing Countries: Methods, Models and Policy*, Lawrence Haddad, John Hoddinott, and Harold Alderman, eds., Baltimore: Johns Hopkins University Press, 1998.

50 George Loewenstein, "Out of Control: Visceral Influences on Behavior," *Organizational Behavior and Human Decision Processes* 65: 3, 1996, 272–92; Colin F. Camerer, George Loewenstein, and Matthew Rabin, eds., *Advances in Behavioral Economics*, Princeton, NJ: Princeton University Press, 2011.

51  Karla Hoff and Priyanka Pandey, "Discrimination, Social Identity, and Durable Inequalities," *American Economic Review* 96: 2, 2006, 206–11; A. Mani, S. Mullainathan, E. Shafir, and H. Zhao, "Poverty Impedes Cognitive Function," *Science* 341: 6149, August 30, 2013, 976–80.

52  Robert J. Shiller, *Irrational Exuberance*, Princeton, NJ: Princeton University Press, 2001.

53  B. S. Frey and S. Meier, "Selfish and Indoctrinated Economists? *European Journal of Law and Economics* 19: 2, 2005, 165–71.

54  Robert J. Leonard, "War as a 'Simple Economic Problem': The Rise of an Economics of Defense," in *Economics and National Security: A History of Their Interaction*, Craufurd D. W. Goodwin, ed., Chapel Hill, NC: Duke University Press, 1991.

55  Jack Hirshleifer, *The Dark Side of the Force: Economic Foundations of Conflict Theory*, New York: Cambridge, 2001; Michelle Garfinkel and Stergios Skarperdas, "Contract or War?" *American Economist* 441: 1, 2000, 5–16; Michelle R. Grossman and Minseong Kim, "Swords or Ploughshares?" *Journal of Political Economy* 103: 6, 1995, 1275–88.

56  Robert Costanza, Rudolf de Groot, Paul Sutton, Sander van der Ploeg, Sharolyn J. Anderson, Ida Kubiszewski, Stephen Farber, and R. Kerry Turner, "Changes in the Global Value of Ecosystem Services," *Global Environmental Change* 26, 2014, 152–58.

57  James J. Heckman, "Skill Formation and the Economics of Investing in Disadvantaged Children," *Science* 312, June 30, 2006, 1900–2; Mark R. Rank, "The Cost of Keeping Children Poor," *New York Times*, April 15, 2018, nytimes.com.

58  Mukesh Eswaran, *Why Gender Matters in Economics*, Princeton, NJ: Princeton University Press, 2014.

59  Nathan Nunn, Alberto F. Alesina, and Paola Giuliano, "On the Origins of Gender Roles: Women and the Plough," *Quarterly Journal of Economics* 128: 2, 2013, 469–530. Their argument draws on an earlier analysis by Ester Boserup, *Women's Role in Economic Development*, London: George Allen and Unwin, 1970.

60  For contrasting views, see Russell Hardin, *All for One: The Logic of Group Conflict*, Princeton, NJ: Princeton University Press, 1995, and Benedict Anderson, *Imagined Communities: Reflections on the Origin and Spread of Nationalism*, New York: Verso, 1983. See also discussions in Richard Jenkins, *Social Identity*, and in Wendy Bottero, *Stratification: Social Division and Inequality*, New York: Routledge, 2005, 249.

61  M. Sherif, O. J. Harvey, B. J. White, W. Hood, and C. W. Sherif, *Intergroup Conflict and Cooperation: The Robbers Cave Experiment*, Norman, OK: The University Book Exchange, 1961.

62  Ta-Nehisi Coates, *Between the World and Me*, New York: Spiegel and Grau, 2015, 7. See also Karen E. Fields and Barbara J. Fields, *Racecraft*, New York: Verso, 2012.

63  David Harvey, *Seventeen Contradictions and the End of Capitalism*, New York: Oxford University Press, 2014.

64  Lise Vogel, "Foreword," in *Social Reproduction Theory*, Tithi Bhattacharya, ed., London: Pluto, 2017, xi.

65  Nancy Fraser, "From Redistribution to Recognition? Dilemmas of Justice in a Post-Socialist Age," *New Left Review* 212, 1995, 68–68; Nancy Fraser and Axel Honneth, *Redistribution or Recognition?* New York: Verso, 2003.

66  Karl Marx, Letter to Meyer and Vogt, cited in Jon Elster, *Making Sense of Marx*, New York: Cambridge University Press, 1985, 21.

67  Vladimir Lenin, *Imperialism: The Highest Stage of Capitalism*, New York: Resistance Books, 1999. (Original work published 1917)

68  Andre Gunder Frank, *The Development of Underdevelopment*, Boston: Free Press, 1966; Arghiri Emmanuel, *Unequal Exchange*, London: New Left Books, 1972.

69  See, for instance, Naila Kabeer, "Globalization, Labor Standards, and Women's Rights: Dilemmas of Collective (In)action in an Interdependent World," *Feminist Economics* 10: 1, 2004, 3–35.

70  W. E. B. DuBois, *The Souls of Black Folk*, Chicago: A. C. McGlurg, 1907 (Original work published 1903); *Black Reconstruction*, New York: Atheneum, 1969. (Original work published 1935)

71  B. R. Ambedkar, *Annihilation of Caste*, New York: Verso, 2004. (Original work published 1936)

72  Charles W. Mills, *The Racial Contract*, Ithaca, NY: Cornell University Press, 1999.

73  William A. Darity, Jr., "Forty Acres and a Mule in the 21st Century," *Social Science Quarterly* 89: 3, 2008, 656–64; William A. Darity Jr., Patrick L. Mason, and James B. Stewart, "The Economics of Identity: The Origin and Persistence of Racial Identity Norms," *Journal of Economic Behavior & Organization* 60, 2006, 283–305.

74  Angela Davis, *Women, Race, and Class*, New York: Vintage, 1983.

75  Kimberlé Williams Crenshaw, "Demarginalizing the Intersection of Race and Sex: A Black Feminist Critique of Antidiscrimination Doctrine, Feminist Theory and Antiracist Politics," *University of Chicago Legal Forum*, 1989, 139–67; "Mapping the Margins: Intersectionality, Identity Politics, and Violence against Women of Color," *Stanford Law Review* 43: 6, 1991, 1241–99; Patricia Hill Collins, *Black Feminist Thought*, New York: Routledge, 1991.

76  William Darity, "Stratification Economics: The Role of Intergroup Inequality," *Journal of Economics and Finance* 29: 2, 2005, 144–53; William A. Darity Jr., Darrick Hamilton, and James B. Stewart, "A Tour de Force in Understanding Intergroup Inequality: An Introduction to Stratification Economics," *Review of Black Political Economy* 42, 2015, 1–6.

77  Vrushali Patil, "From Patriarchy to Intersectionality: A Transnational Feminist Assessment of How Far We've Really Come," *Signs* 38: 4, 2013, 847–67.

78  Mary Romero, "Crossing the Immigration and Race Border: A Critical Race Theory Approach to Immigration Studies." *Contemporary Justice Review* 11, 2008, 23–37.

79  William M. Dugger, ed., *Inequality: Radical Institutionalist Views on Race, Gender, Class, and Nation*, Westport, CT: Greenwood, 1996; Charles Tilly, *Durable Inequalities*, Berkeley: University of California Press, 1999.

80  Mancur Olson, *The Logic of Collective Action*, Cambridge, MA: Harvard University Press, 1965.

81  John R. Commons, "Institutional Economics," *American Economic Review* 21, 1931, 648–57; Geoffrey Hodgson, *Economics and Institutions*, New York: Wiley, 1991.

82  George A. Akerlof and Rachel E. Kranton, "Economics and Identity," *Quarterly Journal of Economics* 115: 3, 2000, 715–53.

83  Marianne Bertrand, Dolly Chugh, and Sendhil Mullainathan, "Implicit Discrimination," *American Economic Review* 95: 2, 2005, 94–98.

84  Marcus Rediker, *Pirates of All Nations*, Boston: Beacon, 2005.

85  Michelle Garfinkel, "Stable Alliance Formation in Distributional Conflict," *European Journal of Political Economy* 20, 2004, 829–52.

86  Robert P. Gilles, *The Cooperative Game Theory of Networks and Hierarchies*, New York: Springer, 2010.

87  Michael Suk-Young Chwe, "Farsighted Coalitional Stability," *Journal of Economic Theory* 63, 1994, 299–325.

88  Henry Hanssman, "When Does Worker Ownership Work?" *The Yale Law Journal* 99: 8, 1990, 1749–815.

89  Alberto Alesina, Reza Baqir, and William Easterly, "Public Goods and Ethnic Divisions," *The Quarterly Journal of Economics* 114: 4, 1999, 1243–84; Brian An, Morris Levy, and Rodney Hero, "It's Not Just Welfare: Racial Inequality and the Local Provision of Public Goods in the United States," *Urban Affairs Review* 54: 5, 2018, 833–65.

90  Lara Cushing, Rachel Morello-Frosch, Madeline Wander, and Manuel Pastor, "The Haves, the Have-nots, and the Health of Everyone: The Relationship Between Social Inequality and Environmental Quality," *Annual Review of Public Health* 36, 2015, 193–209.

91  J. R. Lott and L. W. Kenny, "Did Woman's Suffrage Change the Size and Scope of Government? *Journal of Political Economy* 107, 1999, 1163–98; T. S. Aidt, J. Dutta, and E. Loukoianova, "Democracy Comes to Europe: Franchise Extension and Fiscal Outcomes, 1830–1938," *European Economic Review* 50, 2006, 249–83.

92  Pew Research Center, "Wide Gender Gap, Growing Educational Divide in Voters' Party Identification," March 20, 2018, people-press.org.

93  Amin Maalouf, *In the Name of Identity*, New York: Arcade, 2012, 4.

94  Kimberlé Williams Crenshaw, "Demarginalizing the Intersection of Race and Sex: A Black Feminist Critique of Antidiscrimination Doctrine, Feminist Theory and Antiracist Politics," *University of Chicago Legal Forum*, 1989, 139–67; "Mapping the Margins: Intersectionality, Identity

Politics, and Violence against Women of Color," *Stanford Law Review* 43: 6, 1991, 1241–99; Patricia Hill Collins, *Black Feminist Thought*, New York: Routledge, 1991.

95  Leslie McCall, "The Complexity of Intersectionality," *Signs: Journal of Women, Culture and Society* 30: 3, 2005, 1771–800.

96  See Folbre, *Greed, Lust, and Gender*, Chapter 11.

97  John Stuart Mill, *The Subjection of Women*, with an introduction by Wendell Carr, Cambridge, MA: MIT Press, 1970, 11. (Harriet Taylor was not officially listed as a co-author, but Mill described her as such.)

98  Mill, *The Subjection of Women*, 13.

# Chapter 4. Appropriation, Reproduction, and Production

1  Ulla Grapard, "Robinson Crusoe: The Quintessential Economic Man?" *Feminist Economics* 1: 1, 1995, 33–52.

2  These definitions differ slightly in detail from those I have offered in previous work. They are similar to those specified by Lourdes Benería, in "Reproduction, Production and the Sexual Division of Labour," *Cambridge Journal of Economics* 3, 1979, 203–25.

3  For more discussion, see Nancy Folbre, *Valuing Children*, Cambridge, MA: Harvard University Press, 2008, Chapter 2.

4  Marilyn Power, "Social Provisioning as a Starting Point for Feminist Economics," *Feminist Economics* 10: 3, 2004, 3–19; Antonella Picchio, *Social Reproduction: The Political Economy of the Labor Market*, Cambridge: Cambridge University Press, 1992.

5  See, for instance, Oded Galor and David N. Weil, "Population, Technology, and Growth: From Malthusian Stagnation to the Demographic Transition and beyond," *American Economic Review* 90: 4, 2000, 806–28.

6  Kingsley Davis, "Low Fertility in Evolutionary Perspective," *Population and Development Review* 12, 1986, 48–65.

7  Nancy Folbre, "Chicks, Hawks, and Patriarchal Institutions," in *Handbook of Behavioral Economics*, Morris Altman, ed., Armonk, NY: M. E. Sharpe, 2006, 499–516.

8  John Caldwell, *Theory of Fertility Decline*, New York: Academic Press, 1982; Nancy Folbre, "Of Patriarchy Born: The Political Economy of Fertility Decisions," *Feminist Studies* 9: 2, 1983, 261–84; *Who Pays for the Kids? Gender and the Structures of Constraint*, New York: Routledge, 1994.

9  Nancy Folbre, "Of Patriarchy Born: The Political Economy of Fertility Decisions," *Feminist Studies* 9: 2, 1983, 261–84.

10  Jenny Brown, *Birth Strike*, New York: PM Press, 2019.

11  For instance, Michelle Budig, Joya Misra, and Irene Boeckmann, "The

Motherhood Penalty in Cross-National Perspective: The Importance of Work–Family Policies and Cultural Attitudes," *Social Politics* 19: 2, 2012, 163–93.

12  Exceptions include the imputed value of owner-occupied housing and of agricultural goods produced for one's own consumption.

13  Marilyn Waring, *If Women Counted*, New York: Harper and Row, 1988.

14  Tom Toles, "He Who Dies with the Most Toys Now Loses!" *Washington Post*, October 24, 2016, washingtonpost.com.

15  James K. Boyce, *The Political Economy of the Environment*, Northampton, MA: Elgar, 2002; Jared Diamond, *Collapse*, New York: Penguin, 2006; Geoffrey Heal, *Endangered Economies*, New York: Columbia University Press, 2016.

16  Nancy Folbre and Jooyeoun Suh, "Valuing Unpaid Child Care in the U.S.: A Prototype Satellite Account Using the American Time Use Survey," *Review of Income and Wealth* 62: 4, 2016, 668–85; Robert Costanza, Rudolf de Groot, Paul Sutton, Sander van der Ploeg, Sharolyn J. Anderson, Ida Kubiszewski, Stephen Farber, and R. Kerry Turner, "Changes in the Global Value of Ecosystem Services," *Global Environmental Change* 26, 2014, 152–58.

17  Folbre and Suh, "Valuing Unpaid Child Care."

18  Kenneth Boulding, *The Economy of Love and Fear*, Belmont: Wadsworth, 1973.

19  Raul Caruso, "*The Economy of Love and Fear*, by Kenneth Boulding," *Crossroads* 5: 3, 2005, 109–18.

20  Albert O. Hirschman, *The Passions and the Interests: Political Arguments for Capitalism before Its Triumph*, Princeton, NJ: Princeton University Press, 1977.

21  John Roemer, *A General Theory of Exploitation and Class*, Cambridge, MA: Harvard University Press, 1982; David Harvey, *The New Imperialism*, Oxford: Oxford University Press, 2005.

22  Michelle Garfinkel, "Stable Alliance Formation in Distributional Conflict," *European Journal of Political Economy* 20, 2004, 829–52.

23  Maria Mies, *Patriarchy and Accumulation on a World Scale*, New York: Zed, 1986, 66.

24  Frank Knight, *Risk, Uncertainty, and Profit*, Boston: Houghton Mifflin, 1921, 374–75.

25  Pedro Manuel Carneiro and James J. Heckman, "Human Capital Policy," IZA Discussion Papers, No. 821, Bonn: Institute for the Study of Labor, 2003, econstor.eu.

26  Jane Humphries, "Class Struggle and the Persistence of the Working Class Family," *Cambridge Journal of Economics* 1, 1977, 242–58; Christopher Lasch, *Haven in a Heartless World*, New York: Norton, 1995.

27  Sut Jhally, *Advertising and the End of the World*, Documentary video, 1998.

28  Nancy Folbre, "Children as Public Goods," *American Economic Review* 84:

2, 1994, 86–90; Douglas A. Wolf, Ronald D. Lee, Timothy Miller, Gretchen Donehower, and Alexandre Genest, "Fiscal Externalities of Becoming a Parent," *Population and Development Review* 37: 2, 2011, 241–66.

29  Paul Samuelson, "An Exact Consumption-Loan Model of Interest with or without the Social Contrivance of Money," *Journal of Political Economy* 66: 6, 1958, 468.

30  Mark Lino, Kevin Kuczynski, Nestor Rodriguez, and TusaRebecca Schap, *Expenditures on Children by Families, 2015*, Washington, DC: US Department of Agriculture, Center for Nutrition Policy and Promotion, 2014, isminc.com.

31  In principle, it is possible to specify a "reproduction function," and some twentieth-century skepticism regarding independent measurement of capital in production functions foreshadows the following discussion of difficulties measuring reproductive inputs and outputs.

32  Amartya Sen, "Human Capital and Human Capability," *World Development* 25: 12, 1997, 2; Martha Nussbaum, *Women and Human Development*, New York: Cambridge University Press, 2001; Ingrid Robeyns, "Sen's Capability Approach and Gender Inequality: Selecting Relevant Capabilities," *Feminist Economics* 9: 2–3, 2003, 61–92.

33  Sen, "Human Capital and Human Capability," 2.

34  For a longer discussion of commitments versus investments, see Nancy Folbre, *Valuing Children*, Cambridge, MA: Harvard University Press, 2008, Chapter 3.

35  Nancy Folbre, *Valuing Children: Rethinking the Economics of the Family*, Cambridge, MA: Harvard University Press, 2008.

36  Nancy Folbre and Julie Nelson, "For Love or Money?" *Journal of Economic Perspectives* 14: 4, 2000, 123–40.

37  Diane Elson, "Social Reproduction in the Global Crisis: Rapid Recovery or Long-Lasting Depletion," in *The Global Crisis and Transformative Social Change*, Peter Utting, Shahra Razavi, and Rebecca Varghese Buchholz, eds., New York: Palgrave Macmillan, 2012, 63–80; Tithi Bhattacharya, "What Is Social Reproduction Theory?" *Socialist Worker,* September 10, 2013, socialistworker.org.

38  Nancy Folbre, "Exploitation Comes Home: A Critique of the Marxian Theory of Family Labor," *Cambridge Journal of Economics* 6: 4, 1982, 317–29.

39  Nancy Fraser, "Capitalism's Crisis of Care," *Dissent* 63: 4, 2016, 30.

40  Barbara Laslett and Johanna Brenner, "Gender and Social Reproduction: Historical Perspectives," *Annual Review of Sociology* 15, 1989, 382; Maureen Mackintosh, "Gender and Economics: The Sexual Division of Labor and the Subordination of Women," in *Of Marriage and the Market*, Kate Young, Carol Wolkowitz, and Roslyn McCullagh, eds., London: CSE Books, 1981, 10.

41  Meg Luxton, "Feminist Political Economy in Canada and the Politics of Social Reproduction," in *Social Reproduction*, Kate Bezanson and Meg Luxton, eds., Montreal: McGill-Queen's University Press, 2006, 36.

42  See, for instance, Antonella Picchio, *Social Reproduction: The Political Economy of the Labor Market,* Cambridge: Cambridge University Press, 1992; Jane Humphries and Jill Rubery, "The Reconstitution of the Supply Side of the Labour Market: The Relative Autonomy of Social Reproduction," *Cambridge Journal of Economics* 8: 4, 1984, 331–46. See also Bezanson and Luxton, eds., *Social Reproduction.* Colin Farrelly, "Patriarchy and Historical Materialism," *Hypatia* 26: 1, 2011, 1–21.

43  James Coleman, "Social Capital in the Creation of Human Capital," *American Journal of Sociology* 84, 1988, S95–S120; Shirley Burgraaf, *The Feminine Economy and Economic Man: Revising the Role of Family in the Post-Industrial Age,* Reading, MA: Perseus Books, 1997.

44  Frank Ackerman and Lisa Heinzerling, *Priceless,* New York: New Press, 2004. I differ with their argument that all imputations should be avoided, however, because even a crude estimate of the value of externalities may translate the value of nonmarket processes into a metric that market participants can easily understand.

45  Thomas Princen, "The Shading and Distancing of Commerce: When Internalization Is Not Enough," *Ecological Economics* 20: 3, 1997, 235–53.

46  Nancy Folbre, "Children as Public Goods," *American Economic Review* 84: 2, 1994, 86–90.

47  Employers use carrots in the form of rewards for seniority and sticks in the form of contractual restrictions on worker mobility in order to minimize the potential loss of firm-specific skills. On carrots, see Edward P. Lazear, *Personnel Economics,* Cambridge, MA: MIT Press, 1995. On sticks, see Alan Krueger and Orley Ashenfelter, "Theory and Evidence on Employer Collusion in the Franchise Sector," Department of Economics, Princeton University, Working Paper, September 2017, econpapers.repec.org.

48  Laura Addati, "Extending Maternity Protection to All Women: Trends, Challenges, and Opportunities," *International Social Security Review* 68: 1, 2015, 69–93.

49  Rosemary L. Hopcroft, "Parental Status and Differential Investment in Sons and Daughters: Trivers-Willard Revisited," *Social Forces* 83: 3, 2005, 111–36.

50  For an early discussion of the economic incentives to son preference, see Nancy Folbre, "Comment on Market Opportunities, Genetic Endowments, and Intrafamily Resource Distribution, by Mark Rosenzweig and T. Paul Schultz," *American Economic Review* 74: 3, 1984, 518–20. For an especially powerful case study, see Mead Cain, "The Consequences of Reproductive Failure: Dependence, Mobility, and Mortality Among the Elderly of Rural South Asia," *Population Studies* 40: 3, 1986, 375–88.

51  Lawrence B. Glickman, *A Living Wage. American Workers and the Making of Consumer Society,* Ithaca, NY: Cornell University Press, 1997.

52  Shelly Lundberg, "Sons, Daughters, and Parental Behavior," *Oxford Review of Economic Policy* 21: 3, 2005, 340–56.

53  Kenneth Feinberg, *What Is Life Worth?* New York: Public Affairs, 2005.

54  Jane Waldfogel, "Understanding the 'Family Gap' in Pay for Women with Children," *The Journal of Economic Perspectives* 12: 1, 1998, 137–56.

55  Wendy Sigle-Rushton and Jane Waldfogel, "Motherhood and Women's Earnings in Anglo American, Continental European, and Nordic Countries," *Feminist Economics* 13: 2, 2007, 55–91.

56  Victor Fuchs, *Women's Quest for Economic Equality*, Cambridge, MA: Harvard University Press, 1988.

57  Nancy Folbre, "Should Women Care Less? Intrinsic Motivation and Gender Inequality," *British Journal of Industrial Relations* 50: 4, 2012, 597–619.

58  Evelyn Nakano Glenn, *Forced to Care: Coercion and Caregiving in America*, Cambridge, MA: Harvard University Press, 2010.

59  On social capital, see Glenn Loury, "A Dynamic Theory of Racial Income Differences," in *Women, Minorities, and Employment Discrimination*, P. Wallace and A. Lamond, eds., Lexington, MA: Lexington Books, 1977; James Coleman, "Social Capital in the Creation of Human Capital," *American Journal of Sociology* 84, 1988, S95–S120; Charles Tilly, *Durable Inequalities*, Berkeley: University of California Press, 1999.

60  Ayelet Shachar, *The Birthright Lottery: Citizenship and Global Inequality*, Cambridge, MA: Harvard University Press, 2009.

61  David Roediger, *The Wages of Whiteness*, New York: Verso, 2007; George Lipsitz, *The Possessive Investment in Whiteness*, Philadelphia: Temple University Press, 2006.

62  Lee Badgett and Jeff Frank, eds., *Sexual Orientation Discrimination: An International Perspective*, New York: Routledge, 2007.

63  Nancy Folbre, "The Political Economy of Human Capital," *Review of Radical Political Economics* 44: 3, 2012, 281–92.

64  Annette Lareau, *Unequal Childhoods: Race, Class, and Family Life. A Decade Later*, 2nd ed., Oakland: University of California Press, 2011.

65  Sabino Kornrich and Frank Furstenberg, "Investing in Children: Changes in Parental Spending on Children, 1972–2007," *Demography* 50: 1, 2013, 1–23.

66  Samuel Bowles, Herbert Gintis, and Melissa Osborne Groves, eds., *Unequal Chances: Family Background and Economic Success*, Princeton, NJ: Princeton University Press, 2005.

67  Greg J. Duncan and Jeanne Brooks-Gunn, eds., *The Consequences of Growing Up Poor*, New York: Russell Sage Foundation, 1999.

68  Sara McLanahan and Christine Percheski, "Family Structure and the Reproduction of Inequalities," *Annual Review of Sociology* 34, 2008, 257–76.

69  Motoko Rich, Amanda Cox, and Matthew Bloch, "Money, Race and Success: How Your School District Compares," *New York Times*, April 29, 2016.

70  George Borjas, "Ethnicity, Neighborhoods, and Human-Capital Externalities," *American Economic Review* 85, 1995, 365–90; Shelly J. Lundberg and Richard

Startz, "Inequality and Race: Models and Policy," in *Meritocracy and Economic Inequality*, Kenneth Arrow, Samuel Bowles, and Steven Durlauf, eds., Princeton, NJ: Princeton University Press, 2000.

## Chapter 5. Hierarchy and Exploitation

1  For a broad overview of economists' engagement with group selection, see Jeroen C. J. M. van den Bergh and John M. Gowdy, "A Group Selection Perspective on Economic Behavior, Institutions, and Organizations," *Journal of Economic Behavior and Organization* 72, 2009, 1–20.

2  Robert A. Pollak, "A Transaction Cost Approach to Families and Households," *Journal of Economic Literature* 23: 2, 1985, 581–608.

3  Edward Lazear, "Pay Equality and Industrial Politics," *Journal of Political Economy* 97, 1989, 561–80.

4  Philip J. Cook and Robert H. Frank, *The Winner-Take-All Society*, New York: Free Press, 1995.

5  Richard D. Alexander, *The Biology of Moral Systems*, New York: Aldine de Gruyter, 1987; Kevin MacDonald, "The Establishment and Maintenance of Socially Imposed Monogamy in Western Europe," *Politics and the Life Sciences* 14: 1, 1995, 3–23.

6  Steven A. Frank, "Repression of Competition and the Evolution of Cooperation," *Evolution* 57: 4, 2003, 693–705.

7  Frans de Waal, *Good Natured*, Cambridge, MA: Harvard University Press, 1996.

8  Edward O. Wilson, *The Social Conquest of Earth*, New York: W. W. Norton, 2012.

9  Edward O. Wilson, "Evolution and Our Inner Conflict," *New York Times*, June 24, 2012, opinionator.blogs.nytimes.com.

10 Frans de Waal, *Good Natured*, 30.

11 Herbert Gintis, Samuel Bowles, and Ernst Fehr, "Explaining Altruistic Behavior in Humans," *Evolution in Human Behavior* 24: 3, 2003, 153–72.

12 Samuel Bowles and Herbert Gintis, *A Cooperative Species*, Princeton, NJ: Princeton University Press, 2013.

13 Jung-Kyoo Choi and Samuel Bowles, "The Coevolution of Parochial Altruism and War," *Science* 318: 5850, October 26, 2007, 636–40.

14 Herbert A. Simon, "A Mechanism for Social Selection and Successful Altruism," *Science*, 250: 4988, December 21, 1990, 1665–68.

15 Nancy Folbre, "Should Women Care Less? Intrinsic Motivation and Gender Inequality," *British Journal of Industrial Relations* 50: 4, 2012, 597–619.

16 Nancy Folbre, *Greed, Lust and Gender*, New York: Oxford University Press, 2009.

17 Nancy Folbre, *The Invisible Heart: Economics and Family Values*, New York: New Press, 2001.

18  Mancur Olson, "Dictatorship, Democracy, and Development," *American Political Science Review* 87: 3, 1993, 567–76; Douglass North, "Institutions," *Journal of Economic Perspectives* 5: 1, 1991, 97–112.

19  Mancur Olson, *The Logic of Collective Action*, Cambridge, MA: Harvard University Press, 1965.

20  Paul A. Samuelson, "Social Indifference Curves," *Quarterly Journal of Economics* 70: 1, 1956, 12.

21  J. M. Buchanan, R. D. Tollison, and G. Tullock, *Toward a Theory of the Rent-Seeking Society*, College Station: Texas A and M Press, 1980.

22  Alec Nove, *The Economics of Feasible Socialism*, New York: Taylor and Francis, 1983.

23  Gary Becker, *A Treatise on the Family*, Cambridge, MA: Harvard University Press, 1981.

24  Jack Hirshleifer, "Shakespeare vs. Becker on Altruism: The Importance of Having the Last Word," *Journal of Economic Literature* 15: 2, 1977, 500–2.

25  Nancy Folbre, "Hearts and Spades: Paradigms of Household Economics," *World Development* 14: 2, 1986, 245–55.

26  Mancur Olson, "Dictatorship, Democracy, and Development," Douglass North, John Joseph Wallis, and Barry R. Weingast, *Violence and Social Orders*, New York: Cambridge University Press, 2009; Daron Acemoglu and James Robinson, *Why Nations Fail*, New York: Crown, 2012.

27  One of the most straightforward and easily accessible explanations of these dynamics in terms of Cooperators and Defectors (instead of Doves and Hawks) can be found in Chapter 7, "Beyond Self Interest" of Robert H. Frank, *Microeconomics and Behavior*, New York: McGraw Hill, 1991.

28  Polarities between the masculine and feminine in economic theory tend to assign a strong positive to the former and a weak negative to the latter. See Julie Nelson, "Gender, Metaphor, and the Definition of Economics," *Economics and Philosophy* 8: 1, 1992, 103–25. An example of a bird with feminine connotations that is not a predator, but seldom vulnerable to hawks, would be a swan. An example of a bird with masculine connotations less appealing than a hawk would be a vulture.

29  Douglass North, John Joseph Wallis, and Barry R. Weingast, *Violence and Social Orders*, New York: Cambridge University Press, 2009. Whether such efforts are gradually gaining traction or not remains a subject of debate. For a pessimistic view, see Scheidel, *The Great Leveler*; for an optimistic view, see Steven Pinker, *The Better Angels of Our Nature*, New York: Penguin, 2011.

30  Mancur Olson, "Dictatorship, Democracy, and Development," *American Political Science Review* 87: 3, 1993, 567–76.

31  Steven Marglin, "What Do Bosses Do? The Origins of Hierarchy in Capitalist Production," *Review of Radical Political Economics* 6, 1974, 60–112.

32  Susan Brownmiller, *Against Our Will: Men, Women, and Rape*, New York: Simon and Schuster, 1975; Silvia Federici, *Caliban and the Witch:*

*Women, Capitalism and Primitive Accumulation*, New York: Autonomedia, 2005.

33 Kenneth Arrow, *Social Choice and Individual Values*, New Haven, CT: Yale University Press, 1963; Jane Mansbridge, "What Is Political Science For?" *Perspectives on Politics* 12: 1, 2014, 8–17.

34 Quoted in Phil McKenna, "No Voting System Is Perfect, but Why do We Put Up with One of the Worst?" *New Scientist*, April 12, 2008, 33.

35 For some discussion of the background of this quote, see Richard M. Langworth, "Democracy is the Worst Form of Government . . .," June 26, 2009, richardlangworth.com.

36 For the larger quotation in context, see "(1857) Frederick Douglass, 'If There Is no Struggle, There Is no Progress,'" BlackPast, January 25, 2007, blackpast.org.

37 John Wall, "Why Children and Youth Should Have the Right to Vote: An Argument for Proxy-Claim Suffrage," *Children Youth and Environments* 24: 1, 2014, 108–23.

38 Carol Anderson, "The Five Ways Republicans Will Crack Down on Voting Rights in 2020," *The Guardian*, November 13, 2019, theguardian.com.

39 Martin Gilens, *Affluence and Influence*, Princeton, NJ: Princeton University Press, 2012.

40 Principal-agent models apply a more specific definition of agent than the one used in Chapter 2.

41 The classic formulation remains Armen A. Alchian and Harold Demsetz, "Production, Information Costs, and Economic Organization," *American Economic Review* 62: 5, 1972, 777–95.

42 Samuel Bowles and Herbert Gintis, "A Political and Economic Case for the Democratic Enterprise," *Economics and Philosophy* 9, 1993, 75–100; Gregory K. Dow, *Governing the Firm*, New York: Cambridge University Press, 2003.

43 Joseph R. Blasi, Richard B. Freeman, and Douglas L. Kruse, *The Citizen's Share*, New Haven, CT: Yale University Press, 2014.

44 Samuel Bowles, "The Production Process in a Competitive Economy: Walrasian, Neo-Hobbesian, and Marxian Models," *American Economic Review* 75: 1, 1985, 16–36.

45 Elissa Braunstein and Nancy Folbre, "To Honor or Obey: The Patriarch as Residual Claimant," *Feminist Economics* 7: 1, 2001, 25–54.

46 For a simple but compelling illustration of this point, see Robin Hahnel, *The ABCs of Political Economy*, London: Pluto Press, 2002, 106.

47 On acts against the education of slaves in the US South, see material on the Thirteen Media with Impact Site, pbs.org.

48 Harry Braverman, *Labor and Monopoly Capital*, New York: Monthly Review Press, 1974; Peter Skott and Frederick Guy, "A Model of Power-Biased Technological Change," *Economics Letters* 95: 1, 2007, 124–31.

49 John Rawls, *A Theory of Justice*, Cambridge, MA: Harvard University Press, 1971.

50  Amartya Sen, "Cooperation, Inequality, and the Family," *Population and Development Review* 15, 1989, 61–76.

51  Charles W. Mills, *The Racial Contract*, Ithaca, NY: Cornell University Press, 1999.

52  For a discerning explanation of lock-in, see W. Brian Arthur, "Self-Reinforcing Mechanisms in Economics," in *The Economy as an Evolving Complex System*, Philip W. Anderson, Kenneth J. Arrow, and David Pines, eds., , New York: Addison-Wesley, 1988, 9–31.

53  On rent-seeking, see J. M. Buchanan, R. D. Tollison, and G. Tullock, *Toward a Theory of the Rent-Seeking Society*, College Station: Texas A and M Press, 1980.

54  For a more detailed discussion of "just deserts" and its imbrications in the neoclassical theory of marginal productivity, see Nancy Folbre, "Just Deserts? Earnings Inequality and Bargaining Power in the US Economy," Washington Center for Equitable Growth Working Paper, 2016, equitablegrowth.org.

55  In technical terms, the model outlined here represents a cooperative Nash-bargaining approach, described in more detail in William D. Ferguson, *Collective Action and Exchange*, Stanford, CA: Stanford University Press, 2013, Chapter 4.

56  See discussion in Ferguson, *Collective Action and Exchange*, Chapter 4.

57  In mathematical terms, assume that the relative number of leaders and followers is the same in both groups, and let democratic output be Y and followers' share be $\lambda$; let authoritarian output be Z and followers' share be $\pi$. Followers are equally well-off if $\lambda Y = \pi Z$. As long as the ratio of $Y/Z = \pi/\lambda$, they will be equally well-off even if Z is greater than Y.

58  Albert Hirschman discusses some but not all of these options in *Exit, Voice and Loyalty*, Cambridge: Harvard University Press, 1970.

59  Karl Marx, *Capital*, Vol. 1, Chapter 26, marxists.org.

60  Naila Kabeer, "Gender Equality and Women's Empowerment: A Critical Analysis of the Third Millennium Development Goal 1," *Gender & Development* 13: 1, 2005, 13–24.

61  Leslie McCall, "The Complexity of Intersectionality," *Signs* 30: 3, 2005, 1771–1800.

62  Maria Mazzucato, *The Value of Everything*, New York: Penguin, 2018.

63  Erik Olin Wright, *Class Counts: Comparative Studies in Class Analysis*, New York: Cambridge University Press, 1997, 11.

64  APM Research Lab Staff, "The Color of Coronavirus: Covid-19 Deaths by Race and Ethnicity in the U.S.," APM Research Lab, June 24, 2020, apmresearchlab.org.

65  Benjamin Ferguson, "Exploitation and Disadvantage," *Economics & Philosophy* 32: 3, 2016, 485–509.

66  See, for instance, William Darity Jr. and Darrick Hamilton, "Bold Policies for Economic Justice," *The Review of Black Political Economy* 39: 1, 2012, 79–85.

67  Karl Marx, *Capital*, Vol. 1, Chapter 26, New York: Vintage Books, 1976; David Harvey, "The 'New Imperialism': Accumulation by Dispossession," *Socialist Register* 40, 2004, 63–87.

68  Robert Nozick, *Anarchy, State and Utopia*, Malden, MA: Basic Books, 1974.

69  William Darity, "Forty Acres and a Mule in the 21st Century," *Social Science Quarterly* 89: 3, 2008, 656–64.

70  John Roemer, *A General Theory of Exploitation and Class*, Cambridge, MA: Harvard University Press, 1982. The adjective "alienable" is relevant here because human capital is also a productive asset, but not one that can be redistributed within a single generation.

71  Robert E. Goodin, "Women's Work: Its Irreplaceability and Exploitability," in *Illusion of Consent: Engaging with Carole Pateman*, Daniel I. O'Neill, Mary Lyndon Shanley, and Iris Marion Young, eds., University Park: Pennsylvania State Press, 2008.

72  Erik Wright, *Envisioning Real Utopias*, London: Verso, 2010, 26.

73  See the discussion in Ferguson, *Collective Action and Exchange*, Chapter 4.

74  Marjorie McElroy, "The Empirical Content of Nash-Bargained Household Behavior," *Journal of Human Resources* 25: 4, 1990, 559–83; Nancy Folbre, "Gender Coalitions: Extrafamily Influences on Intrafamily Inequality," in *Intrahousehold Resource Allocation in Developing Countries: Methods, Models and Policy*, Lawrence Haddad, John Hoddinott, and Harold Alderman, eds., Baltimore: Johns Hopkins University Press, 1998; P. A. Chiappori, B. Fortin, and G. Lacroix, "Marriage Market, Divorce Legislation and Household Labor Supply," *Journal of Political Economy* 110, 2002, 37–72.

75  See karrass.com.

76  Samuel Bowles and Herbert Gintis, "The Revenge of Homo Economicus: Contested Exchange and the Revival of Political Economy," *The Journal of Economic Perspectives* 7: 1, 1993, 83–102.

77  Bina Agarwal, "Bargaining and Gender Relations: Within and Beyond the Household," *Feminist Economics* 3: 1, 1997, 1–51.

78  Shelly Lundberg and Robert A. Pollak, "Efficiency in Marriage," *Review of Economics of the Household* 1: 3, 2003, 153–67.

79  For a classic description, see Pierre Bourdieu, *Outline of a Theory of Practice*, New York: Cambridge University Press, 1977. See also Edward Ross, *Social Control: A Survey of the Foundations of Order*, New York: The Macmillan Company, 1901.

80  Edna Ullmann-Margalit, *The Emergence of Norms,* Oxford: Clarendon Press, 1977, 189.

81  Paula Ionide, *The Emotional Politics of Racism*, Stanford, CA: Stanford University Press, 2015; Richard Sennett and Jonathan Cobb, *The Hidden Injuries of Class*, New York: Norton, 1993.

82  See, for instance, Karla Hoff and Priyanka Pandey, "Discrimination, Social Identity, and Durable Inequalities," *American Economic Review* 96: 2, 2006, 206–11.

83  Paula England, "Sometimes the Social Becomes Personal," *American Sociological Review* 81: 1, 2016; Paula England and Irene Browne, "Internalization and Constraint in Women's Subordination," *Current Perspectives in Social Theory* 12, 1992, 97–123. Frantz Fanon, *The Wretched of the Earth*, New York: Grove Press, 1968.

# Chapter 6. Patriarchal Ascents

1  Maria Mies, *Patriarchy and Accumulation on a World Scale*, New York: Zed, 1986; Gerda Lerner, *The Creation of Patriarchy*, New York: Oxford University Press, 1986; Riane Eisler, *The Chalice and the Blade*, New York: Harper, 1988

2  See for instance, Colin Farrelly, "Patriarchy and Historical Materialism," *Hypatia* 26: 1, 2011, 1–21.

3  Relatively recent popular accounts of "big history" that explore gendered themes include Malcolm Potts, Martha Campbell, and Thomas Hayden, *Sex and War*, Dallas: Benbella, 2008; Stephen Pinker, *The Better Angels of Our Nature*, New York: Penguin, 2011; and David Christian, *Maps of Time*, Berkeley: University of California Press, 2011.

4  Kimberly A. Hamlin, *From Eve to Evolution*, Chicago: University of Chicago Press, 2015.

5  Charlotte Perkins Gilman, *Women and Economics*, Carl N. Degler, ed., New York: Harper and Row, 1966. (Original work published 1898)

6  Leta Hollingworth, "Social Devices for Impelling Women to Bear and Rear Children," *American Journal of Sociology* 22: 1, 1916, 19.

7  Frederick Engels, *The Origin of the Family, Private Property and the State*, New York: Pathfinder, 1972. (Original work published 1884)

8  August Bebel, *Woman Under Socialism*, translated from the original German of the 33rd edition by Daniel De Leon, New York: Schocken Books, 1971.

9  James C. Scott, *Against the Grain: A Deep History of the Earliest States*, New Haven, CT: Yale University Press, 2017.

10  Maria Mies, *Patriarchy and Accumulation on a World Scale*, New York: Zed, 1986.

11  Riane Eisler, *The Chalice and the Blade*, New York: Harper, 1988. This book draws from Marija Gimbutas, *The Goddesses and Gods of Old Europe*, Berkeley: University of California Press, 1982.

12  Plutarch, *The Lives of the Noble Grecians and Romans*, translated by John Dryden, New York: Modern Library, 1992.

13  For a fascinating discussion of endogamy and caste systems in modern India, see Janaki Abraham, "Contingent Caste Endogamy and Patriarchy," *Economic and Political Weekly* XLIX: 2, 2014, 56–65.

14 Susan Brooks Thistlewaite, "You May Enjoy the Spoil of Your Enemies: Rape as a Biblical Metaphor for War," *Semeia* 61, 1993, 59–78.

15 Numbers 31, King James Version of the *Old Testament*, biblegateway.com.

16 Sandie Gravett, "Reading 'Rape' in the Hebrew Bible: A Consideration of Language," *Journal for the Study of the Old Testament* 28: 3, 2004, 279–99.

17 Friedrich Nietzsche, *Thus Spoke Zarathustra*, Adrian Del Caro and Robert B. Pippin, eds., translated by Adrian Del Caro, New York: Cambridge University Press, 2006, Chapter 18.

18 Among evolutionary psychologists, see David M. Buss, *Evolutionary Psychology*, 5th ed., New York: Routledge, 2015; Leda Cosmides and John Tooby, "Better than Rational: Evolutionary Psychology and the Invisible Hand," *American Economic Review* 84: 2, 1994, 327–32. Among feminist psychologists, see Alice H. Eagly and Wendy Wood, "The Social Role Theory of Sex Differences," in *Encyclopedia of Gender and Sexuality Studies*, New York: Wiley and Sons, 2016.

19 Bruce Winterhalder and Eric Alden Smith, "Analyzing Adaptive Strategies: Human Behavioral Ecology at Twenty-Five," *Evolutionary Anthropology* 9: 2, 2000, 51–72; R. Boyd and P. J. Richerson, *Culture and the Evolutionary Process*, Chicago: University of Chicago Press, 1985.

20 Elizabeth Kolbert, *The Sixth Extinction*, New York: Henry Holt, 2014.

21 Lars Rodseth and Shannon A. Novak, "The Impact of Primatology on the Study of Human Society," in *Missing the Revolution*, Jerome Barkow, ed., New York: Oxford, 2006, 187–220.

22 Sarah Blaffer Hrdy, *Mother Nature*, New York: Pantheon, 1999.

23 Patricia Adair Gowaty, "Power Asymmetries Between the Sexes, Mate Preferences, and Components of Fitness," in *Evolution, Gender, and Rape*, Cheryl Brown Travis, ed., Cambridge, MA: The MIT Press, 2003, 61–86; "Sexual Dialectics, Sexual Selection, and Variation in Reproductive Behavior," in *Feminism and Evolutionary Biology*, Patricia Adair Gowaty, ed., New York: Chapman and Hall, 1997, 351–84.

24 Barbara Smuts, "Male Aggression Against Women: An Evolutionary Perspective," *Human Nature* 3, 1992, 1–44; "The Evolutionary Origins of Patriarchy," *Human Nature* 6: 1, 1995, 1–32.

25 Kathleen Sterling, "Man the Hunter, Woman the Gatherer? The Impact of Gender Studies on Hunter Gatherer Research (A Retrospective)," in *The Oxford Handbook of the Archaeology and Anthropology of Hunter Gatherers*, Vicki Cummings, Peter Jordan, Marek Zvelebil, eds., New York: Oxford, 2014.

26 Hillard S. Kaplan and Jane B. Lancaster, "An Evolutionary and Ecological Analysis of Human Fertility, Mating Patterns, and Parental Investment," in *Offspring: Human Fertility Behavior in Biodemographic Perspective*, Kenneth W. Wachter and Rodolfo A. Bulatao, eds., Washington: National Research Council, 2003, 170–223.

27 Robert W. Sussman and Roberta L. Hall, "Addendum: Child Transport, Family Size, and Increase in Human Population During the Neolithic,"

*Current Anthropology* 13: 2, 1972, 258–67; George J. Armelagos, Alan H. Goodman, and Kenneth H. Jacobs, "The Origins of Agriculture: Population Growth during a Period of Declining Health," *Population and Environment* 13: 1, 1991, 9–22.

28 Laurence J. Kirmayer, Christopher Fletcher, and Lucy J. Boothroyd, "Suicide Among the Inuit of Canada," in *Suicide in Canada,* Antoon A. Leenaars, Susanne Wenckstern, Isaac Sakinofsky, Ron Dyck, Michael J. Kral, and Roger Bland, eds., Toronto: University of Toronto Press, 1998, 189–211.

29 Eleanor Leacock, "Women's Status in Egalitarian Society: Implications for Social Evolution," *Current Anthropology* 19: 2, 1978, 247–75.

30 Jung–Kyoo Choi and Samuel Bowles, "The Coevolution of Parochial Altruism and War," *Science* 318: 5850, October 26, 2007, 636–40.

31 Pinker, *The Better Angels of Our Nature,* 678.

32 Jared Diamond, *Guns, Germs, and Steel,* New York: W. W. Norton, 1999.

33 Kyle Summers, "The Evolutionary Ecology of Despotism," *Evolution and Human Behavior* 26, 2005, 106–35.

34 Adrienne Mayor, "Animals in Warfare," in *The Oxford Handbook of Animals in Classical Thought and Life,* Gordon Lindsay Campbell, ed., New York: Oxford University Press, 2014.

35 S. C. Gwynne, *Empire of the Summer Moon,* New York: Simon and Schuster, 2010.

36 Adrienne Mayor, *The Amazons,* Princeton, NJ: Princeton University Press, 2014.

37 Claude Lévi-Strauss, *The Elementary Structures of Kinship,* Boston: Beacon, 1969; Claude Meillasoux, *Maidens, Meal and Money,* New York: Cambridge University Press, 1981.

38 Luke Glowacki, Michael L. Wilson, and Richard W. Wrangham, "The Evolutionary Anthropology of War," *Journal of Economic Behavior and Organization,* 2017, sciencedirect.com.

39 Michelle Scalise Sugiyama, "Fitness Costs of Warfare for Women," *Human Nature* 25, 2014, 476–95.

40 William Tulio Divale and Marvin Harris, "Population, Warfare, and the Male Supremacist Complex," *American Anthropologist* 78: 3, 1976, 521–38.

41 See, for instance, David Eaton, *Violence, Revenge and the History of Cattle Raiding along the Kenya–Uganda Border,* Halifax, Nova Scotia: Dalhousie University, 2008.

42 Barbara Rogers, *The Domestication of Women,* New York: Routledge, 2005.

43 Dorothy L. Hodgson, "Pastoralism, Patriarchy and History: Changing Gender Relations among Maasai in Tanganyika, 1890–1940," *The Journal of African History* 40: 1, 1999, 41–65.

44 On male mate-guarding, see David Buss, *The Evolution of Desire,* New York: Basic Books, 2003.

45 Malcolm Potts, Martha Campbell, and Thomas Hayden, *Sex and War,* Dallas: Benbella, 2008.

46 Timothy Earle, *How Chiefs Come to Power*, Stanford, CA: Stanford University Press, 1997; Napoleon Chagnon, *Yanomamo: The Fierce People*, 3rd ed., New York: Holt, Rinehart, and Winston, 1983.

47 Daron Acemoglu and James Robinson, *Why Nations Fail*, New York: Crown, 2012.

48 Eric Alden Smith, Kim Hill, Frank Marlowe, David Nolin, Polly Wiessner, Michael Gurven, Samuel Bowles, Monique Borgerhoff Mulder, Tom Hertz, and Adrian Bell, "Wealth Transmission and Inequality among Hunter-Gatherers," *Current Anthropology* 51: 1, 2010, 19–34; Amy Bogaard, Mattia Fochesato, and Samuel Bowles, "The Farming-Inequality Nexus: New Methods and Evidence from Western Eurasia," 93: 371, 2019, 1129–43.

49 Ian Hodder, "Çatalhöyük: The Leopard Changes its Spots. A Summary of Recent Work," *Anatolian Studies* 64, 2014, 1–22.

50 Ian Hodder, "Women and Men at Çatalhöyük," *Scientific American* 290: 1, 2004, 76–83.

51 Robert Carneiro, "A Theory of the Origin of the State," *Science* 169: 3947, August 21, 1970, 733–38.

52 Ian Frazier, "Invaders," *The New Yorker*, April 5, 2005, newyorker.com.

53 Bo Li and Yin Zheng, *50000 Years of Chinese History*, Inner Mongolia, China: Inner Mongolian People's Publishing, 2001, 925. (in Chinese)

54 Ester Boserup, *The Conditions of Agricultural Growth*, London: Allen and Unwin, 1965; D. B. Grigg, *Population Growth and Agrarian Change*, New York: Cambridge University Press, 1980.

55 Hillard Kaplan, "Evolutionary and Wealth Flows Theories of Fertility: Empirical Tests and New Models," *Population and Development Review* 20: 4, 1994, 753–91.

56 Nancy Folbre, "Of Patriarchy Born: The Political Economy of Fertility Decisions," *Feminist Studies* 9: 2, 1983, 261–84.

57 Judith Blake, "Coercive Pronatalism and American Population Policy," in *Aspects of Population Growth Policy*, R. Parke and C. F. Westoff, eds., Vol. 6 of The Commission on Population Growth and the American Future Research Reports, Washington, DC: US Government Printing Office, 1972, 81–109; Adrienne Rich, "Compulsory Heterosexuality and Lesbian Existence," *Signs* 5: 4, 1980, 631–60.

58 Laura L. Betzig, *Despotism and Differential Reproduction*, New York: Aldine, 1986.

59 Claude Meillassoux, *Maidens, Meal and Money: Capitalism and the Domestic Community*, New York: Cambridge University Press, 1981; Gerda Lerner, *The Creation of Patriarchy*, New York: Oxford University Press, 1986.

60 Esther K. Hicks, *Infibulation: Female Mutilation in Islamic Northeastern Africa*, New York: Transaction, 1993.

61 Lucia Corno, Eliana La Ferrara, and Alessandra Voena, "The Historical Roots of Female Genital Cutting," paper presented at the meetings of the Allied Social Science Association, San Diego, CA, January 3, 2020.

62  Orlando Patterson, *Slavery and Social Death*, Cambridge, MA: Harvard University Press, 1985

63  Karl Marx, "The Life-Destroying Toil of Slaves," in *The Karl Marx Library*, Vol. II: *On America and the Civil War*, Saul K. Padover, ed., New York: McGraw-Hill, 1972; Eric Williams, *Capitalism and Slavery*, Chapel Hill: University of North Carolina Press, 1944; Edward E. Baptist, *The Half Has Never Been Told: Slavery and the Making of American Capitalism*, New York: Basic Books, 2014.

64  Steven Jay Gould, "The Geometer of Race," *Discover*, November 1994, 65–68.

65  Christine B. Hickman, "The Devil and the One Drop Rule: Racial Categories, African Americans, and the U.S. Census," *Michigan Law Review* 95: 5, 1997, 1161–265.

66  Theodore W. Allen, *The Construction of the White Race*, London: Verso, 1997.

67  Pamela D. Bridgewater, "Un/Re/Dis Covering Slave Breeding in Thirteenth Amendment Jurisprudence," *Washington and Lee Journal of Civil Rights and Social Justice* 7: 1, 2001, 11–43.

68  Robert Fogel, *Without Consent or Contract: The Rise and Fall of American Slavery*, New York: W. W. Norton, 1989.

69  Fogel, *Without Consent or Contract*.

70  Andrew F. Hanssen and Robert K. Fleck, "Rulers Ruled by Women: An Economic Analysis of the Rise and Fall of Women's Rights in Ancient Sparta," *Economic Governance* 10 (2009), 221–45.

71  Hanssen and Fleck, "Rulers Ruled by Women."

72  Perry Anderson, *Passages from Antiquity to Feudalism*, London: Verso, 1996.

73  See, for instance, Chris Middleton, "Peasants, Patriarchy and the Feudal Mode of Production in England: 2 Feudal Lords and the Subordination of Peasant Women," *The Sociological Review* 29: 1, 1981, 137–54.

74  Gordon J. Schochet, *Patriarchalism in Political Thought: The Authoritarian Family and Political Speculation and Attitudes, Especially in l7th Century England*, Oxford: Blackwell, 1975.

75  Jean Bodin, *The Six Books of a Commonweal*, Kenneth Douglas McRae, ed., Cambridge: Harvard University Press, 1962, 20–30. (Facsimile reprint of the English translation of 1606)

76  F. L. Carsten, ed., *The New Cambridge Modern History*, Vol. V. *The Ascendancy of France, 1648–88*, Cambridge: Cambridge University Press, 1961, 105.

77  Sir Robert Filmer, "Observations Upon Aristotle's Politics," in *Patriarcha and Other Political Works*, Peter Laslett, ed., Oxford: Basil Blackwell, 1949.

78  Ester Boserup, *The Conditions of Agricultural Growth*, London: Allen & Unwin, 1965.

79  Wally Seccombe, *A Millennium of Family Change*, New York: Verso, 1992.

80 Silvia Federici, *Caliban and the Witch*, New York: Autonomedia, 2004, 189.

81 Federici, *Caliban and the Witch*, 14.

82 Wally Seccombe, *A Millennium of Family Change*, New York: Verso, 1993. See also his *Weathering the Storm*, New York: Verso, 1993.

83 Weijing Lu, "Women, Gender, the Family, and Sexuality," in *A Companion to Chinese History*, Michael Szonyi, ed., New York: John Wiley and Sons, 2017, 207–20.

84 See discussion in Chapter 2 of Steven Cheung, "The Enforcement of Property Rights in Children and the Marriage Contract," *Economic Journal* 82: 326, 1972, 641–57.

85 James Z. Lee and Cameron D. Campbell, *Fate and Fortune in Rural China*, New York: Cambridge University Press, 2007.

86 Gerry Mackie, "Ending Footbinding and Infibulation: A Convention Account," *American Sociological Review* 61: 6, 1996, 999–1017.

87 Uma Chakravarti, "Conceptualising Brahmanical Patriarchy in Early India: Gender, Caste, Class and State," *Economic and Political Weekly* 28: 14, April 3, 1993, 585.

88 Janaki Abraham, "Contingent Caste Endogamy and Patriarchy," *Economic and Political Weekly* 49: 2, 2014, 56–65.

89 Leila Ahmed, *Women and Gender in Islam*, New Haven, CT: Yale University Press, 1992.

90 Lena Edlund, "Cousin Marriage Is Not Choice: Muslim Marriage and Underdevelopment," *American Economic Review* 108, 2018, 353–57.

91 Elissa Braunstein, "Patriarchy versus Islam: Gender and Religion in Economic Growth," *Feminist Economics* 20: 4, 2014, 58–86.

92 Diamond, *Guns, Germs, and Steel*.

93 Douglass North and R. P. Thomas, *The Rise of the Western World: A New Economic History*, Cambridge: Cambridge University Press, 1973; Nathan Rosenberg and L. E. Birdzall, Jr., *How the West Grew Rich, The Economic Transformation of the Industrial World*, New York: Basic Books, 1986.

94 See, for instance, Eric Williams, *Capitalism and Slavery*, Chapel Hill: University of North Carolina Press, 1944; Serap A. Kayateikin, "Between Political Economy and Postcolonial Theory: First Encounters," *Cambridge Journal of Economics* 33: 6, 2009, 1113–18.

95 Dennis O. Flynn, "Fiscal Crisis and the Decline of Spain (Castile)," *Journal of Economic History* 42: 1, 1982, 139–47.

96 For a particularly compelling account of royal corruption, see Adam Hochschild, *King Leopold's Ghost*, New York: Mariner Books, 1998.

97 E. Zein-Elabdin, "Economics, Postcolonial Theory, and the Problem of Culture: Institutional Analysis and Hybridity," *Cambridge Journal of Economics* 33: 6, 2009, 1153–67.

98 John A. Crow, *The Epic of Latin America*, Berkeley: University of California Press, 1992.

99  June Nash, "Aztec Women: The Transition from Status to Class in Empire and Colony," in *Women and Colonization: Anthropological Perspectives*, Mona Etienne and Eleanor Leacock, eds., New York: Bergin and Garvey, 1980, l34–48.

100 Crow, *The Epic of Latin America*, 150.

101 Ann Stoler, "Carnal Knowledge and Imperial Power: Gender, Race, and Morality in Colonial Asia," in *Gender at the Crossroads of Knowledge: Feminist Anthropology in the Postmodern Era*, Micaela di Leonardo, ed., Berkeley: University of California Press, 1991, 58.

102 Stoler, "Carnal Knowledge and Imperial Power," 79.

103 Kenneth Ballhatchet, *Race, Sex, and Class under the Raj*, New York: St. Martin's Press, 1980, 98.

104 Ballhatchet, *Race, Sex, and Class*, 14.

105 Vrushali Patil, "From Patriarchy to Intersectionality: A Transnational Feminist Assessment of How Far We've Really Come," *Signs* 38: 4, 2013, 847–67; Anthony Pagden, *Lords of All the World: Ideologies of Empire in Spain, Britain, and France, c.1500–c.1800*, New Haven, CT: Yale University Press, 1995.

106 Ashis Nandy, *Traditions, Tyranny and Utopias*, Delhi: Oxford University Press, 1987.

107 Evelyn Nakano Glenn, "Settler Colonialism as Structure: A Framework for Comparative Studies of US Race and Gender Formation," *Sociology of Race and Ethnicity* 1: 1, 2015, 52–72.

108 See, for instance, Bernard Magubane, "The Native Reserves (Bantustans) and the Role of the Migrant Labor System in the Political Economy of South Africa," in *The World as a Company Town: Multinational Corporations and Social Change*, Elizabeth Idris-Soven and Mary K. Vaughan, eds., Berlin: de Gruyter, 1978.

109 Luise White, *The Comforts of Home: Prostitution in Colonial Nairobi*, Chicago: University of Chicago Press, 1990.

110 Eleanor Leacock, "Interpreting the Origins of Gender Inequality: Conceptual and Historical Problems," *Dialectical Anthropology* 7: 4, 1983, 263–84.

111 Benedict Carton, *Blood from Your Children: The Colonial Origins of Generational Conflict in South Africa*, Charlottesville: University of Virginia Press, 2000.

112 Dorothy L. Hodgson, "Pastoralism, Patriarchy and History: Changing Gender Relations among Maasai in Tanganyika, 1890–1940," *The Journal of African History* 40: 1, 1999, 41–65.

113 Nancy Folbre, "Patriarchal Social Formations in Zimbabwe," in *Patriarchy and Class in Africa*, Sharon Stichter and Jane Parpart, eds., New York: Sage, 1997, 61–80.

114 Debbie Budlender and Francie Lund, "South Africa: A Legacy of Family Disruption," *Development and Change* 42: 4, 2011, 925–46.

115 Erik Kades, "The Dark Side of Efficiency: Johnson v. M'Intosh and the Expropriation of American Indian Lands," *University of Pennsylvania Law Review* 148: 4, 2000, 1065–190.

116 Suad Joseph, *Gender and Citizenship in the Middle East*, Syracuse, NY: Syracuse University Press, 2000.
117 Max Fisher, "The Real Roots of Sexism in the Middle East (It's Not Islam, Race, or 'Hate')," *Atlantic*, April 25, 2012, theatlantic.com.
118 Ella Shohat, "Area Studies, Transnationalism, and the Feminist Production of Knowledge," *Signs* 26: 4, 2001, 1270.
119 Diskin Clay and Andrea L. Purvis, *Four Island Utopias*, Newburyport, MA: Focus Publications/R. Pullins, 1999.
120 Phillip W. Porter and Eric S. Sheppard, *A World of Difference*, New York: Guilford Press, 1998, 108.

## Chapter 7. Capitalist Trajectories

1 Joseph A. Schumpeter, *Capitalism, Socialism and Democracy*, London: Routledge, 1994, 82–83.
2 Andrew Ure, *The Philosophy of Manufactures*, New York: Augustus M. Kelley, 1967, 475. (Original work published 1835)
3 Nancy Folbre, *Greed, Lust, and Gender*, New York: Oxford University Press, 2009.
4 Chandra Mohanty, "Under Western Eyes, Revisited. Feminist Solidarity Through Anticapitalist Struggles," *Signs* 28: 2, 2003, 499–535.
5 Rhonda M. Williams, "Capital, Competition, and Discrimination: A Reconsideration of Racial Earnings Inequality," *Review of Radical Political Economics* 19: 2, 1987, 1–15; Rhonda M. Williams and Robert E. Kenison, "The Way We Were? Discrimination, Competition, and Inter-Industry Wage Differentials in 1970," *Review of Radical Political Economics* 28: 2, 1996, 1–31.
6 For a thoughtful discussion of varying definitions applied to the US context, see Michael Merrill, "Putting Capitalism in its Place: A Review of Recent Literature," *The William and Mary Quarterly* 52: 2, 1994, 315–26.
7 On the persistence of primitive accumulation, see David Harvey, "The 'New Imperialism': Accumulation by Dispossession," *Socialist Register* 40, 2004, 63–87.
8 See, for instance, Anibal Quijano, "Coloniality of Power and Eurocentrism in Latin America," *International Sociology* 15: 2, 2000, 215–32.
9 Ashley Bohrer, "Intersectionality and Marxism: A Critical Historiography," *Historical Materialism* 26: 2, 2018, historicalmaterialism.org.
10 Tithi Bhattacharya, "Introduction: Mapping Social Reproduction Theory," in *Social Reproduction Theory*, Tithi Bhattacharya, ed., London: Pluto, 2017, 1–20.
11 Susan B. Carter, "Labor," in *Historical Statistics of the United States*, Millennial Edition, Susan B. Carter, Scott S. Gartner, Michael Haines, Alan Olmstead, Richard Sutch, and Gavin Wright, eds., New York:

Cambridge University Press, 2004; Phyllis Deane, *The First Industrial Revolution*, New York: Cambridge University Press, 1979, 162; Ronald Aminzade, "Reinterpreting Capitalist Industrialization: A Study of Nineteenth-Century France," *Social History* 9: 3, 1984, 329–50.

12 Jane Humphries, "Enclosures, Common Rights, and Women: The Proletarianization of Families in the Late Eighteenth and Early Nineteenth Centuries," *Journal of Economic History* 50: 1, 1990, 17–42; Marjorie Abel and Nancy Folbre, "Women's Market Participation in the Late 19th Century: A Methodology for Revising Estimates," *Historical Methods* 23: 4, 1990, 167–76; Nancy Folbre, "Informal Market Work in Massachusetts, 1875–1920," *Social Science History* 17: 1, 1993, 135–60.

13 Nancy Folbre, "The Unproductive Housewife: Her Evolution in Nineteenth-Century Economic Thought," *Signs: Journal of Women in Culture and Society* 16: 3, 1991, 463–84.

14 Steven Ruggles, "Patriarchy, Power, and Pay: The Transformation of American Families, 1800–2015," *Demography* 52: 6, 2015, 1797–823.

15 Nancy Folbre and Barnet Wagman, "Counting Housework: New Estimates of Real Product in the U.S., 1800–1860," *Journal of Economic History* 53: 2, 1993, 275–88. Barnet Wagman and Nancy Folbre, "Household Services and Economic Growth in the U.S., 1870–1930," *Feminist Economics* 2: 1, 1996, 43–66.

16 Steven Ruggles, "Patriarchy, Power, and Pay."

17 Isis Gaddis and Stephan Klasen, "Economic Development, Structural Change, and Women's Labor Force Participation," *Journal of Population Economics* 27: 3, 2014, 639–81.

18 Gary S. Fields, "Self-employment and Poverty in Developing Countries," *IZA World of Labor*, 2019, wol.iza.org.

19 Stephan Klasen and Janneke Pieters, *What Explains the Stagnation of Female Labor Force Participation in Urban India?* Washington, DC: The World Bank, 2015.

20 Denise Hare, "What Accounts for the Decline in Labor Force Participation Among Married Women in Urban China, 1991–2011?" *China Economic Review* 38, 2016, 251–66; Lan Liu, Xiao-yuan Dong, and Xiaoying Zheng. "Parental Care and Married Women's Labor Supply in Urban China," *Feminist Economics* 16: 3, 2010, 169–92.

21 Gargi Bhattacharya, *Rethinking Racial Capitalism*, New York: Rowman and Littlefield, 2018; Kalyan Sanyal, *Rethinking Capitalist Development*, New York: Routledge, 2007.

22 International Labour Office, *Status in Employment*, May 2018, ilo.org. Contributing family workers, mostly women and children, are defined as those employed in a family enterprise who are not considered full partners.

23 International Labour Office, *Labour Market Access—A Persistent Challenge for Youth All Around the World*, Geneva: Author, ilo.org.

24  International Labour Office, *Care Work and Care Jobs*, Geneva: Author, 2018, Table A.3.1. See, for instance, totals for the United States, Canada, United Kingdom, and France. See also Table 1, Time spent in detailed primary activities and percent of the civilian population engaging in each activity, averages per day by sex, 2016 annual averages, American Time Use Survey, US Bureau of Labor Statistics, bls.gov.

25  International Labour Office, *Care Work and Care Jobs*; see totals for China, India, Ecuador, and Ghana.

26  Bina Agarwal, *A Field of One's Own: Gender and Land Rights in South Asia*, New York: Cambridge University Press, 1994.

27  Carmen Diana Deere and Magdalena León de Leal, *Empowering Women: Land and Property Rights in Latin America*, Pittsburgh: University of Pittsburgh Press, 2014. Cheryl Doss, Chiara Kovarik, Amber Peterman, Agnes Quisumbing, and Mara van den Bold, "Gender Inequalities in Ownership and Control of Land in Africa: Myth and Reality," *Agricultural Economics* 46: 3, 2015, 403–34.

28  Christopher Middleton, "The Sexual Division of Labour in Feudal England," *New Left Review* 113, 1979, 147–68.

29  Ivy Pinchbeck, *Women Workers in the Industrial Revolution*, New York: Routledge, 2013. (Original work published 1930) Jane Humphries and Jacob Weisdorf, "The Wages of Women in England, 1260–1850," *The Journal of Economic History* 75: 2, 2015, 405–47.

30  Katherine A. Moos, "The Political Economy of State Regulation: The Case of the English Factory Acts," unpublished manuscript, Department of Economics, University of Massachusetts, Amherst, 2017.

31  Wally Seccombe, "Patriarchy Stabilized: The Construction of the Male Breadwinner Wage Norm," *Social History* 11: 1, 1986, 53–76.

32  Jane Humphries, "Class Struggle and the Persistence of the Working-Class Family," *Cambridge Journal of Economics* 1, 1977, 24–58.

33  Friedrich Engels, *The Condition of the Working Class in England*, 1845.

34  Ibid.

35  Folbre, *Greed, Lust and Gender*.

36  Ibid.

37  Stephanie Seguino, "Accounting for Gender in Asian Economic Growth," *Feminist Economics* 6: 3, 2000, 27–58.

38  Cedric Robinson, *Black Marxism*, Chapel Hill: University of North Carolina Press, 2000; Gargi Bhattacharyya, *Rethinking Racial Capitalism*, New York: Rowman and Littlefield, 2018.

39  Ben Johnson, "Rule Britannia," at Historic UK, historic-uk.com.

40  Roxanne Dunbar-Ortiz, *An Indigenous People's History of the U.S.*. Boston: Beacon Press, 2014; Eric Kades, "The Dark Side of Efficiency: Johnson v. M'Intosh and the Expropriation of American Indian Lands," *University of Pennsylvania Law Review* 148: 4, 2000, 1065–190.

41  William Darity Jr., "Forty Acres and a Mule in the 21st Century," *Social Science Quarterly* 89: 3, 2008, 656–64.

42  Edna Bonacich, "A Theory of Ethnic Antagonism: The Split Labor Market," *American Sociological Review* 37, 1972, 547–59; John Roemer, "Divide and Conquer: Microfoundations of the Marxian Theory of Discrimination," *Bell Journal of Economics* 10, August 1979, 695–705; Michael Reich, *Racial Inequality,* Princeton, NJ: Princeton University Press, 1981.

43  Randy Albelda and Chris Tilly, "Towards a Broader Vision: Race, Gender, and Labor Market Segmentation," in David Kotz, Terrence McDonough, and Michael Reich, eds., *Social Structures of Accumulation: The Political Economy of Growth and Crisis,* New York: Cambridge University Press, 1994.

44  Randy P. Albelda, "Occupational Segregation by Race and Gender, 1958–1981," *Industrial and Labor Relations Review* 39: 3, 1986, 404–11; James S. Cunningham and Nadja Zalokar, "The Economic Progress of Black Women, 1940–1980: Occupational Distribution and Relative Wages," *Industrial and Labor Relations Review* 45: 3, 1992, 540–55.

45  Evelyn Nakano Glenn, "From Servitude to Service Work: Historical Continuities in the Racial Division of Paid Reproductive Labor," *Signs* 1, 1992, 1–43.

46  Samuel Bowles and Herbert Gintis, *Schooling in Capitalist America: Educational Reform and the Contradictions of Economic Life,* New York: Basic Books, 1976; Robert Margo, *Race and Schooling in the South, 1880–1950: An Economic History,* Chicago: University of Chicago Press, 1990.

47  Andre Gunder Frank, *The Development of Underdevelopment,* Boston: Free Press, 1966.

48  Daron Acemoglu and James Robinson, *Why Nations Fail,* New York: Crown, 2012.

49  Alice Amsden, *Asia's Next Giant: South Korea and Late Industrialization,* New York: Oxford University Press, 1989.

50  Michael L. Ross, "Oil, Islam, and Women," *American Political Science Review* 102: 1, 2008, 107–23.

51  Timothy J. Hatton and Jeffrey G. Williamson, *Global Migration and the World Economy: Two Centuries of Policy and Performance,* Cambridge, MA: MIT Press, 2006.

52  Pierrette Hondagneu-Sotelo and Cynthia Cranford, "Gender and Migration," in *Handbook of the Sociology of Gender,* Janet Saltzman Chafetz, ed., New York: Springer, 2008, 105–26.

53  Holly J. McCammon and Karen E. Campbell, "Winning the Vote in the West: The Political Successes of the Women's Suffrage Movements, 1866–1919," *Gender and Society* 15: 1, 2001, 55–82.

54  Thomas Piketty, *Capital in the Twenty-First Century,* Cambridge, MA: Harvard University Press, 2014.

55  Tom Brokaw, *The Greatest Generation,* New York: Random House, 2005.

56  Stephen Marglin and Juliet Schor, eds., *The Golden Age of Capitalism,* Oxford: Clarendon Press, 1991.

57 Ida Kubiszewski, Robert Costanza, Carol Franco, Philip Lawn, John Talberth, Tim Jackson, and Camille Aylmer, "Beyond GDP: Measuring and Achieving Global Genuine Progress," *Ecological Economics* 93, 2013, 57–68.

58 Vrushali Patil, "From Patriarchy to Intersectionality: A Transnational Assessment of How Far We've Really Come," *Signs* 38: 4, 2013, 847–67.

59 Chandra Talpade Mohanty, "Cartographies of Struggle. Third World Women and the Politics of Feminism," in *Third World Women and the Politics of Feminism*, Chandra Talpade Mohanty, Ann Russo, and Lourdes Torres, eds., Bloomington: Indiana University Press, 1991, 1–47.

60 Radha Kumar, *The History of Doing: An Illustrated Account of Movements for Women's Rights and Feminism in India, 1800–1990*, New York: Verso, 1993.

61 Manisha Desai, *Gender and the Politics of Possibilities*, New York: Rowman and Littlefield, 2009.

62 Ashwini Deshpande, *The Grammar of Caste*, New York: Oxford University Press, 2011.

63 Peggy A. Lovell, "Race, Gender, and Development in Brazil," *Latin American Research Review* 29: 3, 1994, 1–36.

64 Amy Chua, *Worlds on Fire*, New York: Doubleday, 2002.

65 Birte Siim and Pauline Stolz, "Particularities of the Nordic: Challenges to Equality Politics in a Globalized World," in *Remapping Gender, Place, and Mobility*, Stine Thidemann Faber and Helene Pristed Nielsen, eds., New York: Routledge, 2016, 19–31.

66 Vera Mackie, *Feminism in Modern Japan*, New York: Cambridge University Press, 2003; Ito Peng, "Gender and Generation: Japanese Child Care and the Demographic Crisis," in *Child Care Policy at the Crossroads: Gender and Welfare State Restructuring*, Sonya Michel and Rianne Mahan, eds., New York: Routledge, 2013, 31–56.

67 Jenny Brown, *Birth Strike: The Hidden Fight over Women's Work*, New York: PM Press, 2019.

68 Joel Mokyr, "Technological Progress and the Decline of European Mortality," *American Economic Review* 83: 2, 1993, 324–30.

69 Wally Seccombe, *Weathering the Storm*, New York: Verso, 1995.

70 Cornelia Usborne, *The Politics of the Body in Weimar Germany: Women's Reproductive Rights and Duties*, New York: Springer, 1992, 9.

71 K. D. Kingsley, "Parents Go On Strike," *The North American Review* 245: 2, 1938, 221–39.

72 Martha J. Bailey, "'Momma's Got the Pill': How Anthony Comstock and Griswold v. Connecticut Shaped US Childbearing," *American Economic Review* 100: 1, 2010, 98–129; Martha J. Bailey, "Fifty Years of Family Planning: New Evidence on the Long-Run Effects of Increasing Access to Contraception," *Brookings Papers on Economic Activity*, Spring 2013, 341–409.

73  Betsy Hartmann, *Reproductive Rights and Wrongs*, Boston: South End Press, 1999; Michelle Goldberg, *The Means of Reproduction*, New York: Penguin, 2009.

74  Stuart Basten and Quanbao Jiang, "Fertility in China: An Uncertain Future," *Population Studies* 69, 2015, S97–S105.

75  George A. Akerlof, Janet L. Yellen, and Michael L. Katz, "An Analysis of Out-of-Wedlock Childbearing in the United States," *Quarterly Journal of Economics* 111: 2, 1996, 277–317.

76  Elissa Braunstein and Nancy Folbre, "To Honor or Obey: The Patriarch as Residual Claimant," *Feminist Economics* 7: 1, 2001, 25–54.

77  R. Geddes and D. Lueck, "The Gains from Self-Ownership and the Expansion of Women's Rights," *American Economic Review* 92: 4, 2002, 1079–92.

78  Matthias Doepke and Michèle Tertilt, "Women's Liberation: What's In It for Men?" *Quarterly Journal of Economics* 124: 4, 2009, 1541.

79  Jocelyn Viterna and Kathleen M. Fallon, "Gender, the State, and Development," in *Handbook of the Sociology of Development*, Gregory Hooks, ed., Berkeley: University of California Press, 2015, 414–39.

80  S. Laurel Weldon and Mala Htun, "Feminist Mobilisation and Progressive Policy Change: Why Governments Take Action to Combat Violence Against Women," *Gender and Development* 21: 2, 2013, 231–47.

81  Barbara Bergmann, *The Economic Emergence of Women*, New York: Basic Books, 1986.

82  Bergmann, *The Economic Emergence of Women*.

83  Nancy Folbre and Julie Nelson, "For Love or Money?" *The Journal of Economic Perspectives* 14: 4, 2000, 123–40.

84  Maria Charles and David B. Grusky, *Occupational Ghettos: The Worldwide Segregation of Women and Men*, Stanford, CA: Stanford University Press, 2004.

85  Charles and Grusky, *Occupational Ghettos*, 204; Paula England, "The Gender Revolution: Uneven and Stalled," *Gender and Society* 24: 2, 2010, 149–66.

86  Susan Pinker, *The Sexual Paradox*, New York: Simon and Schuster, 2009.

87  Piketty, *Capital in the Twenty-First Century*.

88  Samuel Bowles, Herbert Gintis and Melissa Osborne Groves, *Unequal Chances*, Princeton, NJ: Princeton University Press, 2009.

89  On the transmission of human capital, see George Borjas, "Ethnicity, Neighborhoods, and Human-Capital Externalities," *American Economic Review* 85, 1995, 365–90; Shelly J. Lundberg and Richard Startz, "Inequality and Race: Models and Policy," in *Meritocracy and Economic Inequality*, Kenneth Arrow, Samuel Bowles, and Steven Durlauf. eds., Princeton, NJ: Princeton University Press, 2000. On the transmission of financial wealth, see William Darity Jr. and Darrick Hamilton, "Race, Wealth and Intergenerational Poverty," *The American Prospect*, August 14, 2009, prospect.org.

90  William J. Wilson, *The Declining Significance of Race*, Chicago: University of Chicago Press, 1980.

91  Gavin Wright, *Sharing the Prize*, Cambridge, MA: Harvard University Press, 2013.

92  David B. Grusky, Francine D. Blau, and Mary C. Brinton, *The Declining Significance of Gender?* New York: Russell Sage Foundation, 2008.

93  F. D. Blau and L. M. Kahn, "The US Gender Pay Gap in the 1990s: Slowing Convergence," *Industrial and Labor Relations Review* 60, 2006, 45–66; Hadas Mandel and Moshe Semyonov, "Gender Pay Gap and Employment Sector: Sources of Earnings Disparities in the United States, 1970–2010," *Demography* 51, 2014, 1597–618.

94  D. H. Autor, "Skills, Education, and the Rise of Earnings Inequality Among the 'Other 99 Percent.'" *Science* 344: 6186, May 22, 2014, 843–51; Rachel E. Dwyer, "The Care Economy? Gender, Economic Restructuring, and Job Polarization in the U.S. Labor Market," *American Sociological Review* 78: 3, 2013, 390–416.

95  Gail Lapidus, *Women in Soviet Society*, Berkeley: University of California Press, 1978.

96  Lapidus, *Women in Soviet Society*.

97  Diane P. Koenker, "Men against Women on the Shop Floor in Early Soviet Russia: Gender and Class in the Socialist Workplace," *American Historical Review* 100: 5, 1995, 1438–64.

98  Gail Lapidus, "Occupational Segregation and Public Policy: A Comparative Analysis of American and Soviet Patterns," *Signs* 1: 3, Part 2, 1976, 136.

99  "Vladimir Putin Embraces the Russian Church," *The Economist*, February 3, 2018, economist.com.

100 Miriam Elder, "Pussy Riot Sentenced to Two Years in Prison Colony over Anti-Putin Protest," *The Guardian*, August 17, 2012, theguardian.com.

101 Lawrence King, Patrick Hamm, and David Stuckler, "Rapid Large-scale Privatization and Death Rates in Ex-communist Countries: An Analysis of Stress-Related and Health System Mechanisms," *International Journal of Health Services* 39: 3, 2009, 461–89.

102 Andrea Atencio and Josefina Posadas, *Gender Gap in Pay in the Russian Federation: Twenty Years Later, Still a Concern*, Washington, DC: The World Bank, 2015.

103 Eva Fodor and Daniel Horn, "Economic Development and Gender Equality: Explaining Variations in the Gender Poverty Gap after Socialism," *Social Problems* 62: 2, 2015, 286–308.

104 Judith Stacey, "When Patriarchy Kowtows: The Significance of the Chinese Family Revolution for Feminist Theory," *Feminist Studies* 2: 2, 1975, 64–112.

105 Elizabeth Croll, "The Exchange of Women and Property: Marriage in Post-Revolutionary China," in *Women and Property—Women as Property*, Renee Hirschon, ed., London: Croom Helm, 1984, 44–61.

106 H. Liaw, "Women's Land Rights in Rural China: Transforming Existing Laws Into a Source of Property Rights," *Pacific Rim Law and Policy* 17, 2008, 237–64.

107 John Knight, "China as a Developmental State," *World Economy* 37: 10, 2014, 1335–47.

108 Avraham Ebenstein, "The 'Missing Girls' of China and the Unintended Consequences of the One Child Policy," *Journal of Human Resources* 45: 1, 2010, 87–115; Y. Zhang and F. W. Goza, "Who Will Care for the Elderly in China? A Review of the Problems Caused by China's One-Child Policy and Their Potential Solutions," *Journal of Aging Studies* 20: 2, 2006, 151–64; Yu Changyong, Dai Zhiming, and Ma Ruili, "Reality and Expectation: An Empirical Study of Shrinking Family Support for the Elderly in Rural China," *China Rural Survey* 2, 2017, en.cnki.com.cn.

109 Edward Wong, "A Chinese Virtue Is Now the Law," *New York Times*, July 13, 2013, nytimes.com.

110 Vanessa L. Fong, "China's One-Child Policy and the Empowerment of Urban Daughters," *American Anthropologist* 104: 4, 2002, 1098–109.

111 Timothy Hildebrandt, "The One-Child Policy, Elder Care, and LGB Chinese: A Social Policy Explanation for Family Pressure," *Journal of Homosexuality*, 2018, 1–19.

112 Cindy Fan, *China on the Move: Migration, the State, and the Household*, New York: Routledge, 2007.

113 Sarah Cook and Xiao-yuan Dong, "Harsh Choices: Chinese Women's Paid Work and Unpaid Care Responsibilities Under Economic Reform," *Development and Change* 42: 4, 2011, 947–65; Yingchun Ji, Xiaogang Wu, Shengwei Sun, and Guangye He, "Unequal Care, Unequal Work: Toward a More Comprehensive Understanding of Gender Inequality in Post-reform Urban China," *Sex Roles* 77: 11–12, 2017, 765–78.

114 Amy Qin, "A Prosperous China Says 'Men Preferred,' and Women Lose," *New York Times*, July 16, 2019, nytimes.com.

115 Claude Diebolt and Faustine Perrin, "From Stagnation to Sustained Growth: The Role of Female Empowerment," *American Economic Review* 103: 3, 2013, 545–49.

116 George Lee, "Rosa Luxemburg and the Impact of Imperialism," *The Economic Journal* 81: 324, 1971, 847–62.

117 Daron Acemoglu and James Robinson develop a similar argument in *Why Nations Fail*, New York: Crown, 2012. However, they devote little attention to the role of military power, race/ethnicity, or gender and offer a benign view of "inclusive capitalism" as primarily generating growth in GDP.

# Chapter 8. Welfare State Tensions

1 A set of interesting and well-footnoted examples of references to the nanny state can be found on the "Nanny state" entry on Wikipedia, accessed March 18, 2019, at en.wikipedia.org/wiki/Nanny_state; on public patriarchy, see Sylvia Walby, *Theorizing Patriarchy*, London: Basil Blackwell, 1990.

2 Peter H. Lindert, *Growing Public,* Vols. I and II, New York: Cambridge University Press, 2004; Ito Peng, "Social Investment Policies in Canada, Australia, Japan, and South Korea," *International Journal of Child Care and Education Policy* 5: 1, 2011, 41–53.

3 My argument here builds on Dani Rodrik, "Populism and the Economics of Globalization," *Journal of International Business Policy* 1: 1–2, 2018, 12–33.

4 Diane Elson, *Male Bias in the Development Process*, Manchester, UK: Manchester University Press, 1995; Maria Karamessini and Jill Rubery, eds., *Women and Austerity: The Economic Crisis and the Future for Gender Equality*, New York: Routledge, 2013; Irene Gedalof, *Difference in an Age of Austerity*, New York: Springer, 2017.

5 Joseph E. Stiglitz, *Economics of the Public Sector*, New York: Norton, 2000; J. M. Buchanan, R. D. Tollison, and G. Tullock, *Toward a Theory of the Rent-Seeking Society*, College Station: Texas A and M Press, 1980.

6 Ian Gough, *The Political Economy of the Welfare State*, New York: Macmillan, 1979; James O'Connor, *The Fiscal Crisis of the State*, New York: St. Martin's Press, 1973.

7 Vladimir S. Tikunov and Olga Yu Chereshnya, "Public Health Index in Russian Federation from 1990 to 2012," *Social Indicators Research* 129: 2, 2016, 775–86.

8 Alec Nove, *The Economics of Feasible Socialism*, New York: Harper Collins, 1991. For an important exception to this generalization, see Peter Bohmer, Savvina Chowdhury, and Robin Hahnel, "Reproductive Labor and Participatory Economics," manuscript, Department of Economics, Portland State University, Portland, Oregon.

9 Nancy Folbre, "Roemer's Market Socialism: A Feminist Critique," *Politics and Society* 22: 4, 1995, 595–606.

10 M. Boldrin, M. D. Nardi, and L. E. Jones, "Fertility and Social Security," *Journal of Demographic Economics* 81, 2015, 261–99; Gary S. Becker, "A Theory of Social Interactions," *Journal of Political Economy* 82, 1974, 1063–93.

11 Martin Feldstein, "Social Security, Induced Retirement, and Aggregate Capital Accumulation," *Journal of Political Economy* 82: 5, 1974, 905–26. This argument is sometimes labeled "Ricardian equivalence," but its derivation from the work of David Ricardo has been questioned.

12 For a mainstream defense of this proposition, see Robert Shiller, *The New*

*Financial Order: Risk in the Twenty-First Century*, Princeton, NJ: Princeton University Press, 2004.

13 James M. Buchanan, "The Samaritan's Dilemma," in *Altruism, Morality and Economic Theory*, Edmund S. Phelps, ed., New York: Russell Sage Foundation, 1975, 71–85.

14 John Stuart Mill, *Principles of Political Economy: And Chapters on Socialism*, New York: Oxford Classics, 1999, 350.

15 Bruno S. Frey, "How Intrinsic Motivation Is Crowded Out and In," *Rationality and Society* 6: 3, 1994, 334–52; David U. Himmelstein, Dan Ariely, and Steffie Woolhandler, "Pay-for-Performance: Toxic to Quality? Insights from Behavioral Economics," *International Journal of Health Services* 44: 2, 2014, 203–14.

16 George A. Akerlof, "Labor Contracts as Partial Gift Exchange," *Quarterly Journal of Economics* 97: 4, 1982, 543–69.

17 For a formal model explaining how self-enforcing rules for intergenerational transfers can unravel, see Alessandro Cigno, "Intergenerational Transfers Without Altruism: Family, Market and State," *European Journal of Political Economy* 9: 4, 1993, 505–18.

18 On "decommodification," see G. Esping-Andersen, *The Three Worlds of Welfare Capitalism*, Cambridge, England: Polity Press, 1990. For an early critique, see Jane Lewis, "Gender and the Development of Welfare Regimes: Further Thoughts," *Social Politics* 4: 2, 1997, 160–77.

19 For more discussion, see Folbre, *Valuing Children: Rethinking the Economics of the Family*, Cambridge, MA: Harvard University Press, 2009, and Nancy Folbre, "Varieties of Patriarchal Capitalism," *Social Politics* 16: 2, 2009, 204–9.

20 Gøsta Esping-Anderson, *Social Foundations of Postindustrial Economies*, New York: Oxford University Press, 1999, 45.

21 Diane Elson, "Gender Awareness in Modeling Structural Adjustment," *World Development* 23: 11, 1995, 1851–68.

22 Peter H. Lindert, *Growing Public,* Vols. I and II, New York: Cambridge University Press, 2004; Ito Peng, "Social Investment Policies in Canada, Australia, Japan, and South Korea," *International Journal of Child Care and Education Policy* 5: 1, 2011, 41–53.

23 United Nations, *Human Development Report 2016: Human Development for Everyone,* New York: United Nations Development Programme, 2016, hdr.undp.org.

24 Mauricio Avendano and Ichiro Kawachi, "Why Do Americans Have Shorter Life Expectancy and Worse Health Than Do People in Other High-Income Countries?" *Annual Review of Public Health* 35, 2014, 307–25.

25 James J. Heckman, "Skill Formation and the Economics of Investing in Disadvantaged Children," *Science* 312, 2006, 1900–2. See also the special issue of the *Journal of Human Development and Capabilities* 17: 4, 2016, "Investing in Early Childhood Development."

26  David E. Bloom, David Canning, and Jaypee Sevilla, "The Effect of Health on Economic Growth: A Production Function Approach," *World Development* 32: 1, 2004, 1–13.

27  Jane Jenson, "Lost in Translation: The Social Investment Perspective and Gender Equality," *Social Politics* 16: 4, 2009, 446–83.

28  Jenson, "Lost in Translation."

29  Chris Leck, Dominic Upton, and Nick Evans, "Social Return on Investment: Valuing Health Outcomes or Promoting Economic Values?" *Journal of Health Psychology* 21: 7, 2016, 1481–90.

30  Kate Pickett and Richard G. Wilkinson, *The Spirit Level: Why Greater Equality Makes Societies Stronger,* London: Bloomsbury, 2009.

31  Campbell Robertson and Robert Gebeloff, "How Millions of Women Became the Most Essential Workers in America," *New York Times,* April 18, 2020, nytimes.com.

32  Steven Saxonberg, "From Defamilialization to Degenderization: Toward a New Welfare Typology," *Social Policy & Administration* 47: 1, 2013, 26–49; Sophie Mathieu, "From the Defamilialization to the 'Demotherization' of Care Work," *Social Politics: International Studies in Gender, State & Society* 23: 4, 2016, 576–91.

33  Nancy Folbre, *Greed, Lust and Gender: A History of Economic Ideas,* New York: Oxford, 2009.

34  Jane Humphries, "Enclosures, Common Rights, and Women: The Proletarianization of Families in the Late Eighteenth and Early Nineteenth Centuries," *Journal of Economic History* 50: 1, 1990, 17–42.

35  Folbre, *Greed, Lust and Gender.*

36  Donald O. Parsons, "On the Economics of Intergenerational Control," *Population and Development Review* 10: 1, 1984, 41–54; Nancy Folbre, "'The Wealth of Patriarchs': Deerfield, Massachusetts, 1720–1840," *Journal of Interdisciplinary History* 16: 2, 1985, 199–220.

37  Jack Caldwell, "On Net Intergenerational Wealth Flows: An Update," *Population and Development Review* 31: 4, 2005, 721–40.

38  Laura L. Lovett, *Conceiving the Future: Pronatalism, Reproduction, and the Family in the United States, 1890–1938,* Chapel Hill: University of North Carolina Press, 2009.

39  Hilary Land, "The Family Wage," *Feminist Review* 6, 1980, 55–77.

40  Alice Kessler-Harris, *A Woman's Wage: Historical Meanings and Social Consequences,* Lexington: University Press of Kentucky, 2014.

41  Susan Pederson, *Family, Dependence, and the Origins of the Welfare State,* New York: Cambridge University Press, 1995.

42  Folbre, *Greed, Lust and Gender.*

43  Jay Winter, *The Great War and the British People,* 2d ed., New York: Springer, 2003.

44  Jennifer Mittelstadt, *The Rise of the Military Welfare State,* Cambridge, MA: Harvard University Press, 2015.

45  Eleanor F. Rathbone, *The Disinherited Family,* London: Edward Arnold, 1924.

46 Joya Misra, "Mothers or Workers? The Value of Women's Labor: Women and the Emergence of Family Allowance Policy," *Gender and Society* 12: 4, 1998, 376–99.

47 Folbre, *Valuing Children*.

48 Edward J. McCaffery, *Taxing Women*, Chicago: University of Chicago Press, 1999.

49 For a discussion of the empirical implications, see Nancy Folbre, Marta Murray-Close, and Jooyeoun Suh. "Equivalence Scales for Extended Income in the US," *Review of Economics of the Household* 16: 2, 2018, 189–227.

50 Lawrence B. Glickman, *A Living Wage*, Ithaca, NY: Cornell University Press, 1999.

51 See the definitions offered by the Economic Policy Institute at epi.org/publication/what-families-need-to-get-by-epis-2015-family-budget-calculator/ and by the MIT Living Wage Project at livingwage.mit.edu/articles/27-new-data-up-calculation-of-the-living-wage.

52 See MIT Living Wage Project at livingwage.mit.edu/articles/27-new-data-up-calculation-of-the-living-wage.

53 See the website of the Global Living Wage Coalition at globallivingwage.org.

54 Richard Anker and Martha Anker, *Living Wages Around the World*, Cheltenham: Edward Elgar, 2017.

55 Michelle Adato and John Hoddinott, eds., *Conditional Cash Transfers in Latin America*, Washington, DC: Institute for Food Policy Research, 2010, ifpri.org.

56 Hans-Werner Sinn, "The Pay-as-You-Go Pension System as Fertility Insurance and an Enforcement Device," *Journal of Public Economics* 88, 2004, 1336.

57 David M. Cutler and Richard Johnson, "The Birth and Growth of the Social-Insurance State: Explaining Old-Age and Medical Insurance Across Countries," Research Division, Federal Reserve Bank of Kansas City, 2001.

58 Theda Skocpol, *Protecting Soldiers and Mothers*, Cambridge, MA: Belknap Press, 1995.

59 Gary S. Becker and Kevin M. Murphy, "Family and the State," *Journal of Law and Economics* 31, 1988, 1–18.

60 Seymour Moskowitz, "Filial Responsibility Statutes: Legal and Policy Considerations," *Journal of Law and Policy* 9, 2000, 709–36.

61 Shirley Burgraaf, *The Feminine Economy and Economic Man. Revising the Role of Family in the Post-Industrial Age*, Reading, MA: Perseus Books, 1997. It is worth noting many other flaws in this proposal. How would such private transfers be distributed between mothers and fathers who part ways? As with public transfers, crowding out could come into play as in "I'm not paying you a dime over your 15 percent," or "I've paid you the legal requirement, so don't expect me to visit you in the hospital."

62 Rita Jing-Ann Chou, "Filial Piety by Contract? The Emergence, Implementation, and Implications of the 'Family Support Agreement' in China," *Gerontologist* 51: 1, 2011, 3–16.

63 Organization for Economic Cooperation and Development, *Pensions at a Glance 2015*, Washington, DC: Author.

64 David E. Bloom and Roddy McKinnon, "The Design and Implementation of Public Pension Systems in Developing Countries: Issues and Options," IZA Policy Paper No. 59, May 2013, econstor.eu.

65 Stein Ringen and Kinglun Stein, "What Kind of Welfare State Is Emerging in China?" Working Paper No. 2013–2, United Nations UNRISD, 2013, econstor.eu.

66 Gary Becker and Kevin Murphy, "The Family and the State," *Journal of Law and Economics* 31: 1, 1988, 1–18.

67 Claudia Dale Goldin and Lawrence Katz, *The Race Between Education and Technology*, Cambridge, MA: Harvard University Press, 2007.

68 Samuel Bowles and Herbert Gintis, *Schooling in Capitalist America*, New York: Basic Books, 1976.

69 Jacob S. Hacker, "The Historical Logic of National Health Insurance: Structure and Sequence in the Development of British, Canadian, and US Medical Policy," *Studies in American Political Development* 12: 1, 1998, 57–130.

70 David M. Cutler and Richard Johnson, "The Birth and Growth of the Social-Insurance State: Explaining Old-Age and Medical Insurance Across Countries," Research Division, Federal Reserve Bank of Kansas City, 2001.

71 "Both in Rich and Poor Countries Universal Health Care Brings Huge Benefits," *The Economist*, April 26, 2018, economist.com.

72 Guy Carrin and Chris James, "Social Health Insurance: Key Factors Affecting the Transition Towards Universal Coverage," *International Social Security Review* 58: 1, 2005, 45–64.

73 World Bank and World Health Organization, *Tracking Universal Health Coverage: The 2017 Global Monitoring Report*, December 13, 2017, world-bank.org.

74 Robert W. Patterson, "What Happened to the America in Corporate America?" *National Review*, July 31, 2013, nationalreview.com.

75 Skocpol, *Soldiers and Mothers*.

76 Grant Miller, "Women's Suffrage, Political Responsiveness, and Child Survival in American History," *Quarterly Journal of Economics* 123: 3, 2008, 1287–327.

77 Claudia Goldin, *Understanding the Gender Gap*, New York: Oxford, 1990.

78 Suzanne Mettler, *Dividing Citizens: Gender and Federalism in New Deal Public Policy*, Ithaca, NY: Cornell University Press, 1998.

79 Ira Katznelson, *When Affirmative Action Was White*, New York: W. W. Norton, 2005.

80 Eileen Boris and Jennifer Klein, *Caring for America*, New York: Oxford University Press, 2012.

81  Robert Margo, *Race and Schooling in the South, 1880–1950,* Chicago: University of Chicago Press, 2007.

82  Jill Quadagno, *The Color of Welfare. How Racism Undermined the War on Poverty,* New York: Oxford University Press, 1994; John E. Roemer, Woojin Lee, and Karine van der Straeten, *Racism, Xenophobia and Distribution,* Cambridge, MA: Harvard University Press, 2007.

83  Martin Gilens, *Why Americans Hate Welfare,* Chicago: University of Chicago Press, 2009.

84  Christopher Howard, *The Hidden Welfare State,* Princeton, NJ: Princeton University Press, 1999.

85  National Academies of Sciences, Engineering, and Medicine, *The Economic and Fiscal Consequences of Immigration,* Washington, DC: National Academies Press, 2017.

86  Suzanne Mettler, "The Transformed Welfare State and the Redistribution of Political Voice," in *The Transformation of American Politics: Activist Government and the Rise of Conservatism,* Paul Pierson and Theda Skocpol, eds., Princeton, NJ: Princeton University Press, 2007, 191–222.

87  Nancy Folbre, "The Resentment Zone: Losing Means-Tested Benefits," *New York Times,* March 22, 2010, economix.blogs.nytimes.com.

88  Jane Mayer, *Dark Money: The Hidden History of the Billionaires behind the Rise of the Radical Right,* New York: Doubleday, 2016; Nancy McClean, *Democracy in Chains,* New York: Penguin, 2017.

89  Larry Bartels, *Unequal Democracy,* Princeton, NJ: Princeton University Press, 2009.

90  Alberto Alesina, Reza Baqir, and William Easterly, "Public Goods and Ethnic Divisions," *The Quarterly Journal of Economics* 114: 4, 1999, 1243–84; Michael Bleaney and Arcangelo Dimico, "Ethnic Diversity and Conflict," *Journal of Institutional Economics* 13: 2, 2017, 357–78.

91  Lena Edlund and Rohini Pande, "Why Have Women Become Left-Wing? The Political Gender Gap and the Decline in Marriage," *Quarterly Journal of Economics* 117: 3, 2002, 917–61; Lena Edlund, Laila Haider, and Rohini Pande, "Unmarried Parenthood and Redistributive Politics," *Journal of the European Economic Association* 3: 1, 2005, 95–119.

92  Monika L. McDermott, *Masculinity, Femininity, and American Political Behavior,* New York: Oxford University Press, 2016.

93  "The Health Care Bill's Insults to Women," *New York Times,* May 12, 2017, nytimes.com.

94  Amanda Clayton and Pär Zetterberg, "Quota Shocks: Electoral Gender Quotas and Government Spending Priorities Worldwide," *The Journal of Politics* 80: 3, 2018, 916–32.

95  Raghabendra Chattopadhyay and Esther Duflo, "Women as Policy Makers: Evidence from a Randomized Policy Experiment in India," *Econometrica* 72: 5, 2004, 1409–43; Lori Beaman, Esther Duflo, Rohini Pande, and Petia Topalova, "Female Leadership Raises Aspirations and

Educational Attainment for Girls: A Policy Experiment in India," *Science* 335: 6068, 2012, 582–86.

96 Anne Marie Goetz, "The New Cold War on Women's Rights," United Nations Research Institute for Social Development, June 22, 2015, unrisd. org.

97 William Grieder, *One World, Ready or Not*, New York: Simon and Schuster, 1998; Alan Tonelson, *The Race to the Bottom*, New York: Basic Books, 2000.

98 Hongbin Cai and Daniel Treisman, "Does Competition for Capital Discipline Governments? Decentralization, Globalization, and Public Policy," *American Economic Review* 95: 3, 2005, 817–30.

99 Dani Rodrik, *The Globalization Paradox: Democracy and the Future of the World Economy*, New York: W. W. Norton, 2011.

100 Peter Abrahamson, "Future Welfare. An Uneven Race to the Top and/or a Polarized World?" in *The Routledge International Handbook to Welfare State Systems*, Christian Aspalter, ed., New York: Routledge, 2017, 41–70.

101 James K. Boyce and Léonce Ndikumana, "Is Africa a Net Creditor? New Estimates of Capital Flight from Severely Indebted Sub-Saharan African Countries, 1970–96," *Journal of Development Studies* 38: 2, 2001, 27–56.

102 Nicholas Shaxson, *Treasure Islands*, London: Bodley Head, 2011; Gabriel Zucman, "Taxing Across Borders: Tracking Personal Wealth and Corporate Profits," *Journal of Economic Perspectives* 28: 4, 2014, 121–48.

103 Alan S. Blinder, "Offshoring: The Next Industrial Revolution?" *Foreign Affairs* 85: 2, 2006, 113–28.

104 Greg LeRoy, *The Great American Jobs Scam*, Oakland, CA: Berrett-Koehler, 2005.

105 Claudia Goldin and Lawrence Katz, *The Race Between Education and Technology*, Cambridge, MA: Harvard University Press, 2009.

106 Richard Freeman, "The Great Doubling: The Challenge of the New Global Labor Market," unpublished manuscript, 2006, emlab.berkeley.edu. See also his "What Does Global Expansion of Higher Education Mean for the U.S.?" in *American Universities in a Global Market*, Charles T. Clotfelter, ed., Chicago: University of Chicago Press, 2010, 373–404.

107 Nancy Folbre, *Saving State U: Fixing Public Higher Education*, New York: New Press, 2010.

108 Richard Morin, "Indentured Servitude in the Persian Gulf," *New York Times*, April 12, 2014, nytimes.com.

109 Susan Ferguson and David McNally, "Precarious Migrants: Gender, Race, and the Social Reproduction of a Global Working Class," *Socialist Register* 51, 2015, 1–23; Bridget Anderson, "Migration, Immigration Controls and the Fashioning of Precarious Workers," *Work, Employment, and Society* 24: 2, 2010, 300–17.

110 Rhacel Parreñas, *Servants of Globalization*, Stanford, CA: Stanford University Press, 2015.

111 Nancy Folbre and Douglas Wolf, "The Intergenerational Welfare State," *Population and Development Review* 38, 2012, 36–51.

112  Douglas A. Wolf, Ronald D. Lee, Timothy Miller, Gretchen Donehower, and Alexandre Genest, "Fiscal Externalities of Becoming a Parent," *Population and Development Review* 37: 2, 2011, 241–66.

113  Ronald Demos Lee and Andrew Mason, eds., *Population Aging and the Generational Economy: A Global Perspective*, Cheltenham, UK: Edward Elgar, 2011.

114  Adam Tooze, "Germany," in *Families and States in Western Europe*, Quintin Skinner, ed., New York: Cambridge University Press, 2011, 81.

115  Folbre and Wolf, "The Intergenerational Welfare State."

116  Samuel H. Preston "Children and the Elderly: Divergent Paths for America's Dependents," *Demography* 21: 4, 1984, 435–57; Heather Hahn, "Federal Expenditures on Children," *Society for Research in Child Development Social Policy Report* 29: 1, 2015, 1–26, files.eric.ed.gov.

117  Ron Lee and Andy Mason, "National Transfer Accounts and Intergenerational Transfers," in *International Handbook on Aging and Public Policy*, Sarah Harper and Kath Hamblin, eds., Northampton, MA: Edward Elgar, 2014, Chapter 12.

118  Sandra L. Colby and Jennifer M. Ortman, *Projections of the Size and Composition of the U.S. Population: 2014 to 2060*, Washington, DC: U.S. Census Bureau Report P25-1143; March 3, 2015, census.gov.

119  James M. Poterba, "Demographic Structure and the Political Economy of Public Education," *Journal of Policy Analysis and Management* 16: 1, 1997, 48–66; David N. Figlio and Deborah Fletcher, "Suburbanization, Demographic Change, and the Consequences for School Finance," *Journal of Public Economics* 96: 11–12, 2012, 1144–53.

120  Liz Alderman, "After Economic Crisis, Low Birthrates Challenge Southern Europe," *New York Times*, April 16, 2017, nytimes.com.

121  Zhongwei Zhao, Quinzi Xu, and Xin Yuan, "Far Below Replacement Fertility in Urban China," *Journal of Biosocial Science* 49, 2017, S4–S19.

122  Nicholas Bakalar, "U.S. Fertility Rate Reaches a Record Low," *New York Times*, July 3, 2017, nytimes.com.

123  Gøsta Esping-Anderson, *Social Foundations of Postindustrial Economies*, New York: Oxford, 1999.

124  Jenny Brown, *Birth Strike: The Hidden Fight over Women's Work*, Oakland, CA: PM Press, 2019.

125  Michelle Goldberg, *The Means of Reproduction*, New York: Penguin, 2009.

126  Diane Elson, "Recognize, Reduce, and Redistribute Unpaid Care Work: How to Close the Gender Gap," *New Labor Forum* 26: 2, 2017, 52–61.

## Chapter 9. Gender and Care Costs

1  Ingrid Palmer, "Public Finance from a Gender Perspective," *World Development* 23: 11, 1995, 1981–86; Robert I. Lerma, "Policy Watch: Child Support Policies," *Journal of Economic Perspectives* 7: 1, 1993, 171–82.

2 For a more extended discussion of the Chicken Game, see Nancy Folbre and Thomas Weisskopf, "The Rise and Decline of Patriarchal Capitalism," in *Capitalism on Trial: Explorations in the Tradition of Thomas E. Weisskopf*, Robert Pollin and Jeannette Wicks-Lim, eds., Cheltenham, UK: Edward Elgar, 2013.

3 Sara Cantillon, "Measuring Differences in Living Standards Within Households," *Journal of Marriage and Family* 75: 3, 2013, 598–610.

4 Anne L. Alstott, *No Exit: What Parents Owe Their Children and What Society Owes Parents*, New York: Oxford University Press, 2005.

5 For a prescient discussion of differences in the fungibility of the services that intimate partners provide one another, see Paula England and George Farkas, *Households, Employment and Gender*, New York: Aldine, 1986.

6 Michelle J. Budig and Paula England, "The Wage Penalty for Motherhood," *American Sociological Review* 66: 2, 2001, 204–25; Jane Waldfogel, "Understanding the 'Family Gap' in Pay for Women with Children," *The Journal of Economic Perspectives* 12: 1, 1998, 137–56; Michelle J. Budig, Joya Misra, and Irene Boeckman, "The Motherhood Penalty in Cross-National Perspective: The Importance of Work–Family Policies and Cultural Attitudes," *Social Policy* 19: 2, 2012, 163–93; Yoon Kyung Chung, Barbara Downs, Danielle H. Sandler, and Robert Sienkiewicz, "The Parental Gender Earnings Gap in the United States," 2017, Working Papers 17–68, Center for Economic Studies, US Census Bureau; Henrik Kleven, Camille Landais, and Jakob Egholt Søgaard, "Children and Gender Inequality: Evidence from Denmark," *American Economic Journal: Applied Economics* 11: 4, 2019, 181–209.

7 LeeAnne DeRigne and Shirley L. Porterfield, "Employment Change Among Married Parents of Children with Special Health Care Needs," *Journal of Family Issues* 3: 5, 2017, 579–606.

8 Paula England, Jonathan Bearak, Michelle Budig, and Melissa Hodges, "Do Highly Paid, Highly Skilled Women Experience the Largest Motherhood Penalty?" *American Sociological Review* 81: 6, 2016, 1161–89.

9 Eliza K. Pavalko and Joseph D. Wolfe, "Do Women Still Care? Cohort Changes in US Women's Care for the Ill or Disabled," *Social Forces* 94: 3, 2015, 1359–84. Hiroyuki Yamada and Satoshi Shimizutani, "Labor Market Outcomes of Informal Care Provision in Japan," *The Journal of the Economics of Ageing* 6, 2015, 79–88.

10 Donald Cox and Beth Soldo, "Motives for Care that Adult Children Provide to Parents: Evidence from 'Point Blank' Survey Questions," *Journal of Comparative Family Studies* 44: 4, 2013, 491–518.

11 Angelina Grigoryeva, "Own Gender, Sibling's Gender, Parent's Gender: The Division of Elderly Parent Care Among Adult Children," *American Sociological Review* 82: 1, 2017,116–46.

12 Anna Aizer, "The Gender Wage Gap and Domestic Violence," *American Economic Review* 100:4, 2010, 1847–59.

13  Dan Anderberg, Helmut Rainer, Jonathan Wadsworth, and Tanya Wilson, "Unemployment and Domestic Violence: Theory and Evidence," *Economic Journal* 126: 597, 2016, 1947–79.

14  Gustavo J. Bobonis, Melissa González-Brenes, and Roberto Castro, "Public Transfers and Domestic Violence: The Roles of Private Information and Spousal Control," *American Economic Journal: Economic Policy* 5: 1, 2013, 179–205.

15  Sara Cantillon and Brian Nolan, "Poverty Within Households: Measuring Gender Differences Using Nonmonetary Indicators," *Feminist Economics* 7: 1, 2001, 5–23.

16  Two studies are particularly influential: Duncan Thomas, "Intra-household Resource Allocation: An Inferential Approach," *Journal of Human Resources* 25: 4, 1990, 635–64; and Shelly Lundberg and Robert A. Pollak, "Separate Spheres Bargaining and the Marriage Market," *Journal of Political Economy* 101: 6, 1993, 988–1010.

17  Nancy Folbre, Jayoung Yoon, Kade Finnoff, and Allison Sidle Fuligni, "By What Measure? Family Time Devoted to Children in the United States," *Demography* 42: 2, 2005, 373–90.

18  Michael Burda, Daniel S. Hamermesh, and Philippe Weil, "Total Work and Gender: Facts and Possible Explanations," *Journal of Population Economics* 26: 1, 2013, 239–61.

19  Suzanne M. Bianchi, John P. Robinson, and Melissa A. Milke, *The Changing Rhythms of American Family Life*, New York: Russell Sage, 2006; Avanti Mukherjee, *Three Essays on 'Doing Care,' Gender Differences in the Work Day, and Women's Care Work in the Household,"* Ph.D. dissertation, University of Massachusetts Amherst, 2017, scholarworks.umass.edu.

20  Mukherjee, *Three Essays*.

21  Nancy Folbre, "Developing Care," 2018, Policy Brief, International Development Research Centre. Ottawa, Canada, https://idl-bnc-idrc.dspacedirect.org.

22  Sanjiv Gupta and Michael Ash, "Whose Money, Whose Time? A Nonparametric Approach to Modeling Time Spent on Housework in the United States," *Feminist Economics* 14: 1, 2008, 93–120.

23  Michael Bittman, Paula England, Liana Sayer, Nancy Folbre, and George Matheson "When Does Gender Trump Money? Bargaining and Time in Household Work," *American Journal of Sociology* 109: 1, 2003, 186–214; Marianne Bertrand, Emir Kamenica, and Jessica Pan, "Gender Identity and Relative Income within Households," *Quarterly Journal of Economics* 130: 2, 2015, 571–614.

24  Lundberg and Pollak. "Separate Spheres Bargaining and the Marriage Market."

25  Victor R. Fuchs, "Sex Differences in Economic Well-being," *Science* 232: 4749, April 25, 1986, 459–64.

26  Karen C. Holden and Pamela J. Smock, "The Economic Costs of Marital Dissolution: Why Do Women Bear a Disproportionate Cost?" *Annual Review of Sociology* 17, 1991, 51–78.

27  Laura M. Tach and Alicia Eads, "Trends in the Economic Consequences of Marital and Cohabitation Dissolution in the U.S.," *Demography* 52: 2, 2015, 401–32.

28  J. Jarvis and S. P. Jenkins, "Marital Splits and Income Changes: Evidence From the British Household Panel Survey," *Population Studies* 53: 2, 1999, 237–54; R. Finnie, "Women, Men, and the Economic Consequences of Divorce: Evidence from Canadian Longitudinal Data," *Canadian Journal of Sociology and Anthropology* 30, 1993, 205–41; R. V. Burkhauser, G. J. Duncan, and R. Berntsen, "Wife or Frau, Women do Worse: A Comparison of Women and Men in the United States and Germany after Marital Dissolution," *Demography* 28: 3, 1991, 353–60.

29  Andrew J. Cherlin, *The Marriage Go-Round*, New York: Knopf, 2010.

30  Tach and Eads, "Trends in the Economic Consequences of Marital and Cohabitation Dissolution."

31  George A. Akerlof, "Men Without Children," *The Economic Journal* 108, 1998, 287–309.

32  U.S. Census, CH-1. *Living Arrangements of Children Under 18 Years Old: 1960 to Present*, cps.ipums.org.

33  Ursula Henz, "Long-Term Trends of Men's Co-Residence with Children in England and Wales," *Demographic Research* 30: 23, 2014, 685.

34  J. Bart Stykes, Wendy D. Manning, and Susan L. Brown, "Nonresident Fathers and Formal Child Support: Evidence from the CPS, the NSFG and the SIPP," *Demographic Research* 29: 46, 2013, 1299–1330.

35  Emily Higgs, Cristina Gomez-Vidal, and Michael J. Austin, "Low-Income Nonresident Fatherhood: A Literature Review with Implications for Practice and Research," *Families in Society* 99: 2, 2018, 115.

36  Nancy Folbre, *Valuing Children*, Cambridge, MA: Harvard University Press, 2008.

37  Ariel Kalil, Rebecca Ryan, and Elise Chor, "Time Investments in Children Across Family Structures," *The Annals of the American Academy of Political and Social Science* 654: 1, June 9, 2014, 150–168.

38  Sara McLanahan, "Diverging Destinies: How Children Are Faring Under the Second Demographic Transition," *Demography* 41: 4, 2004, 607–27.

39  Sara McLanahan and Wade Jacobsen, "Diverging Destinies Revisited," in *Families in an Era of Increasing Inequality*, Paul R. Amato, Alan Booth, Susan M. McHale, and Jennifer Van Hook, eds., New York: Springer, 2015, 3–23.

40  Sarah Bradshaw, Sylvia Chant, and Brian Linneker, "Challenges and Changes in Gendered Poverty: The Feminization, De-feminization and Re-feminization of Poverty in Latin America," *Feminist Economics* 25: 1, 2019, 119–44.

41  Laurie DeRose and W. Bradford Wilcox, "The Cohabitation-Go-Round: Cohabitation and Family Instability Across the Globe," New York: Social Trends Institute and Institute for Family Studies, 2017, worldfamilymap.

ifstudies.org. Chia Liu, Albert Esteve, and Rocío Treviño, "Female Headed Households and Living Conditions in Latin America," *World Development* 90, 2017, 311–28.

42 Nancy Folbre, "Measuring Care: Gender, Empowerment, and the Care Economy," *Journal of Human Development* 7: 2, 2006, 183–200.

43 Sylvia Chant, *Gender and Generation and Poverty: Exploring the 'Feminization of Poverty' in Africa, Asia and Latin America,* Northampton, MA: Edward Elgar, 2007.

44 Nancy Folbre, "The Pauperization of Mothers: Patriarchy and Public Policy in the US," *Review of Radical Political Economics* 16: 4, 1985, 72–88.

45 Sarah Bradshaw, Sylvia Chant, and Brian Linneker, "Gender and Poverty: What We Know, Don't Know, and Need to Know for Agenda 2030," *Gender, Place & Culture*, 2017, 1–22.

46 Recent studies that focus on female headship, broadly defined, include Liu, Esteve, and Treviño, "Female-headed Households and Living Conditions in Latin America"; Annamaria Milazzo and Dominique van de Walle, "Women Left Behind? Poverty and Headship in Africa," *Demography* 54: 3, 2017, 1119–45; Stephan Klasen, Tobias Lechtenfeld, and Felix Povel, "A Feminization of Vulnerability? Female Headship, Poverty, and Vulnerability in Thailand and Vietnam," *World Development* 71, 2015, 36–53.

47 Nancy Folbre, Marta Murray-Close, and Jooyeoun Suh, "Equivalence Scales for Extended Income in the US," *Review of Economics of the Household* 16: 2, 2018, 189–227.

48 David Newhouse, Pablo Suárez Becerra, and Martin Evans, "New Global Estimates of Child Poverty and Their Sensitivity to Alternative Equivalence Scales," *Economics Letters* 157, 2017, 125–28.

49 Mary Romero, "Reflections on Globalized Care Chains and Migrant Women Workers," *Critical Sociology* 44: 7–8, 2018, 1179–89.

50 Nancy Folbre, "Gender and the Care Penalty," in *Oxford Handbook of Women in the Economy*, Laura Argys, Susan Averett, and Saul Hoffman, eds., New York: Oxford University Press, 2018; Heidi Hartmann and Steve Rose, "Still a Man's Labor Market: The Long-Term Earnings Gap," Washington, DC: Institute for Women's Policy Research, 2004, iwpr.org.

51 Youngjoo Cha and Kim A. Weeden, "Overwork and the Slow Convergence in the Gender Gap in Wages," *American Sociological Review* 79: 3, 2014, 457–84.

52 Ipshita Pal and Jane Waldfogel, "The Family Gap in Pay: New Evidence for 1967 to 2013," *RSF: The Russell Sage Foundation Journal of the Social Sciences* 2: 4, 2016, 104–27.

53 Daniel Horn, "The Pandemic Could Put Your Doctor out of Business," *The Washington Post*, April 24, 2020, washingtonpost.com.

54 Torben Iverson and Frances Rosenbluth, *Women, Work and Politics*, New Haven, CT: Yale University Press, 2010.

55  Shelley J. Correll, Stephen Benard, and In Paik, "Getting a Job: Is There a Motherhood Penalty?" *American Journal of Sociology* 112: 5, 2007, 1297–1339.

56  Marianne Bertrand and Sendhil Mullainathan, "Are Emily and Greg More Employable than Lakisha and Jamal? A Field Experiment on Labor Market Discrimination," *American Economic Review* 94: 4, 2004, 991–1013; András Tilcsik, "Pride and Prejudice: Employment Discrimination Against Openly Gay Men in the United States," *American Journal of Sociology* 117: 2, 2011, 586–626.

57  Joan C. Williams and Stephanie Bornstein, "Evolution of FReD: Family Responsibilities Discrimination and Developments in the Law of Stereotyping and Implicit Bias," *Hastings Law Journal* 59, 2007, 1311.

58  United States Federal Equal Employment Opportunity Commission family discrimination guidelines, eeoc.gov.

59  Joan C. Williams and Nancy Segal, "Beyond the Maternal Wall: Relief for Family Caregivers Who Are Discriminated Against on the Job," *Harvard Women's Law Journal* 26, 2003, 77–162.

60  Claudia Goldin and Lawrence F. Katz, "A Most Egalitarian Profession: Pharmacy and the Evolution of a Family-Friendly Occupation," *Journal of Labor Economics* 34: 3, 2016, 705–46.

61  Joan Williams, *Unbending Gender,* New York: Oxford University Press, 2001; Damian Grimshaw and Jill Rubery, "The Motherhood Pay Gap: A Review of the Issues, Theory and International Evidence," Working Paper No. 1/2015, Geneva: International Labour Organization, Gender equality and diversity branch, 2015.

62  Nancy Folbre, "A Theory of the Misallocation of Time," in *Family Time,* Nancy Folbre and Michael Bittman, eds., New York: Routledge, 2004.

63  Dan Clawson and Naomi Gerstel, *Unequal Time,* New York: Russell Sage, 2014; Lonnie Golden, "Irregular Work Scheduling and Its Consequences," Economic Policy Institute Briefing Paper No. 394, April 9, 2015, ssrn.com.

64  B. Gault, H. Hartmann, A. Hegewisch, J. Milli, and L. Reichlin, *Paid Parental Leave in the United States: What the Data Tell Us About Access, Usage, and Economic and Health Benefits,* Washington, DC: Institute for Women's Policy Research, 2014; Elaine McCrate, "Work Flexibility for Whom? Control over Work Schedule Variability in the U.S.," *Feminist Economics* 18: 1, 2012, 39–72; Naomi Gerstel and Dan Clawson, "Class Advantage and the Gender Divide: Flexibility on the Job and at Home," *American Journal of Sociology* 120: 2, 2014, 395–431.

65  Harriet B. Presser, "Shift Work and Child Care Among Young Dual-Earner American Parents," *Journal of Marriage and the Family* 50: 1, 1988, 133–48.

66  Greta Friedemann-Sánchez, *Assembling Flowers and Cultivating Homes,* New York: Lexington Books, 2006.

67  Jessica Pan, "Gender Segregation in Occupations: The Role of Tipping and Social Interactions," *Journal of Labor Economics* 33: 2, 2015, 365–408; Paula England, Paul Allison, and Yuxiao Wu, "Does Bad Pay Cause

Occupations to Feminize, Does Feminization Reduce Pay, and How Can We Tell with Longitudinal Data?," *Social Science Research* 36: 3, 2007, 1237–56.

68 Áine Cain, Anaele Pelisson, and Shayanne Gal, "9 Places in the US Where Job Candidates May Never Have to Answer the Dreaded Salary Question Again," *Business Insider*, April 10, 2018, businessinsider.com.

69 Maria Charles and David B. Grusky, *Occupational Ghettos: The Worldwide Segregation of Women and Men*, Stanford, CA: Stanford University Press, 2004.

70 Heather McLaughlin, Christopher Uggen, and Amy Blackstone, "The Economic and Career Effects of Sexual Harassment on Working Women," *Gender & Society* 3: 3, 2017, 333–58.

71 Kristin J. Kleinjans, Karl Fritjof Krassel, and Anthony Dukes, "Occupational Prestige and the Gender Wage Gap," *Kyklos*, February 2017; Susan Pinker, *The Sexual Paradox*, New York: Simon and Schuster, 2009.

72 Lee Badgett and Nancy Folbre, "Job Gendering: Occupational Choice and the Labor Market," *Industrial Relations* 42: 2, 2003, 270–98.

73 L. Bursztyn, T. Fujiwara, and A. Pallais, "Acting Wife: Marriage Market Incentives and Labor Market Investments," *American Economic Review* 107: 11, 2017, 3288–319.

74 M. V. Lee Badgett, "The Wage Effects of Sexual Orientation Discrimination," *Industrial and Labor Relations Review* 48: 4, 1995, 726–39.

75 Nancy Folbre, ed., *For Love and Money: Care Provision in the U.S.*, New York: Russell Sage.

76 Nicole M. Fortin, "The Gender Wage Gap Among Young Adults in the United States: The Importance of Money Versus People," *Journal of Human Resources* 43: 4, 2008, 884–918.

77 Nancy Folbre, "When a Commodity Is not Exactly a Commodity," *Science* 319: 5871, 2008, 1769–70.

78 Paula England, Michelle Budig, and Nancy Folbre, "Wages of Virtue: The Relative Pay of Care Work," *Social Problems* 49: 4, 2002, 455–73; David N. Barron and Elizabeth West, "The Financial Costs of Caring in the British Labor Market: Is There a Wage Penalty for Workers in Caring Occupations?" *British Journal of Industrial Relations* 51: 1, 2013, 104–23; Barry T. Hirsch and Julia Manzella, Who Cares—And Does it Matter? Measuring the Wage Penalty for Caring Work," in *Research in Labor Economics: Why Are Women Becoming More Like Men (and Men More Like Women) in the Labor Market?* 40 (2015), 213–75; Michelle Budig, Melissa Hodges, and Paula England, "Wages of Nurturant and Reproductive Care Workers: Adjudicating Individual and Structural Mechanisms Producing the Care Pay Penalty," *Social Problems* 66:2, 2018, 294–319; Bruce Pietrykowski, "The Return to Caring Skills: Gender, Class, and Occupational Wages in the US," *Feminist Economics* 23: 4, 2017, 32–61.

79 According to the May 2017 Occupation and Employment Survey of the Bureau of Labor Statistics, the median hourly wage of child care workers

was $10.72 compared to $10.97 for parking lot attendants. See bls.gov/oes/current/oes_stru.htm.

80 Paula England, *Comparable Worth*, Rutgers, NJ: Transaction, 1992.

81 Michelle J. Budig and Joya Misra, "How Care–Work Employment Shapes Earnings in Cross-National Perspective," *International Labor Review*, Special Issue: Workers in the Care Economy, 149: 4, 2010, 441–60.

82 Folbre, ed., *For Love and Money*; Shereen Hussein, Mohamed Ismail, and Jill Manthorpe, "Changes in Turnover and Vacancy Rates of Care Workers in England from 2008 to 2010: Panel Analysis of National Workforce Data," *Health & Social Care in the Community* 24: 5, 2016, 547–56.

83 Nancy Folbre and Julie Nelson, "Why a Well Paid Nurse Is a Better Nurse," *Journal of Nursing Economics* 24: 3, 2006, 127–30.

84 Maelan Le Goff, "Feminization of Migration and Trends in Remittances," IZA World of Labor, January 2016, wol.iza.org.

85 Patricia Cortés and José Tessada, "Low-Skilled Immigration and the Labor Supply of Highly Skilled Women," *American Economic Journal: Applied Economics* 3: 3, 2011, 88–123; Delia Furtado and Heinrich Hock, "Low Skilled Immigration and Work–Fertility Tradeoffs Among High Skilled US Natives," *American Economic Review* 100: 2, 2010, 224–28.

86 Lídia Farré, Libertad González Luna, and Francesca Ortega, "Immigration, Family Responsibilities and the Labor Supply of Skilled Native Women," 2009, IZA Discussion Paper No. 4265; Guglielmo Barone and Sauro Mocetti, "With a Little Help from Abroad: The Effect of Low-skilled Immigration on the Female Labour Supply," *Labour Economics* 18: 5, 2011, 664–75; Patricia Cortés and Jessica Pan, "Outsourcing Household Production: Foreign Domestic Workers and Native Labor Supply in Hong Kong," *Journal of Labor Economics* 31: 2, 2013, 327–71.

87 Francesca Bettio, Annamaria Simonazzi, and Paola Villa, "Change in Care Regimes and Female Migration: The 'Care Drain' in the Mediterranean," *Journal of European Social Policy* 16: 3, 2006, 271–85; Isabel Shutes and Carlos Chiatti, "Migrant Labour and the Marketisation of Care for Older People: The Employment of Migrant Care Workers by Families and Service Providers," *Journal of European Social Policy* 22: 4, 2012, 392–405.

88 David J. Deming, "The Growing Importance of Social Skills in the Labor Market," National Bureau of Economic Research, Working Paper 2147, 2015, nber.org.

89 Jennifer Utrata, *Women Without Men*, Ithaca, NY: Cornell University Press, 2015, 16.

90 M. V. Lee Badgett, *When Gay People Get Married*, New York: New York University Press, 2009.

91 Michelle Goldberg, *The Means of Reproduction*, New York: Penguin, 2010.

92 Guttmacher Institute, "Unintended Pregnancy in the U.S., Guttmacher Institute, January 2019," https://www.guttmacher.org/fact-sheet/unintended-pregnancy-united-states; Robin H. Pugh Yi, "Abortionomics: When Choice Is a Necessity. The Impact of Recession on Abortion,"

Prepared by Akeso Consulting, LLC, for Turner Strategies December 2011, ontheissuesmagazine.com.

93  Ronnie Cohen, "Denial of Abortion Leads to Economic Hardship for Low-Income Women," Reuters, January 2018, reuters.com.

94  Olanike Adelakun-Odewale, "Recovery of Child Support in Nigeria," in *The Recovery of Maintenance in the E.U. and Worldwide*, Paul Beaumont, Burkhard Hess, Lara Walker, and Stefanie Spancken, eds., Oxford: Hart, 2014, 244, 241–60.

95  Vanessa Rios-Salas and Daniel R. Meyer, "Single Mothers and Child Support Receipt in Peru," *Journal of Family Studies* 20: 3, 2014, 298–310. See also Laura Cuesta, "Child Support Policy Schemes in Latin America and Their Potential Consequences on the Economic Wellbeing of Children and Families," paper presented at the Latin American Studies Association annual conference, Boston, MA, May 2019.

96  OECD Family Database, "PF1.5: Child Support," Table PF1.5.B, oecd.org.

97  Michael Rush, *Between Two Worlds of Father Politics: USA or Sweden?* New York: Oxford University Press, 2015, 113.

98  Paula England and Nancy Folbre, "Involving Dads: Parental Bargaining and Family Well Being," in *Handbook of Father Involvement: Multidisciplinary Perspectives*, Catherine S. Tamis-LeMonda and Natasha Cabrera, eds., Mahwah, NJ: Lawrence Erlbaum, 2002.

99  Ultrata, *Women Without Men*.

100  Rush, *Between Two Worlds*, 113.

101  Beaumont et al., *The Recovery of Maintenance*.

102  Maria Cancian and Daniel R. Meyer, "Reforming Policy for Single-Parent Families to Reduce Child Poverty," *RSF: The Russell Sage Foundation Journal of the Social Sciences* 4: 2, 2018, 91–112.

103  Helena Bergman and Barbara Hobson, "Compulsory Fatherhood: The Coding of Fatherhood in the Swedish Welfare State," in *Making Men into Fathers*, Barbara Hobson, ed., New York: Cambridge University Press, 2002, 92–124.

104  Peter McDonald, "Very Low Fertility: Consequences, Causes and Policy Approaches," *Japanese Journal of Population* 6: 1, 2008, 19–23.

105  Peter McDonald, "Gender Equality, Social Institutions and the Future of Fertility," *Journal of Population Research* 17, 2000, 1–16; Goldberg, *Means of Reproduction*.

106  Janet Gornick and Marcia Meyers, *Families that Work: Policies for Reconciling Parenthood and Employment*, New York: Russell Sage, 2003; Claudia Olivetti and Barbara Petrongolo, "The Economic Consequences of Family Policies: Lessons from a Century of Legislation in High-Income Countries," *Journal of Economic Perspectives* 31: 1, 2017, 205–30.

107  Ann-Zofie Duvander and Mats Johansson, "Parental Leave Use for Different Fathers: A Study of the Impact of Three Swedish Leave Reforms," in *Fatherhood in the Nordic Welfare States*, Guðný Björk Eydal and Tine Rostgaard, eds., Bristol, UK: Policy Press, 2016.

108 Signe Hald Andersen, "Paternity Leave and the Motherhood Penalty: New Causal Evidence," *Journal of Marriage and Family* 80: 5, 2018, 1125–43.

109 Guðný Björk Eydal, Ingólfur V. Gíslason, Tine Rostgaard, Berit Brandth, Ann-Zofie Duvander, and Johanna Lammi-Taskula, "Trends in Parental Leave in the Nordic Countries: Has the Forward March of Gender Equality Halted?" *Community, Work & Family* 18: 2, 2015, 167–81.

110 A. S. Orloff, "Gendering the Comparative Analysis of Welfare States: An Unfinished Agenda," *Sociological Theory*, 27: 3, 2009, 317–43.

111 Carmen Castro-García and Maria Pazos-Moran, "Parental Leave Policy and Gender Equality in Europe," *Feminist Economics* 22: 3, 2016, 51.

112 Mary Daly and Emanuele Ferragina. "Family Policy in High-Income Countries: Five Decades of Development," *Journal of European Social Policy* 28:3 (2017), 255–270.

113 Merike Blofield and Juliana Martínez Franzoni, "Maternalism, Co-responsibility, and Social Equity: A Typology of Work–Family Policies," *Social Politics* 22: 1, 2014, 38–59.

114 Rachel Connelly, Xiao-yuan Dong, Joyce Jacobsen, and Yaohui Zhao, "The Care Economy in Post-Reform China: Feminist Research on Unpaid and Paid Work and Well-Being," *Feminist Economics* 24:2 (2018), 1–30.

115 Ito Peng, "The 'New' Social Investment Policies in Japan and South Korea," in *Inclusive Growth, Development and Welfare Policy: A Critical Assessment*, Reza Hasmath, ed., New York: Routledge, 2015, 142–60.

116 Folbre, *Valuing Children*.

117 Zhanna Chernova, "New Pronatalism? Family Policy in Post–Soviet Russia," *Region* 1: 1, 2012, 75–92.

118 Fabián Slonimyczyk and Anna Yurko, "Assessing the Impact of the Maternity Capital Policy in Russia," *Labour Economics* 30, 2014, 265–81; Ekaterina Borozdina, Anna Rotkirch, Anna Temkina, and Elena Zdravomyslova, "Using Maternity Capital: Citizen Distrust of Russian Family Policy," *European Journal of Women's Studies* 23: 1, 2016, 60–75.

119 Ruth Milkman and Eileen Appelbaum, *Unfinished Business*, Ithaca, NY: Cornell University Press, 2013.

120 Folbre, *Valuing Children*.

121 For a more detailed illustration, see Nancy Folbre, "Valuing Houses but not Housewives," *New York Times Economix Blog*, September 9, 2013, economix.blogs.nytimes.com.

122 Robert A. Moffitt, "The Deserving Poor, the Family, and the U.S. Welfare System," *Demography* 52: 3, 2015, 729–49.

123 Nicholas Bakalar, "U.S. Fertility Rate Reaches a Record Low," *New York Times*, July 3, 2017, nytimes.com.

124 Thomas Baudin, David De la Croix, and Paula E. Gobbi, "Fertility and Childlessness in the United States," *American Economic Review* 105: 6, 2015, 1852–82.

125 Francine D. Blau and Lawrence M. Kahn, "The Gender Wage Gap: Extent, Trends, and Explanations," *Journal of Economic Literature* 55: 3, 2017, 789–865.

126 Jay Ginn and Ken MacIntyre, "UK Pension Reforms: Is Gender Still an Issue? *Social Policy and Society* 12: 1, 2013, 91–103; John Jankowski, "Caregiver Credits in France, Germany, and Sweden: Lessons for the United States," *Social Security Bulletin* 71: 4, 2011, 61–76.

127 Katrine V. Løken, Shelly Lundberg, and Julie Riise, "Lifting the Burden: Formal Care of the Elderly and Labor Supply of Adult Children," *Journal of Human Resources* 52: 1, 2017, 247–71.

128 Howes, "Living Wages and Retention of Home-Care Workers."

129 Kanika Arora and Douglas A. Wolf, "Does Paid Family Leave Reduce Nursing Home Use? The California Experience," *Journal of Policy Analysis and Management* 37: 1, 2018, 38–62.

130 Nancy Folbre and Douglas Wolf, eds., *Universal Long-Term Care in the U.S.: Can We Get There from Here?* New York: Russell Sage, 2012.

131 For a consumer-oriented discussion of these issues, see "Receive Payment ad a Caregiver: Cash and Counseling and Other Options," payingforseniorcare.com.

132 A study of California In-Home Supportive Services found that workers hired directly by consumers (primarily kin) were paid less and were less likely to receive fringe benefits than agency workers. A. E. Benjamin and R. Matthias, "Work–Life Differences and Outcomes for Agency and Consumer-Directed Home-Care Workers," *Gerontologist* 44: 4, 2004, 479–88. A survey of Medicaid-financed home-care workers in Arkansas, Florida, and New Jersey between 2000 and 2003 found that those directly hired by consumers were typically paid for less than half of the care hours they provided: Leslie Foster, Stacy B. Dale, and Randall Brown, "How Caregivers and Workers Fared in Cash and Counseling," *Health Services Research* 42, February 2007, 510–32.

133 B. Douglas Bernheim, Andrei Shleifer, and Lawrence H. Summers, "The Strategic Bequest Motive," *Journal of Political Economy* 93: 6, 1985, 1045–76; Max Groneck, "Bequests and Informal Long-Term Care: Evidence from HRS Exit Interviews," *Journal of Human Resources* 52: 2, 2017, 531–72; John Hoddinott, "Rotten Kids or Manipulative Parents: Are Children Old Age Security in Western Kenya?" *Economic Development and Cultural Change* 40: 3, 1992, 545–65.

134 Nancy Folbre and Douglas Wolf, "The Intergenerational Welfare State," *Population and Development Review* 38, 2012, 36–51.

135 Liliana E. Pezzin and Barbara Steinberg Schone, "Parental Marital Disruption and Intergenerational Transfers: An Analysis of Lone Elderly Parents and Their Children," *Demography* 36: 3, 1999, 287–97.

136 Ronald Demos Lee and Andrew Mason, eds., *Population Aging and the Generational Economy: A Global Perspective*, Cheltenham, UK: Edward Elgar, 2011.

137 Alessio Cangiano, "Elder Care and Migrant Labor in Europe: A Demographic Outlook," *Population and Development Review* 40: 1, 2014, 131–54.

138 Mitchell P. LaPlante, "The Woodwork Effect in Medicaid Long-Term Services and Supports," *Journal of Aging and Social Policy* 25, 2013, 161–80.

139 Organisation for Economic Co-operation and Development, *Growing Unequal? Income Distribution and Poverty in OECD Countries*, Paris: Author, 2008.

140 Joint Economic Committee, US Congress, "The Impact of Coronavirus on the Working Poor and People of Color,"n.d., jec.senate.gov.

141 Raewyn Connell, *Gender*, New York: Policy Press, 2009.

142 M. V. Lee Badgett "Gender, Sexuality, and Sexual Orientation: All in the Feminist Family?" *Feminist Economics* 1: 1, 1995, 121–39.

143 Promundo mission statement, promundoglobal.org.

144 Rosemary Crompton, ed., *Restructuring Gender Relations and Employment: The Decline of the Male Breadwinner*, New York: Oxford University Press, 1999; Gornick and Meyers, *Families that Work*; Nancy Fraser, "After the Family Wage: Gender Equality and the Welfare State," *Political Theory* 22: 4, 2004, 591–618.

145 David S. Pedulla and Sarah Thébaud, "Can We Finish the Revolution? Gender, Work–Family Ideals, and Institutional Constraint," *American Sociological Review* 80: 1, 2015, 116–39.

146 Iverson and Rosenbluth, *Women, Work and Politics*, 169.

147 Nicola Yeates, *Globalizing Care Economies and Migrant Workers: Explorations in Global Care Chains,* New York: Palgrave Macmillan, 2009.

148 Rhacel Parreñas, *Servants of Globalization*, 2d ed., Stanford, CA: Stanford University Press, 2015.

149 Lowell Jaeger, "At the Monk-a-stery": Bending the Facts to Tell the Truth from Issue 297.4, *North American Review*, northamericanreview.org.

## Chapter 10. Division and Alliance

1 Susan Watkins, "Which Feminisms?" *New Left Review* 109, 2018, 5–76.

2 Radhika Balakrishnan, James Heintz, and Diane Elson, *Rethinking Economic Policy for Social Justice,* New York: Routledge, 2016.

3 UN Women, *Progress of the World's Women 2019–2020: Families in a Changing World,* 2019, unwomen.org.

4 Helaine Olen, "5 Years Later, 'Lean In' Seems Like a Relic from Another Time," *The Nation*, March 21, 2018, thenation.com.

5 Ashley Fern, "23 Times Women Decided They Could Become the Men They Want to Marry," June 10, 2015, elitedaily.com.

6 William Thompson, *Appeal of One Half the Human Race: Women, Against the Pretensions of the Other Half, Men, to Retain Them in Political, and Hence in Civil and Domestic, Slavery; in Reply to a Paragraph of Mr. Mill's*

*Celebrated Article on Government,* London: Longman, Hurst, Rees, Orme, Brown and Green, 1825.

7   See Nancy Folbre, *Greed, Lust and Gender: A History of Economic Ideas,* New York: Oxford, 2009, Chapter 11.

8   Joel Bleifuss, "A Care Socialist Speaks Out," *In These Times,* November 13, 2011, inthesetimes.com.

9   Ruth Pearson and Diane Elson, "Transcending the Impact of the Financial Crisis in the United Kingdom: Towards Plan F—a Feminist Economic Strategy," *Feminist Review* 109, 2015, 8–30.

10  UN Women, *Progress of the World's Women 2019–2020.*.

11  International Labour Office, *Care Work and Care Jobs,* Geneva: Author, 2018; Nancy Folbre, "Demanding Quality: Worker/Consumer Coalitions and 'High Road' Strategies in the Care Sector," *Politics and Society* 34: 1, 2005, 1–21.

12  Candace Howes, "Living Wages and Retention of Homecare Workers in San Francisco," *Industrial Relations* 44: 1, 2005, 139–63; Dana Goldstein, "Teacher Walkouts: What to Know and What to Expect," *New York Times,* April 3, 2018, nytimes.com; Isaac Davison and Claire Trevett, "Government Announces Historic Pay Equity Deal for Care Workers," *New Zealand Herald,* April 18, 2017, nzherald.co.nz.

13  Francine Deutsch, *Halving It All,* Cambridge, MA: Harvard University Press, 2000.

14  David S. Pedulla and Sarah Thébaud, "Can We Finish the Revolution? Gender, Work–Family Ideals, and Institutional Constraint," *American Sociological Review* 80: 1, 2015, 116–39.

15  M. V. Lee Badgett, *When Gay People Get Married,* New York: New York University Press, 2010.

16  Karl Polanyi, *The Great Transformation,* Boston: Beacon Press, 1957.

17  Thomas Piketty, *Capital in the Twenty-First Century,* Cambridge, MA: Harvard University Press, 2014.

18  Richard V. Reeves, *Dream Hoarders,* Washington, DC: Brookings Institutions Press, 2017.

19  Economic models of the effect of human-capital externalities on racial differences are easily extended to class differences. See George Borjas, "Ethnicity, Neighborhoods, and Human-Capital Externalities," *American Economic Review* 85, 1995, 365–90; Shelly J. Lundberg and Richard Startz, "Inequality and Race: Models and Policy," in *Meritocracy and Economic Inequality,* Kenneth Arrow, Samuel Bowles, and Steven Durlauf. eds., Princeton, NJ: Princeton University Press, 2000.

20  Branko Milanovic, *The Haves and the Have-Nots,* New York: Basic Books, 2010.

21  Lauren Markham, "A Warming World Creates Desperate People," *New York Times,* June 29, 2018, nytimes.com.

22  Riane Eisler, *The Real Wealth of Nations,* San Francisco: Berrett-Koehler, 2008.

23  Alberto Minujin and Shailen Nandy, eds., *Global Child Poverty and Well-being: Measurement, Concepts, Policy and Action*, Bristol: Policy Press, 2012.

24  Anne Case and Angus Deaton, "Mortality and Morbidity in the 21st Century," *Brookings Papers on Economic Activity*, 2017, 397–476; Richard G. Wilkinson and Kate E. Pickett, "The Enemy Between Us: The Psychological and Social Costs of Inequality," *European Journal of Social Psychology* 47: 1, 2017, 11–24.

25  James K. Boyce, "Inequality as a Cause of Environmental Degradation," *Ecological Economics* 11: 3, 1994, 169–78; Moritz A. Drupp, Jasper N. Meya, Stefan Baumgärtner, and Martin F. Quaas, "Economic Inequality and the Value of Nature," *Ecological Economics* 150, 2018, 340–45.

26  K. J. Gibson-Graham, *The End of Capitalism (As We Knew It)*, Cambridge, MA: Blackwell, 1996.

27  Stuart Andreason, "COVID-19, Workers, and Policy," *Workforce Currents*, March 18, 2020, frbatlanta.org.

28  Titan M. Alon, Matthias Doepke, Jane Olmstead-Rumsey, and Michèle Tertilt, "The Impact of COVID-19 on Gender Equality," National Bureau of Economic Research Working Paper No. W26947, March 2020, https://www.nber.org/papers/w26947.

29  Campbell Robertson and Robert Gebeloff, "How Millions of Women Became the Most Essential Workers in America," *New York Times*, April 18, 2020, nytimes.com.

30  Caitlin E. Cox, "Healthcare Workers With COVID-19 Relatively Young, Mostly Female: CDC," TCD/MD The Heartbeat, April 15, 2020, tctmd.com.

31  Jeffery C. Mays and Andy Newman, "Virus Is Twice as Deadly for Black and Latino People Than Whites in New York City, *New York Times,* April 14, 2020, nytimes.com.

32  Gerald Posner, "Big Pharma May Pose an Obstacle to Vaccine Development," *New York Times*, March 2, 2020, nytimes.com.

33  See description and complete lyrics, https://genius.com/Billy-bragg-the-internationale-lyrics.

34  Arlie Russell Hochschild, *Strangers in Their Own Land*, New York: New Press, 2016, 224.

35  John Roemer, Woojin Lee, and Katrine Van Der Straeten, *Racism, Xenophobia, and Distribution*, Cambridge, MA: Harvard University Press, 2007.

36  N. Gregory Mankiw, "Spreading the Wealth Around: Reflections on Joe the Plumber," *Eastern Economic Journal* 210: 36, 2010, 291.

37  Erik Olin Wright, *Envisioning Real Utopias*, New York: Verso, 2010.

38  Janet C. Gornick and Marcia K. Meyers, eds., *Gender Equality*, New York: Verso, 2009.

39  Julie Matthaei, "Feminism and Revolution: Looking Back, Looking Ahead," Resilience, July 2, 2018, resilience.org.

40  Linda Alcoff, Cinzia Arruzza, Tithi Bhattacharya, Rosa Clemente, Angela Davis, Zillah Eisenstein, Liza Featherstone, Nancy Fraser, Barbara Smith, and Keeanga-Yamahtta Taylor, "We Need a Feminism for the 99%. That's Why Women Will Strike This Year," *The Guardian*, January 27, 2018, theguardian.com.

41  For a list of the UN Sustainable Development goals, see un.org.

42  Langston Hughes, "Let America be America Again," poets.org.

43  Leila J. Rupp and Verta Taylor, "Forging Feminist Identity in an International Movement: A Collective Identity Approach to Twentieth-Century Feminism," *Signs: Journal of Women in Culture and Society* 24: 2, 1999, 363–86.

44  See letter of James Madison to Thomas Jefferson of October 24, 1787, in *The Founder's Constitution*, Philip B. Kurland and Ralph Lerner, eds., Chicago: University of Chicago Press, and James Madison, Federalist Paper #10, Bill of Rights Institute, hialeahhigh.org.

45  I owe this formulation to Wally Seccombe.

46  Corey Robin, *The Reactionary Mind*, New York: Oxford University Press, 2018, 4.

47  Carolyn Forché, Introduction to *Against Forgetting*, New York: W. W. Norton, 1993, 43.

# Index